D0768735

DIXIE'S DIRTY SECRET

Also by the Author

North To Canada:
Men and Woman Against the Vietnam War

Women On Top:
The Quiet Revolution That's Rocking the American Music Industry

That's Alright, Elvis:
The Untold Story of Elvis's First Guitarist and Manager, Scotty Moore
(with Scotty Moore)

Goin' Back to Memphis:
A Century of Blues, Rock 'n' Roll, and Glorious Soul

Coming Home:
21 Conversations About Memphis Music

DIXIE'S DIRTY SECRET

The True Story of How the Government,
the Media, and the Mob Conspired to Combat
Integration and the Vietnam Antiwar Movement

James Dickerson

M.E. Sharpe
Armonk, New York
London, England

Library of Congress Cataloging-in-Publication Data

Dickerson, James.
Dixie's dirty secret : the true story of how the government, the media, and the mob conspired to combat integration and the Vietnam antiwar movement / James Dickerson.
p. cm.
Includes bibliographical references and index.
ISBN 0–7656–0340–3 (alk. paper)
1. Mississippi—Race relations. 2. Civil rights movements—Mississippi—History—
20th century. 3. Afro-Americans—Civil rights—Mississippi—History—20th century.
4. Mississippi State Sovereignty Commission. 5. Political persecution—Mississippi—
History—20th century. 6. Vietnamese Conflict, 1961–1975—Protest movements—
Mississippi. 7. Civil rights—Mississippi—History—20th century. I. Title.
E185.93.M6D54   1998
323.1'196073'009045—dc21
98–3165

CIP

Printed in the United States of America

The paper used in this publication meets the minimum requirements of
American National Standard for Information Sciences—
Permanence of Paper for Printed Library Materials,
ANSI Z 39.48-1984.

♾

BM (c)   10   9   8   7   6   5   4   3   2   1

In memory of my grandparents

Audie and Rada Turner

Contents

Acknowledgments   ix
Photographs follow page 118

Chapter   1.   1955–1956   3
Chapter   2.   1957–1959   21
Chapter   3.   1960   36
Chapter   4.   1961–1962   50
Chapter   5.   1963–1964   69
Chapter   6.   1965–1966   100
Chapter   7.   1967   130
• *Chapter   8.*   1968   157
Chapter   9.   1969–1979   182
Chapter 10.   1980–1989   205
Chapter 11.   1990–1998   214

Notes   231
Select Bibliography   239
Index   245

Acknowledgments

I would like to thank the following for help during the twenty years-plus it took to research and write this book: Charles Sudduth, who was an eyewitness to most of it; Rick Abraham, who served on the front lines; John Waits and his father, the late Hilton Waits; Hal DeCell Jr.; Charles Evers; William Winter; William Waller; David Ingebretesen; Dr. Barbara Flanary at the Memphis/Shelby County Public Library; Ed Frank and Cathy Evans of the Mississippi Valley Collection at the University of Memphis; my editor, Peter Coveney; Brown Burnett, Susan Garcia, and the Reverend Ed King, editors at the *Clarion-Ledger* ; the Jean and Alexander Heard Library at Vanderbilt University Library; Mike Parrish at the Lyndon B. Johnson Library and Museum; David Hampton, Rims Barber, George Rogers, and H.T. Holmes at the Mississippi Department of Archives and History; Kerrie Taylor at the University of Mississippi Library; Debra Buccolo at the United States Farm Credit Administration; Bill Dugan at the Office of the Assistant to the Secretary of Defense for Intelligence Oversight; Dr. Bob Tusa of McCain Library and Archives at the University of Southern Mississippi; the Nashville and Davidson County Public Library; James Best, legal counsel for the Hinds County Sheriff's Department; the late Audie and Rada Turner; my mother; and my son, Jonathan.

DIXIE'S DIRTY SECRET

CHAPTER 1

1955 – 1956

It was the week after Christmas 1955.

Memphis had fallen into one of those gray, winter funks that traditionally precedes New Year's Eve celebrations in the city. It was in the midst of that stubborn lethargy that James Gunter, a reporter for the city's morning newspaper, the *Commercial Appeal,* received a tip that something big was in the works. Senator James Eastland of Mississippi had been spotted in the city, along with Senator Strom Thurmond of South Carolina and dozens of other prominent Southerners.

Gunter made a few telephone calls and tracked Eastland and Thurmond to the Peabody Hotel, a monument to a bygone era of Southern gentility. Arriving at the posh hotel, he found himself blocked from entering the room where the meeting was taking place. He was told that the gathering was private and was strongly advised to stay away.

Gunter stood his ground, taking note of who entered the room. When he cornered one delegate in the hallway and asked who would be speaking that day, one of the organizers punched the delegate before he could answer. What Gunter saw that afternoon astonished him. Political leaders from twelve Southern states were at the hotel. It was the largest gathering of its kind since before the Civil War.

When the four-hour meeting broke up at 6 P.M., Gunter was able to talk to enough people to piece together a story. The group, which had named itself the Federation for Constitutional Government, had gathered to devise a plan to fight racial desegregation in the South. In the weeks following the

Memphis gathering, the group established offices in Louisiana and remained in operation well into the 1960s.

Gunter rushed back to the newsroom with a list of thirty-five men he had
recognized at the hotel. In addition to Thurmond and Eastland, the organizers of the meeting, he identified former governor Fielding L. Wright (Mississippi), U.S. Representative John Bell Williams (Mississippi), state
Representative Walter Sillers (Speaker of the Mississippi House of Representatives), Attorney General Eugene Cook (Georgia), Governor Marvin
Griffin (Georgia), Representative Mendel Rivers (South Carolina), Representative F. Edward Hebert (Louisiana), former governor Sam Jones (Louisiana), and former governor Coke Stevenson (Texas).

The next morning the *Commercial Appeal* exposed the secret gathering
with a page-one story and a headline that read: "Federation For Constitutional Government Is Designed to Build Up Effective Force Against Integration." The story made much of the fact that the meeting was held in
secret and identified John U. Barr, a wealthy industrialist from New Orleans, as the chairman.

"This organization is restricted to the South now, but we have found
supporters all over the nation," Barr explained to Gunter during a brief
exchange. "We've kept this thing under wraps until we knew our strength."

When editors at the *New York Times* spotted the story on the national wire
that morning, they asked an aggressive young reporter, Anthony Lewis, to
look into it. After speaking to Barr and others by telephone, Lewis wrote a
story his editors thought was important enough to put on the front page.

Lewis's story quoted Eastland as saying that the new group was designed to "fight the Supreme Court, fight the CIO, fight the NAACP, and
fight all conscienceless pressure groups who are attempting our destruction." Barr told Lewis the group would "fight anything" that tried to destroy the Constitution.

Clearly, everyone at the meeting was in a fighting mood.

Once the veil of secrecy was lifted on the two-day gathering, the *New
York Times* and the *Commercial Appeal* were able to gather the names of
most of those in attendance. The two most powerful backers of the group,
aside from Eastland and his supporters, were Barr, a director of the National
Association of Manufacturers, and Leander Perez, a wealthy and politically
powerful Louisiana racist. "Do you know what the Negro is?" Perez once
asked. "Animals right out of the jungle. Passion. Welfare. Easy life. That's
the Negro. And if you don't know that, you're naive."

What emerged from the newspaper coverage of the Memphis meeting
was a portrait of the most vehement collection of right-wing activists in the
nation. What was not so obvious to reporters at the time was the strategy the

federation had devised to fight integration. The best tactic, the group concluded, was for the states to establish watchdog commissions capable of going head-to-head with the federal government—something akin to a secret police force answerable only to good white men of the South.

Also at the meeting, but keeping a lower profile, were hard-core racists such as William J. Simmons, leader of the notorious Mississippi Association of Citizens' Councils, a white supremacist organization second only to the Ku Klux Klan in its opposition to integration. Leaders from other Citizens' Council groups from around the country were there, as were representatives from right-wing organizations in New York and New Jersey. Before the Memphis group adjourned, Eastland, his emotions surging, called on his fellow Southerners to wage "a great crusade" for the "untainted racial heritage . . . of the Anglo-Saxon race."

In a follow-up story, the *New York Times* quoted Russell Crawford, president of the New York branch of the NAACP, as calling on the U.S. attorney general to investigate the Memphis group as a "subversive" organization. That investigation never took place. As would later become clear, the Memphis group had powerful backers in the federal government.

———

For as long as anyone could remember, Mississippians have regarded Memphis as the "capital of Mississippi." Some of the reasons are obvious. Its geographic location at the northwest corner of the Tennessee–Mississippi state line made it the gatekeeper for interstate travel and commerce. Culturally, Memphis's majority black population owes its roots almost entirely to immigrants from the Mississippi Delta. The same could be said of the city's white population, which is composed of significant percentages of white immigrants from the red-clay hills of northern Mississippi.

A reason not so obvious is the fact that from the 1920s to the present, Memphis has supported one of the most powerful organized crime cartels in the nation. The cartel's origins can be traced back to the 1920s, when white businessmen on and around Beale Street discovered they could make more money selling cocaine and morphine under the counter than they could from the operation of their legitimate businesses. At the turn of the century, cocaine use was reported to be at epidemic levels in Memphis. Police spokesmen told reporters at the time that they estimated that up to 60 percent of the black population was addicted to the drug. As might be expected, drug use at that level had undesirable consequences.

By the 1920s, Memphis was known as the "murder capital" of the nation, a label first attached by the Prudential Insurance Company of America. For the decade ending in 1910 Memphis had the highest homicide rate of any city surveyed by Prudential. It was a distinction that stuck with the city up through the 1950s. Newspapers regularly ran stories with headlines such as "Memphis Battles Attacks On Name."

Second to murder were the problems caused by the hundreds of young girls who left their Mississippi and Arkansas homes for the bright lights of Memphis. Unable to find jobs—and afraid to return home—they started working in brothels and nightclubs, providing a major new market for cocaine peddlers. The girls were so troublesome that city officials organized a special agency to deal with them. The Woman's Protective Bureau processed more than a thousand young girls a year, most of them charged with prostitution, addiction, and theft.

Because the founders of the Memphis cartel were all experienced businessmen, they organized their operations in a businesslike manner. They had learned from crime families in New York and Chicago that the cost of bribing beat cops was a normal expense of doing business. They also had learned that large sums of cash could be a liability if not distributed among cartel members in a manner not to attract attention.

By investing their gains from vice into scores of legitimate storefront businesses, retail stores, insurance agencies, real estate operations, and construction companies, Memphis crime families refined the techniques of money laundering used today by drug cartels the world over. They used political power as a coercive tool, much as crime families in New York and Chicago used the cruder methods of extortion and murder. The Memphis cartel did have muscle, which it occasionally relied on, but its real strength was derived from its domination of the political process. Today elected officials call such money "campaign contributions." In the 1920s and 1930s, they called it the "sugar-tit," a Southern colloquialism for pay-off money.

By the early 1950s, according to sources, the Memphis cartel had utilized the expertise of the blossoming Memphis recording industry to introduce the use of sophisticated electronic listening devices to spy on business competitors (and probably the feds themselves) long before the G-men ever thought about getting court-ordered wiretaps to eavesdrop on the cartel. Although the FBI had used wiretaps since the early 1940s, the targets were war-related and not crime-related since at that time the FBI did not admit the existence of organized crime. In the 1950s, the bureau targeted the Communist Party for wiretaps. Not until the late 1950s, when hidden microphones in Chicago mob locations revealed the existence of a secret Mafia organization called the "Commission," did the bureau target organized crime for wiretaps on a regular basis. By then, Elvis Presley, Carl Perkins, Johnny Cash, Jerry Lee Lewis, and others had attracted enough microphone experts to the Memphis recording industry to make the city a mecca for students of electronic surveillance. Certainly, the Memphis businessmen who financed the cartel knew more about the science of recording than did the FBI.

~~~

With the support of Memphis businessmen, E.H. "Boss" Crump, a gangly, redheaded huckster from the same red-clay hills of northern Mississippi that nurtured the seed of Elvis Aron Presley, was able to build a political and financial empire in the 1920s that dominated local, regional, and even national politics for nearly half a century. For the most part, "Boss" Crump did not accomplish that while serving in office—although he was elected mayor of Memphis three times and served two terms in Congress—but as a private citizen, working from his real estate and insurance office in the North Memphis Savings Bank Building on Main Street.

Crump's right-hand man was Tennessee senator Kenneth McKellar, an Alabamian who moved to Memphis in 1892 and served in the United States Senate from 1916 until 1952, when he was defeated for reelection by Albert Gore, father of Vice President Al Gore. Throughout the 1930s and 1940s, McKellar was a powerhouse in the Senate. He controlled hundreds of patronage jobs and millions of dollars in government contracts, a good percentage of which were directed into Memphis businesses.

Crump and McKellar communicated on a daily basis. Often they exchanged two or three letters a day, and sometimes just as many telegrams. Crump told McKellar how to vote on issues large and small. Together, they decided who received every government job in the state, from clerk to U.S. marshal.

Sometimes they may have broken the law, as when they tried to force the Internal Revenue Service, under threat of a Senate investigation, into pressing criminal charges against a business rival. When Joseph Nunan, the IRS commissioner, refused to do as Crump and McKellar ordered, McKellar wrote Nunan a letter saying he thought Nunan had made a "mistake" in judgment. "I imagine I will have to introduce a resolution to have [you] investigated," said McKellar, adding, "These investigations are long, tiresome and expensive." To Nunan's credit, he refused to give in to McKellar's demands.

In February 1942, Crump saw the following news story:

> LOS ANGELES—During her recent stay in the Angel City, the glamorous Tallulah Bankhead, Broadway actress, at a press interview named the three

greatest men in the nation today in order, as being President Roosevelt, Joe Louis and Wendell Wilkie. Referring to the Brown Bomber, she said: "There's a man who has everything! He's a gentleman."

Outraged by the actress's reference to the black fighter, Crump dashed off a letter to McKellar. "Tallulah is either in love with Joe or evidently has some negro lover to make a statement of that kind," he wrote. He blamed Tallulah's boldness on the president's wife. "Mrs. Roosevelt has done this country more harm than any other individual, and the people are doing a lot of wondering about her husband, which is so unfortunate at this time." McKellar responded: "It is inconceivable that a white girl could have made a statement of that kind. I am tremendously worried over this situation."

Roosevelt and Crump may have been miles apart on the race issue, but that did not stop them from working together. Proof of their meetings eluded investigators until 1996, when the author found evidence of the meetings tucked away in McKellar's private papers. In a "Dear Kenneth" note dated January 18, 1944, and signed by the president, Roosevelt sent McKellar an acknowledgment on White House stationery of a meeting scheduled for himself, Crump, and McKellar at the White House on the following Friday. McKellar's relationship with Roosevelt extended as far back as 1932, when the future president was governor of New York. In a note dated February 5, McKellar instructed Roosevelt of his intention to "run over there [to the governor's mansion] and have a little conversation with [him]."

What was happening in Memphis did not go unnoticed by the national media. On January 26, 1935, *Collier's* magazine published a scathing portrait of Memphis's "commercialized" vice trade entitled "Sinners in Dixie." The reporter noted that Crump's organization controlled every facet of life in the city and he pointed out particularly that the insurance agency owned by Crump received all of the county's insurance business. "In Memphis this is such a well-known fact that no one denies it," said the magazine. "If, for example, a man in that town who is running a hotel, a bank, a garage or a bakery is a supporter of the Democratic organization there are two things he never need worry about: One is service, the other contributions. So long as he votes right—which means in favor of a wide-open town—no business-man in Memphis who needs the aid of the agencies of his local government ever calls upon it in vain."

Following the article's publication in *Collier's,* Crump wrote McKellar a letter in which he described the piece as a "conglomeration of misfit words." Oddly, he was not disturbed over being linked to organized crime. "We must expect these things in life," he wrote. "After all, there are some very good lines. They say we are not grafters and of course, we are not, give a good government, stick with our friends and are winners. . . . The writer's outstanding lie—that we have all the county's insurance."

In 1946, the *Washington Post* used Memphis as an example of how unsuspecting Americans could be enticed into fascism. "The city is a perfect example of the ease with which Americans with a philosophy of efficiency and materialism can succumb to fascism and like it," said the newspaper. "The majority of the citizens of Memphis lick the boots of their notorious tyrant, Mr. E.H. Crump, not because they have to. They lick his boots because it pays. Like all fascist rulers, Crump has the support and admiration of big business." Although Crump had "no organized forces of Brown Shirts," wrote historian V.O. Key, Jr., author of *Southern Politics,* critics of his policies had reason to fear for their lives while visiting the city.

Upon the death of President Franklin Roosevelt in 1945, Vice President Harry Truman became president of the United States. The line of succession set out in the Constitution made Senator McKellar, the president pro tempore of the Senate, the acting vice president. Although the Speaker of the House would have become president if Truman died—and McKellar was second in line—it was McKellar, not the Speaker, who enjoyed the constitutional powers of the office of vice president.

For the next three years, Crump's right-hand man would stand only a couple of heartbeats away from occupying the Oval Office. McKellar attended all the Cabinet meetings and reported back to Crump on the inner workings of the White House. The post-war boom was on, and those three years marked a period of remarkable growth for the Memphis cartel, which reportedly shifted the bulk of its operations away from vice to the more lucrative area of government grants and contracts.

To Crump's surprise, Truman would not do business with the cartel. So in 1948 when Truman ran for election in his own right, Crump broke from the Democratic Party and supported the newly formed right-wing Dixiecrat Party. Truman's subsequent victory was a blow to Crump for several reasons.

First, it ushered into office a new Tennessee senator named Estes Kefauver. He was pro-Truman, anti-Crump, and anti-cartel. Crump's worst fears about Kefauver were realized in 1950 when the senator chaired the Senate Special Committee to Investigate Crime in Interstate Commerce. The hearings conducted by Kefauver's committee were televised and literally blew the lid off organized crime in America.

Second, Truman's election meant McKellar was no longer acting vice president and no longer privy to the secrets of the White House. But there was another, more important reason. Crump and McKellar had maintained a close working relationship with President Roosevelt. As a congressman Crump had voted for every Roosevelt initiative that came along, and as a political boss he had raised money for the president and delivered votes to him on an as-needed basis. As a result—or more likely as insurance for a continuing relationship—Roosevelt had boosted the political career of Memphis's golden boy, Abe Fortas, by appointing him to the Farm Bureau.

Truman's election meant that Fortas was out of a job. Born on June 19, 1910, to Orthodox Jewish immigrants who had moved to Memphis from England only a few years prior to his birth, Fortas was raised on Pontotoc Street in the wild and woolly Beale Street district that suckled the Memphis cartel. There is no evidence his father, a pawnbroker and jeweler, was ever a card-carrying member of the cartel, but since the family were neighbors of the founding members of the cartel it may be assumed they were at least acquainted.

Fortas grew up in a neighborhood in which prostitution, cocaine addiction, extortion, and murder were a normal part of the business atmosphere. As a Jew living on the perimeter of a black neighborhood, he was considered neither white nor black by most Memphians. To break out of that mold, he took advantage of his musical talents and put together a band named the Blue Melody Boys. Whatever his limitations as a fiddle player, Fortas had a brilliant mind and he landed a scholarship, first at Southwestern College in Memphis, then at Yale University, where he obtained a law degree.

By 1933, Fortas was on a fast track with the Roosevelt administration. That year, at the age of twenty-two, he was given a post in the Farm Bureau. Later, his new wife, Carolyn Agger, was offered a job with the National Labor Relations Board, then she quickly moved over to the tax division of the Department of Justice. Fortas was subsequently hired as the assistant director of the Securities and Exchange Commission. By 1946 he had served as an attorney with the Treasury Department and as undersecretary of the Interior.

In January 1946, Fortas wrote a letter to a Memphis friend, confiding his ambition to make money now that he was no longer in government service. "It was difficult to decide to leave the government at this time, when I might perhaps make some contribution," he wrote. "But I believe that by leaving now I may be able to be of greater service in the future." It is an interesting letter, for it leaves the reader wondering if the beneficiaries of the "greater service" he wants to render will be the government or his Memphis benefactors.

By 1948, Fortas was firmly entrenched with a prominent Washington law firm. That year he took on a case that would change his life. A Texan named Lyndon Johnson was accused of voter fraud in a Senate primary election. Fortas won the case for Johnson and thereby ensured his victory in the general election. Johnson was not so much impressed by Fortas's juristic dexterity as by the way he manipulated a legal technicality to his advantage. It was a slick move that handed Johnson victory on a silver platter.

As the Federation for Constitutional Government was meeting in Memphis in late 1955, the city's political front was falling into disarray. McKellar had been defeated for reelection in 1952. Crump, now eighty years of age and in poor health, was still a power broker, but his days were numbered. The new senator from Tennessee, Estes Kefauver, despised Crump and the Memphis cartel, and he was quickly becoming an American folk hero.

As dismal as the political prospects looked, the Memphis cartel was stronger than ever financially. It had investments to protect and no political base from which to operate. In 1955, the cartel looked toward the turmoil seething in Mississippi and saw a golden opportunity.

Watching the Memphis gathering from a distance were FBI director J. Edgar Hoover and New Orleans power broker Carlos "Little Man" Marcello, kingpin of the so-called Dixie Mafia. Hoover and Marcello had at least two things in common: both maintained a friendship with New York mobster Frank Costello—and both were unrepentant racists.

Hoover's relationship with Costello was not brought to light until 1975, three years after the FBI chief's death, when *Time* magazine reported that Hoover and Costello often met in New York's Central Park. In 1988, William Hundley, former chief of the Justice Department's organized crime section, told historian Arthur Schlesinger, Jr., that he believed Hoover and Costello saw each other throughout the 1950s and possibly into the 1960s. This was during a period in which Hoover vehemently denied the existence of organized crime in America.

Hoover's antiblack attitudes had been simmering for years, but it was not until October 1955 that they came to full boil. In 1946, at the request of Walter White, national director of the NAACP, Hoover had sent the organization a letter saying that the NAACP had done much to preserve the principles of "equality, freedom, and tolerance." It was a routine letter, and Hoover didn't give it much thought at the time. However, when he received a memo on October 19, 1955, quoting a Memphis source as saying the NAACP was using that old letter to refute charges it had ties to the Communist Party, Hoover was furious. He ordered an investigation into the NAACP's activities.

Two days later, FBI assistant director Alan Belmont responded with a detailed memorandum that purported to outline the NAACP's "subversive" activities. Thus, it was in the weeks preceding the Memphis gathering that Hoover launched his ruthless campaign against the civil rights movement. From its inception, the Federation for Constitutional Government and J. Edgar Hoover had walked in step.

Tapping into that racial animosity was Carlos Marcello. From his office behind the Town and Country Motel in Jefferson Parish, just below New Orleans, he operated a vegetable produce company that fronted, according to FBI reports, a wide range of illegal activities such as prostitution, narcotic sales, and gambling. Although his reputation as a mobster was such that he could never play a public role in politics, he proved himself a consummate behind-the-scenes strategist. As early as 1948, the New Orleans field office of the FBI had reported that Marcello "had the keys" to the front door of Governor Earl K. Long's office in Angola. The FBI field office regularly submitted evidence that Governor Long had connections to Costello and to typical mob activities such as gambling and prostitution.

That presented a dilemma for Marcello, who did not share Long's more moderate racial views or his support of the national Democratic Party. According to biographer John H. Davis, Marcello was a generous contributor to anti–civil rights organizations and an enthusiastic supporter of the Ku Klux Klan. Philosophically, that put him in agreement with Long's primary foes—Leander Perez, John U. Barr, and former governor Sam Jones, all founding members of the Federation for Constitutional Government. The organization had established its headquarters in the American Bank Building where Perez had his law office. Perez was to Louisiana what Crump was to Tennessee and Mississippi: a political godfather who seemed incapable of separating politics from business. He ruled with absolute power in his home base of Plaquemines Parish until his death in 1969.

Under his leadership the federation maintained a storefront presence until well after the passage of the Civil Rights Act of 1964 (the federation's most prominent political defeat), but that seems to have been only for appearances. By 1964 the work of the federation was being conducted mostly by behind-the-scene players in only three states—Louisiana, Tennessee, and Mississippi. Perez had a financial stake in states' rights, as did Marcello. At issue in Louisiana were valuable oil and land leases worth millions, which had been targeted for federal takeover. Perez wanted the leases to stay under state control, where he had considerable influence. Two things set the Memphis cartel apart from its brethren in Louisiana: its ethnic roots, which were distinctly not Italian, and its ability to wield politics as a razor-sharp weapon.

In 1933, Senator McKellar had submitted a list of names for appointment as FBI agents. Hoover rejected those named and McKellar complained to the U.S. attorney general. In retaliation, Hoover fired three special agents who had been assigned to Tennessee. Three years later, when Hoover appeared before the Senate subcommittee responsible for FBI appropriations, the committee's chairman, Senator McKellar, was lying in wait. He listened to Hoover explain why the FBI needed additional funds, then he publicly boxed the director's ears by criticizing him for allowing his photograph to be used in Hollywood motion pictures. To Hoover's surprise, McKellar said he didn't think the bureau needed additional funds. "It seems to me that your Department is just running wild, Mr. Hoover," said McKellar. "I just think that, Mr. Hoover, with all the money in your hands you are just extravagant."

"Will you let me make a statement?" asked Hoover.

McKellar cut him off. "I think that is the statement," he said.

When Hoover rebounded, using statistics to show just how efficient the FBI had been, how the bureau had brought in $38 million in fines and cost taxpayers only $4.5 million in appropriations, McKellar countered with a solid punch below the belt. Asked McKellar: "How many people have been killed by your Department since you have been allowed to use guns?"

"I think there have been eight desperadoes killed by our agents and we have had four agents in our service killed by them."

McKellar looked at the FBI director with disdain. "In other words the net effect of turning guns over to your department has been the killing of eight desperadoes and four G-men."

Hoover was shaken. He explained that his agents were under orders to apprehend suspects alive, if possible, and were only authorized to use weapons if their lives were in danger.

McKellar was relentless. "I doubt very much whether you ought to have a law that permits you to go around the country armed as an army would, and shoot down all the people that you suspect of being criminals," said McKellar, who was saving his best for last. He asked Hoover point-blank: "Did you ever make an arrest?"

Hoover said that he had never made an actual arrest himself. It was his most humiliating moment, his biographers subsequently wrote; he felt his manhood had been impugned by the question. McKellar's rough treatment of the FBI director did not go unnoticed by America's newly emerging crime families. Everyone knew Crump was "Boss" of Tennessee just as Perez was "Boss" of Louisiana. And everyone knew McKellar was Crump's right-hand man. The McKellar–Hoover confrontation showed that Memphis was a force to be reckoned with. For McKellar to take on Hoover in such a public way was machismo of the highest order in the eyes of the nation's crime bosses.

By 1950, Hoover found himself in the awkward position of shielding America's crime families from an investigation conducted by Senator Estes Kefauver, the archenemy of the Memphis cartel. Not only did Hoover refuse to assist the Senate committee's investigation, he issued a statement denying the existence of organized crime in America.

In a series of televised hearings, Kefauver proved Hoover wrong and exposed a vast network of organized crime in cities from New York to Los Angeles. He called more than eight hundred witnesses before the committee, including Hoover's acquaintance Frank Costello, who agreed to appear only if his face was not photographed.

When Carlos Marcello was called before the committee at a hearing in New Orleans, Kefauver labeled him "the evil genius of organized crime in Louisiana."

Kefauver asked Marcello if he was a member of the Mafia.

"I refuse to answer the question on the ground it might intend to criminate [*sic*] me," said Marcello.

Kefauver was not impressed by Marcello's tough-guy answers. At the conclusion of the hearings, he recommended to the attorney general that Marcello, who was not an American citizen, be deported as soon as possible.

Although the hearings were an enormous success, they drove a wedge even deeper between Hoover and Kefauver. At one point, when two witnesses scheduled to appear before the committee were murdered, Kefauver asked the FBI for help in protecting future witnesses. Hoover's response was brief and to the point: "I regret to advise the Federal Bureau of Investigation is not empowered to perform guard duties."

By 1955, Marcello was hitting full stride in Louisiana. After surviving the Kefauver hearings, he went public for the first time, buying the Town and Country Motel and other high-profile legitimate businesses. He didn't exactly flaunt his wealth, but he didn't hide it either. The unchallenged political boss of Mississippi at that time was Senator James Eastland. Control of Mississippi's profitable underworld operations was in the hands of two organizations: the Memphis cartel and Marcello's Dixie Mafia, with the dividing line between the two set at Highway 80, a two-lane road that ran east to west, from Grenada to Greenville. Everything south of the road belonged to Marcello; everything north of the road belonged to the Memphis cartel. Eastland's cotton plantation was located just north of the road near Doddsville.

Marcello's relationship with the Memphis cartel, according to sources, was friendly but often strained. The Memphis organization had a more liberal view of race relations than that of other crime families across the country. Blacks were never given positions of leadership in the Memphis cartel, but since they were viewed as essential for continued political influence, they were afforded a nominal amount of protection. That would not have gone over too well with Marcello.

When federal troops were used in 1954 to enforce a Supreme Court decision ordering the desegregation of public schools in Little Rock, Arkansas, it sent a shock wave throughout the South, where racial segregation was the law of the land. African Americans were required by statute to attend separate schools. They were prohibited to use any state or private facilities that were not designated for "coloreds."

Public buildings open to African Americans displayed "colored" signs on separate restrooms and water fountains, but many other buildings, such as public libraries, were off limits to citizens of color. African Americans bold enough to enter those buildings were promptly arrested and taken off to jail. The mood of white voters was made clear during the 1955 gubernatorial campaign: White Mississippians were fighting mad. Not since the Civil War had federal troops pointed guns in their direction.

J.P. Coleman had begun his political career in 1946 as a circuit court judge in Ackerman, a small town ninety miles northeast of Jackson. A barrel-chested glad-hander as much at home chewing the fat with the cotton farmers of his rural district as debating the subtleties of the Constitution with legal scholars, he merged a love of the law with a passion for down-home politics and adopted the nickname, "Choctaw County plowboy," which stuck with him his entire career.

When he ran for governor in 1955, he had already been elected to the office of state attorney general, but he was nowhere near being the most powerful political leader in the state. That distinction rested with Senator James Eastland, or "Big Jim" as he was affectionately known to his constituents. Eastland, who owned a 5,000–acre cotton plantation in Sunflower County, a rural district known also as home to bluesman B.B. King, was a big man who smoked a big cigar. He had a slovenly appearance and an oversized beet-red face that always seemed at full moon. Despite his appearance—or perhaps because of it—when he spoke, ordinary people listened.

That election year, Eastland took to the stump, spreading the word from one end of the state to the other. "You are not required to obey any court which passes out such a ruling," he said, referring to the Supreme Court. "In fact, you are obligated to defy it."

The High Court was guilty of a "monstrous crime," Eastland said, and was a "clear threat and present danger to the very foundation of our Republican form of government." The federal government had one goal in mind: "the mongrelization of the white race."

Once, during a Senate subcommittee hearing to discuss bills to require registration of communist organizations, the six-foot, heavy-jowled Eastland tangled with C.B. Baldwin, a former administrator of the Farm Security Administration, after Baldwin testified that Eastland represented the "Cotton Council" and was "fighting against Negro rights."

"You goddamned son of a bitch," Eastland angrily shouted.

Baldwin shouted back that Eastland was "a narrow-minded bigot." Both men were fighting mad, but before they came to physical blows, the police were called and Baldwin stormed out of the committee room.

By the time J.P. Coleman grasped the reins of Mississippi gubernatorial power in January 1956, they were hitched to a runaway team of wild-eyed racial purists hell-bent on revolution. Realistically, Coleman had only two choices: he was either "for 'em or against 'em." He confided to friends that he didn't care for either choice, but, like most white Mississippians, he was opposed to forced integration—and he didn't have the courage to stand up to the hatemongers.

Early in December 1955, in the weeks leading up to his inauguration, he was critical of Senator Eastland's proposals to fight the Supreme Court, calling his ideas "foolish" and "legal poppycock," but in the week following the Memphis gathering, he abruptly changed his position. He told reporters that his stand on segregation would provide a "bombshell" that could be heard "from the Atlantic to the Pacific."

Rather than risk losing any of the hard-fought power he had gained as governor, Coleman came down squarely on the side of Big Jim Eastland, who earlier that year had become chairman of the powerful Senate Judiciary Committee. It was Eastland's position that states had a legal right to pass "acts of nullification" to void Supreme Court decisions that violated the Constitution.

When Eastland advocated the creation of a commission funded by taxpayers to fight the federal government, Coleman embraced the idea as if it were his own. Eastland was a raging bull who had the clout in Memphis and New Orleans to make good on his threats. There was no way Coleman was going to risk confrontation with a man like that.

Early in 1956, Coleman sent a bill to the Mississippi Legislature that would create a supersecret spy agency designed to protect the state against the encroaching power of the federal government. The new agency he proposed would be named the Mississippi State Sovereignty Commission.

The bill was clearly a product of the gathering that had taken place in Memphis the previous December. Under the provisions set forth in the bill, the Commission would be empowered to "perform any and all acts and things deemed necessary and proper to protect the sovereignty of the State of Mississippi, and her sister states, from encroachment" by the federal government. The Commission was given the authority to examine the records and documents of any citizen or organization dealing with matters "about which the commission is authorized to conduct an investigation."

The language of the bill was explicit: "The commission shall have the power and authority to require all persons, firms and corporations having such books, records, documents and other papers in their possession or under their control to produce same within this state at such time and place as the commission may designate, and to permit an inspection and examination thereof by the members of said commission or its authorized representatives and employees."

To enforce that authority, the Commission was provided with a broad-ranging subpoena power that included the authority to enforce obedience "by fine or imprisonment" at the discretion of the Commission. In addition, the Commission was authorized to receive contributions and donations from private groups or individuals. It was designed to operate independently of state government, when necessary, and to utilize private funds to carry out covert operations.

Among the 49 senators and 140 members of the House present for the session that considered the bill were Representative William Winter, who went on to hold several state offices, including governor, lieutenant governor, and tax collector; Representative Hilton Waits; and Representative George Rogers, who eventually left Mississippi politics to work for the Central Intelligence Agency.

If Coleman thought support for the proposal would be unanimous, he was mistaken. "Those of us who were Coleman supporters in the Legislature viewed the proposal for the Sovereignty Commission with a lot of misgiving," says Winter today. "It was viewed then, I think, as a body that in the wrong hands could create a lot of mischief."

There was little debate on the bill. Most of the discussion was done in back rooms, where talk of the "nigger" problem could be done in a more informal atmosphere. At that time, it was considered in bad taste for Southern gentlemen to refer to the "nigger" problem in public, especially now that the Supreme Court had taken an interest in civil rights.

When the bill came to a vote, it passed by a margin of 130 to 2, with 8 representatives not voting. Representative George Rogers and Representative Woody Hewitt cast the only two votes in opposition to the Commission.

Interviewed in 1996 by the author, Rogers said he voted against the bill because there was talk that public money would be used to finance the activities of the Citizens' Council. "I thought that was an improper—if not unconstitutional—use of public funds," he said. "I wasn't in sympathy with all the activities of the Citizens' Council anyway, so I voted against it."

Rogers's opposition to the bill is interesting because of his later involvement with the CIA. Rogers represented Warren County, a Mississippi River district adjacent to Issaquena County. In the years following World War II, both counties were used by the CIA as a safe haven for agents put out to pasture due to retirement, stress, or illness. Rogers ran for reelection in 1969 and won. He remained in the legislature until 1977, when he resigned to work for the CIA.

Rogers worked on the Intelligence Community staff, a division of the CIA that coordinated the intelligence-gathering activities of more than thirteen governmental agencies, including the Defense and Justice departments. "I was in the part that dealt with computers," he said. "It was fascinating work." Whether he read the information or not, subsequent reports on the very Commission he voted to defeat surely passed through his CIA office.

Waits was one of the most influential men in the House because of his expertise on tax issues. He voted for the bill, but was not too happy about it. He declined to have his name on the bill as a sponsor.

"After it was passed, some of us talked about it and developed increased misgivings about it," says Winter. Those misgivings resulted in a motion to reconsider. By the time the bill came up for the final vote, forty-nine lawmakers had backed away from it, including Winter, who this time around voted against it.

The final vote was 91 in favor of the bill, with 23 against and 26 not voting. It sailed through the Senate without a dissenting vote.

The Mississippi Capitol rotunda offers a splendid example of the richness of the architecture of public buildings constructed at the turn of the century. In many ways, the building is a replica of the national capitol in Washington, D.C. A three-story edifice with matching east and west wings, the Mississippi Capitol has a blue and gold dome punctuated with large, colorful panels of stained glass that hover over the rotunda and connect the east and west wings.

The airy space beneath the rotunda is open from the ground floor to the apex of the dome, providing a spectacular sight to anyone who stands on the ground floor and looks straight up. On the second floor, between the east and west wings, is the governor's office. Eight marble pillars reach from the second floor to the third floor, setting off the governor's suite with an imposing aura of power and historical continuity.

It was behind the heavily varnished oak door of the governor's private chambers that J.P. Coleman organized the Mississippi State Sovereignty Commission on May 2, 1956. Under the new law, the governor and lieutenant governor were responsible for its operation. To exert that oversight, the governor was empowered to appoint an overall director as well as a director of public relations.

Four months earlier, upon taking the oath of office, Coleman had observed: "I have not the slightest fear that four years hence when my successor assumes his official oath that the separation of races in Mississippi will be left intact."

The Commission was there to make sure of that.

Coleman appointed a member of the legislature, Representative Ney Gore of Quitman County, to be the Commission's first director. Leonard Hicks, a former head of the Mississippi highway patrol, was put in charge of the investigative department. An ex-FBI agent, Zack Van Landingham, was hired as an investigator.

For the important post of public relations director, Coleman chose the man who had served as his publicity manager in the 1955 campaign—Hal DeCell, editor of the weekly *Deer Creek Pilot.* The title "public relations director" was little more than a euphemism for the person chosen to manage the news media.

Boasting an all-star cast with prior associations not only with the Mississippi political hierarchy but with J. Edgar Hoover, the Commission was given office space on the senate side of the capitol in rooms adjacent to the governor's office.

Even as the Commission's secretaries were arranging empty filing cabinets and desks, and preparing for the flood of paperwork they were told would be coming their way, the FBI was undertaking a secret domestic surveillance program, code named "Cointelpro." Its original purpose was to disrupt and neutralize the activities of the American Communist Party, but it quickly became something else.

Hoover launched the secret operation as a response to earlier Supreme Court rulings that had limited the bureau's power to monitor dissident groups. Twenty years later, when Cointelpro—an acronym for counterintelligence program—came under congressional scrutiny, it would be described by a Senate committee as a "vigilante operation aimed squarely at preventing exercise of First Amendment rights of speech and association."

On May 16, 1956, ten days after stories about the Commission's creation appeared in newspapers across the state, Byron De La Beckwith, a thirty-five-year-old tobacco salesman from Greenwood, Mississippi, typed out a letter to Governor Coleman.

"Nothing I know of would give me greater pleasure than to be allowed to serve as an investigator for the purpose of assisting Chief L.C. Hicks in uncovering plots by the NAACP to integrate our beloved State," said Beckwith in the letter. "I am long and strong for maintaining segregation."

As part of his employment application, Beckwith cited his experience as an ex-Marine at Guadalcanal, where he received the Purple Heart, his membership in both the National Rifle Association and the Greenwood Citizens' Council, and his proficiency with firearms. He said he was "expert with a pistol, good with a rifle and fair with a shotgun . . . and RABID ON THE SUBJECT OF SEGREGATION."

CHAPTER 2

1957 – 1959

Hal DeCell was one of the most talented newspaper editors in Mississippi. Since 1949, he and his wife, Carolyn, had published the *Deer Creek Pilot,* a small-circulation, ad-starved weekly in Rolling Fork, a small town in the Delta best known as the home of bluesman Muddy Waters and former governor Fielding L. Wright, who had played a prominent role at the Memphis gathering.

During the 1955 gubernatorial campaign, DeCell had worked as J.P. Coleman's public relations director, so when a similar-sounding position at the Sovereignty Commission opened up, DeCell, with his connections to both Coleman and Wright, was the logical choice. By today's standards, DeCell's $7,294.41 annual salary at the Commission would place him at poverty level, but in 1956 dollars it was a significant sum, especially for the publisher of a struggling newspaper put out on a hand-operated, hot-lead-typeset printing press.

When he reported to the offices of the Commission on May 15 to begin his duties, DeCell was overwhelmed by the contrast between his dusty, paper-cluttered cubicle at the newspaper and his elegant new workspace. His new job would keep him in the limelight and put him just a handshake away from the governor.

The first thing DeCell did was to organize a series of out-of-state trips for himself and Carolyn. In a report to Ney Gore, the Commission director, he explained his purpose was "to get our side of the story to the hometown newspapers outside the South." He launched that mission in July 1956 with a trip to the annual meeting of the National Editorial Association, held that year in Louisville, Kentucky. At the meeting, he distributed Commission literature and networked with editors he thought would be useful to the cause. "Personal contact adds immensely to the effect and impact of the direct mailings," he explained in a report. "I took my wife with me to work the women's groups, since such women are often extremely influential in the formulation of editorial policy, and, in addition, the fact that she is with me allows me to move more freely among the other couples, since most of those in attendance are also accompanied by their wives."

That summer, the Citizens' Council in Clarksdale, Mississippi, complained to the Commission that NBC television had sent a film crew to the city to interview people about school desegregation. DeCell made some inquiries and learned that the interviews would be aired on a program called "Outlook."

After explaining to Ney that NBC "could ruin [them]" by the manner in which they edited the film, he reserved a room at the Hotel Commodore for himself and Carolyn, and flew to New York, where he talked his way into the NBC studios. To his surprise, the producers permitted him to sit in the editing room as an advisor while engineers worked on the film. Whenever he saw comments he thought unflattering to Mississippi, he asked the editors to set aside those portions of the film.

When he returned to Jackson, he filed a report that explained why he thought his mission had been an unqualified success: "Although they didn't know it at the time, I stuck the removed film clippings in my briefcase and later destroyed them. When we left New York, the film was scheduled to appear on August 26th. However, immediately upon my return I heard from New York that Reuven Frank of NBC had canceled it because he said it would make him look like a segregationist. I imagine it was because he couldn't find the clipped portions of the film. . . ."

Racially, the situation in Mississippi that spring and summer was rancid—and potentially explosive. That April, *Look* magazine published an article entitled "The Shocking Story of Approved Murder in Mississippi." The story focused on Emmett Till, the fourteen-year-old black youth who was killed in the summer of 1955 for whistling at a pretty white woman in a small community just outside Greenwood.

Till, who had come to Mississippi only two weeks earlier from Chicago, was dragged from his great-uncle's cabin, severely beaten and shot once in the head. His killers tied a 70–pound cotton-gin fan around his neck with barbed wire and tossed his body into the Tallahatchie River.

Two white men, J.W. Milam and Roy Bryant, the husband of the woman with whom Till had flirted, were charged with the murder. After a trial that lasted only four days, both men were acquitted by an all-white, all-male jury. Till was not the only black murdered that summer. The Reverend George Washington Lee was killed in the Delta town of Belzoni by a shotgun blast after he became the first black in that community to register to vote. No one was ever arrested for his murder.

In Brookhaven, a black man, who had been campaigning for the defeat of a white incumbent, was murdered on the courthouse lawn in broad daylight. The sheriff witnessed the shooting, but refused to arrest the killer.

The national media responded with horror at events in Mississippi, as did the NAACP. *Life* magazine published a full-page editorial, "In Memoriam: Emmett Till," that said Till's father had died in Italy fighting for his country during World War II. In response, the *Jackson Daily News,* which under the editorial leadership of Jimmy Ward had become one of the most staunchly segregationist dailies in the South, sent a reporter to Chicago to interview Till's mother. Based on that interview, the *Jackson Daily News* ran a story stating that Till's father actually had been hanged in Italy for murder and rape. The war of words over Emmett Till continued well into the summer of 1956.

Shortly after DeCell's visit to New York, states' rights activists from seven states (the same individuals who had formed the Federation for Constitutional Government) met in Jackson to discuss ways of combining their efforts. A few weeks later they met again in Memphis, where representatives of right-wing groups from twenty-five states gathered to listen to John U. Barr's plans for Southern domination.

DeCell missed the Memphis meeting because he already had made plans to attend the New England Press Association meeting on Cape Cod in Massachusetts. Carolyn accompanied him on the trip (at DeCell's expense) and they stayed at the Belmont Hotel in West Harwich-by-the-Sea. While there, DeCell was successful in setting up a guided tour of Mississippi for twenty-two New England editors and publishers. "Each of those invited were handpicked [by] me after private and public conversations to ascertain their fairness in approach and their sentiments," DeCell reported. "It is possible that I may wind up with one or two lemons in the crowd, but no more than that. I also was successful in getting most of the officials in the association and the president of the National Editorial Association."

While DeCell was in Massachusetts screening editors, Ney Gore undertook a two-day, 598–mile road trip through Mississippi in an effort to recruit support for the Commission. He met with cohorts in Greenwood on September 15, but it is not known if he spoke with Byron De La Beckwith on that date. It may be assumed that he did, since Beckwith was on the membership committee of the Greenwood Citizens' Council and his letter to Governor Coleman had been hand-delivered to Gore by the governor's secretary, a gesture that, however intended, provided Gore with a contact person in Greenwood.

The week after DeCell returned to Jackson, he and Gore drove to New Orleans to meet with members of the Federation for Constitutional Government. It was their most important meeting to date. DeCell and Gore shared a room at the elegant Roosevelt Hotel, staying four days in an effort to establish with the federation a plan of attack acceptable to representatives from the other states.

When they returned to Jackson, Gore submitted a report to the governor in which he sheepishly explained the "excess expense" for entertainment costs: "Since we were the originators of the meeting it fell our due to serve as hosts." The weekend after they came back, DeCell returned to New Orleans for a second meeting to organize a group he called the "Voice of the South." Like Gore, he apologized for excessive entertainment expenses.

Later that fall, DeCell made two more trips, the first to the National Editorial Association meeting in Chicago, where he was able to persuade an editorial writer for the *Chicago Daily News* to see things Mississippi's way. On his second trip he went to Los Angeles, where he spent a week or so with the producers of a film about race relations in Mississippi.

"When I left, I told the producers I would help them get the film footage they needed from Mississippi showing our side of the situation if they would promise to include it, among other things," DeCell told Gore upon his return. "They agreed so I'm kind of hopeful at this point."

By October 1956, passions were veering out of control in Mississippi, Tennessee, and Louisiana—partly because of a year-long barrage of national publicity about race relations in the South, but also because it was a presidential election year.

Squared off against Republicans Dwight Eisenhower and Richard Nixon were Democrats Adlai Stevenson and Estes Kefauver. It was a nightmare choice for right-wing radicals, racists, the bosses of organized crime, and states' righters across the South. Most of them did not even *know* a Republican, much less have a business history with one. Their political and economic empires had been built entirely within the framework of the Democratic Party.

The Eisenhower–Nixon ticket scared them to death. But even more frightening was the prospect of having Estes Kefauver as vice president.

Kefauver's most vocal enemies in Mississippi were Senator Eastland, who made no secret of his dislike of the senator from Tennessee, and U.S. Representative John Bell Williams, who announced three weeks before the election that he was going to support the States' Rights ticket.

Williams's announcement brought an uncharacteristically harsh response from Governor Coleman, who supported the Democratic ticket. Coleman told reporters Williams was "taking off" on a "political snipehunt." The reference to a snipehunt—a well-known outdoor game in which the victim is purposely left "holding the bag"—was designed to make Williams appear a buffoon in his opposition to the Democratic ticket.

The Memphis cartel was fearful of Kefauver. It knew from long experience how beneficial—and how potentially disastrous—political power was to their long-range goals. Before his defeat in 1952, Senator McKellar had pumped millions into Memphis, much of it going into the coffers of the cartel, which had long since switched its focus to construction, land development, and various legitimate storefront businesses. To the outside observer, cartel members had gone legitimate, but beneath that veneer of respectability operated the same old network of graft, extortion, and political corruption.

By McKellar's own tally he had secured federal funds for a $6.5 million harbor development in Memphis, a naval air base at nearby Millington that grew into one of the Navy's premier training centers for pilots, a bridge across the Mississippi River, a veterans hospital, and hundreds of housing projects. Not every business that benefited from those multimillion dollar projects was in the cartel, but organized crime families certainly received their share.

By the 1950s, according to confidential sources, the Memphis cartel had established business links with the New Orleans mob by setting up legitimate companies in the Crescent City designed to benefit from McKellar's political influence, especially in the area of government construction loans. Memphis reciprocated, as would become apparent to Drug Enforcement Agency (DEA) officials in later years, by allowing New Orleans to form a joint venture with Florida crime families for the transportation and sale of illegal drugs in Memphis.

The Memphis cartel was opposed to Kefauver for financial reasons, but it had no intentions of establishing connections with Eisenhower and the Republican Party. That was too risky. Its plan was simple: defeat Kefauver and establish a new influence within the Democratic Party.

Working out of his Washington law firm, Abe Fortas cemented his relationship with Lyndon Johnson and looked for new opportunities wherever he could find them. One of his first cases was to represent Federated Department Stores in a lawsuit with the Federal Trade Commission, which had challenged the company's acquisition of a store in Houston. Before the decade ended, Fortas used his Memphis connections to facilitate a merger between Federated and Goldsmiths, Memphis's oldest department store.

By 1955, the entire world knew of Carlos Marcello's hatred of Kefauver. For defying Kefauver's committee, Marcello was convicted of contempt of Congress and sentenced to serve six months in prison. However, that conviction would later be overturned by an appeals court, which ruled he was within his rights to plead the Fifth Amendment 152 times. The federal government had issued its first deportation order against Marcello in 1953. Two years later, Marcello was still fighting that order while seeing Kefauver's face each day on television and in the newspapers. It would be four years before he would find someone he hated more. Meanwhile, any individuals or organizations that were opposed to Kefauver could count on Marcello's help, clandestine or otherwise.

The 1956 presidential election was a disaster for the Democratic Party— Eisenhower beat Stevenson by a margin of only seven million popular votes, but because he received 442 electoral votes to Stevenson's 89, the victory was of landslide dimensions—and it spawned a fearsome new coalition that would dominate Southern politics for decades to come. The coalition had solidified earlier in the year when the "Southern Manifesto," co-authored by Senator James Eastland and signed by ninety-six congressmen, declared the Supreme Court decrees on integration "unconstitutional."

On one side of the new coalition were James Eastland, John Bell Williams, John U. Barr, Leander Perez, Carlos Marcello, the Memphis cartel, the Mississippi Sovereignty Commission, and dozens of right-wing political action groups scattered across the country. On the other side was . . . the rest of humanity.

The coalition caused a rift in Mississippi's leadership, with some leaders such as Governor Coleman remaining loyal to the Democratic Party and others calling for the creation of a new states' rights party. The rift had a cooling effect on the Sovereignty Commission, which was reluctant to take sides. Once the fallout from the election subsided, the Commission sprang back into action. By early 1957, racial violence had subsided and the new focus of attention was on education. Everyone understood that that was the racial battleground of the future.

Early in the year, Governor Coleman made headlines when he said he thought it "inevitable" that Mississippi would close its colleges if an African American were admitted by court order. He blamed all the "trouble" on "professional agitators" who were getting the state's uneducated masses all riled up. At times, he seemed schizophrenic in his policy statements. One day he was threatening to close the state's schools; the next he was attacking hard-core racists such as John Bell Williams, who advocated the same thing. Eventually, Coleman's vacillations would jeopardize the effectiveness of the Commission and ultimately lead to its takeover by extremists; but for the moment, at least, the secret agency struggled along, making up the rules as it went.

By early 1957, it was apparent that DeCell's strategy to use the national media to the Commission's advantage was showing results. When eighteen editors and publishers from New England traveled to Mississippi at state expense late in 1956, most of those polled by local media said they were keeping an open mind about segregation.

Coleman met with the editors and answered their questions about race relations in the state. Said the governor: "As far as I am concerned, there will be no integration in Mississippi. I don't say that boastfully, but because it is for the best interests of the state." Asked by Richard Robertson of the *Darien* (Connecticut) *Review* how he saw the strife ending, Coleman answered that he thought it would be a source of "unrest and unhappiness" for four or five years, then would "settle itself of its own weight."

On the surface, the Commission was doing its job. Its first year in operation it co-opted (bribed, cajoled, outsmarted) enough newspaper editors and reporters outside the South to strongly influence a significant amount of media coverage of what was happening in the state. That was important not just for its public relations benefits, which were obvious, but because the recruitment of members of the news media for work in the Commission's inner sanctum was a top priority.

It was what was happening beneath the surface that increasingly began to take on sinister overtones. Quietly, without fanfare or public recognition, the Commission's investigative unit—ex-police chief Hicks and ex-FBI agent Van Landingham—organized an extensive filing system based on the one used by the FBI for Cointelpro.

No one knows what information went into the Commission files that first year, but vouchers filed with the state auditor's office indicate that Hicks traveled over 2,000 miles the first year. The vouchers also show that the Commission wasted no time in recruiting black informants. The first two black leaders to receive money from the Commission, according to records kept by the state auditor, were the Reverend H.H. Hume and Percy Green, both of whom told interviewers for a television documentary about Mississippi that they believed in segregation. For their endorsements of racial separation, Hume received $150 and Green received $35.

To make sure the documentary, which was produced by the Fund for the Republic of the South, conveyed the proper message, DeCell went to Atlanta, where the film was now being edited. It was the same film that had drawn him to Los Angeles the previous year. His concern was that it would be too critical of the South's efforts to maintain segregation. When he returned to Jackson, he submitted a report to Gore that glowed with enthusiasm.

"When they first started this film they entitled it *Crises in the South*," DeCell said. "Nowhere in the film did they have anyone giving our side of the situation, and it included such detrimental stories as the Till case, [and] interviews with NAACP leaders. . . . Fortunately, our efforts have been successful almost 100 percent. I have managed to get them to remove the Till case and the NAACP leaders and to insert sections on Conwell Sykes, chairman of the Greenville Citizens Council; Leroy Percy, past president of the Delta Council; Rev. H.H. Humes and another negro who believes in segregation; excerpts from the governor's inaugural address; and in general to tone down the original implications of the film, including changing the title to *Segregation and the South*. . . . Personally I am thoroughly satisfied with our progress in dealing with what could have been a block-buster against us."

In late March 1957, DeCell and his wife went to New York City for a meeting of the National Editorial Association. While there, he established contacts with network newsmen from CBS and NBC television, and he met with an editor at J.B. Lippincott, a publisher that had plans to release a book entitled *Mississippi Dialogue*. In his report to Gore, DeCell described the book as one that was "not at all kind to the state," but he advised him not to worry about it: "The book will not be published."

On their way back to Mississippi, DeCell and his wife stopped off in Washington, D.C., where he met with Al Friendly, managing editor of the *Washington Post*. Friendly was writing a series of articles about a recent visit to Mississippi and the South. "I may have tempered his viewpoint a little, but won't know until his articles begin to appear," DeCell said in his report. "He will send me copies."

Gore had met DeCell in New York and gone with him to the National Editorial Association meeting, but he stayed on six days, at Governor Coleman's request, so that he could meet privately with television executives. In his report to the governor, Gore said he thought the executives would be interested in a tour of Mississippi. As was customary in his reports, he apologized for excessive expenses. He said the extra money was spent on "entertaining individuals from NBC, CBS, and ABC television."

DeCell's last trip before the fiscal year ended in June was to Los Angeles and San Francisco, where he attended another meeting of the National

Editorial Association. "We made some friends and planted the seeds for a lot more," he said in his report. "I also worked the chief editorial writer of the *Call Bulletin* in San Francisco, and he promised to give us some beneficial editorial mention in the future."

DeCell and Gore were not the only members of the Commission who traveled extensively that year. Also on the Commission account were the trips of six state lawmakers, three appointees of Governor Coleman, and Lieutenant Governor Carroll Gartin, all of whom drove a total of 16,551 miles on Commission business the first fiscal year. The most dedicated Commission members, according to records of per diem payments made for attendance at the monthly meetings, were Senator William Burgin of Columbus, Senator Earl Evans of Canton, Representative William Johnson of Decatur, and W.S. Henley, a lawyer from Hazlehurst.

Politically, Mississippi entered a short-lived cooling off period in 1957, as did the other states in the Federation for Constitutional Government. With no elections to excite the politicians, they found other outlets for their energies. If the truth be known, Mississippians were running out of ideas on how to fight integration.

Coleman already had signed a bill repealing the state's compulsory school attendance laws. The legislature had passed a "breach of the peace" bill aimed at the NAACP, the purpose of which was to make it a crime for anyone to encourage disobedience of state laws, customs, or traditions. In south Mississippi, a grand jury called for statewide screening of all school and library books for the purpose of banning any books deemed critical of the Southern way of life.

Most of the race-baiting that occurred in Mississippi that year came from the Citizens' Councils. Under the leadership of William J. Simmons, this racist organization formed countless cells in small communities throughout the state. One of the most novel approaches taken by the Council during this time was to support the allegation that the "racial revolution" taking place in America was the result of a Communist conspiracy hatched in the Soviet Union. Thus, to be in favor of integration was to be against mom, apple pie, and the American flag. Close friends of Simmons, such as Medford Evans, editor of the Council's magazine, *The Citizen,* or Louis Hollis, national director of the Council, would not have been surprised by that approach. All three men were also members of the super-secret John Birch Society, a right-wing organization that had a large national following and a reputation for extremist dialogue.

The founder of the Association of Citizens' Councils, which coordinated efforts among the various state groups, was Louisiana's Leander Perez, who once attracted national attention with his characterization of the "two types" of blacks he had observed: "Bad ones are niggers and good ones are darkies." What made Perez dangerous was not so much his racist attitudes, which unfortunately were shared by a substantial percentage of the population, but his enormous wealth and political influence, most notably with Senator Eastland, the potent political link between New Orleans and Memphis.

The most active company with which Perez was associated was the Delta Development Company, which specialized in oil leases. At one time, it was said that every major oil company in the country did business with Delta. In 1941 the Louisiana corporation was dissolved and its assets were transferred to a new company, the Delta Development Company of Delaware. Most of Perez's business dealings with Memphis were through Delta, various construction companies, and the *Plaquemines Gazette,* a newspaper in his home parish that did some of its printing in Memphis.

The Mississippi media in the 1950s, with a few notable exceptions, was a monolithic force united behind the efforts of the Commission. The state's two largest newspapers were the morning *Clarion-Ledger,* and the afternoon *Jackson Daily News,* both published in Jackson by the influential Hederman family.

Editorially, the two newspapers were archconservative. Their opinion pieces parroted the right-wing rhetoric of the day and aggressively defended the "Southern" way of life. Unfortunately, the newspapers' sentiments extended to their news reporting, resulting in embarrassing lapses in news judgment. Both newspapers could be counted on to kill stories favorable to integration and to slant other stories to promote segregation.

Tom Hederman, editor of the *Clarion-Ledger,* was a strong supporter of the Citizens' Councils as well as the Commission. His editorials praised the work of the Councils and the Commission, and behind the scenes he used his considerable influence to promote their agenda. As a result, he was privy to Commission dossiers and was provided with reports on its activity. DeCell didn't have to resort to manipulating the Hederman media (they also owned an interest in television station WJTV); their support was understood.

By 1957, when he took over the editorship of the *Jackson Daily News,* Jimmy Ward had established a national reputation as a spokesman for conservative causes. Ward was taller than Hederman and, unlike Hederman who was a teetotaler, a hard drinker. He had an infectious sense of humor that contrasted vividly with Hederman's grim-faced lack of levity. While Hederman's power had derived from his personal wealth, which was considerable by Mississippi standards, Ward's influence was a direct result of his news instincts and his ability to use the English language as a weapon. His daily front-page column, "Covering the Crossroads," was popular with readers across the state, and often attracted praise from radio commentator Paul Harvey, who for years referred to Ward in his broadcasts as "Jackson Jimmy." Ward was a firm believer in the effectiveness of humor in politics and he permitted *Daily News* cartoonist Bob Howie to moonlight for Citizens' Council publications, though Howie never signed the work he did for them.

In contrast to the Hederman press were four smaller circulation Mississippi newspapers that urged a more moderate approach to politics: the *Delta Democrat-Times* in Greenville, edited by Hodding Carter; the *Lexington Times* and *Durant News,* edited by Hazel Brannon Smith; and the Jackson *State Times,* edited by J. Oliver Emmerich, who subsequently published newspapers in McComb and Greenwood.

Carter and Smith were both awarded Pulitzer Prizes for their work. Carter's 1946 award was for editorials that eloquently pleaded for justice for Japanese Americans interned in prison camps during World War II. Smith's 1964 award was for editorials that called for racial understanding.

After Carter accepted his award, Theodore Bilbo, who served two terms as governor and three as United States senator, threatened to go to Greenville to give Carter a good "skinning." Bilbo lambasted Carter for accepting "a Poolitzer-blitzer prize given by a bunch of nigger-loving Yankeefied communists for advocating the mongrelization of the races." In reply, Carter wrote an editorial that defined a "bilbo" as a "reckless, intolerant vilifier." The Mississippi legislature responded by passing a resolution that branded Carter a liar. And so it went.

In 1957, FBI director J. Edgar Hoover ordered his agents to monitor the activities of Martin Luther King and the Southern Christian Leadership Conference (SCLC). FBI memos indicate Hoover was disturbed by a Washington, D.C., rally that drew 35,000 demonstrators. King, who had been elected president of SCLC, mesmerized the crowd by shouting over and over again, "Give us the ballot."

At that time, the bureau's top secret Cointelpro program, which allowed agents to spy on American citizens, had been in operation for little more than a year. King had been on the national scene for only two years, but Hoover was obsessed with the civil rights leader. Although the FBI did not launch a formal investigation of King and SCLC until 1962, Hoover had ordered agents to break into the SCLC offices in Atlanta as early as January 1959 to gather information. Over the next five years, FBI agents would break into the offices of the civil rights organization at least twenty times, often to install electronic listening devices. Hoover later cited Attorney General Robert Kennedy's 1962 approval of electronic surveillance of King and SCLC headquarters as the authorization for the break-ins. The fact that break-ins were involved to install the listening devices is indicated in a 1966 memo from FBI assistant director Charles Brennan to William Sullivan, another assistant FBI director, in which it was disclosed that Kennedy's successor Nicholas Katzenbach was advised that "trespass" was involved in the surveillance.

When Hoover's agents illegally obtained information about American citizens, it was kept in a special filing system. For example, if an FBI agent broke into an individual's home and discovered a letter critical of Hoover, he would forward the contents of that letter to FBI headquarters under a code name such as Cointelpro. That way it could be filed without giving any apparent indication of the contents of the file. If the individual named in the file discovered the break-in and filed a lawsuit, he would find, after a court-ordered search of the files, that there was no file in his name in the vast FBI vault. It is the same type of filing system ex-FBI agent Van Landingham used in setting up the Mississippi Sovereignty Commission.

After more than a year of relative quiet on the racial battleground, an event occurred on April 24, 1959, that threw Mississippi into turmoil. On that night, a mob of gun-packing and club-toting men burst into the jail at Poplarville and dragged Mack Charles Parker from the third-floor cell block and down the steps into the street.

Parker, a black man who had been charged with raping a pregnant young white woman, was beaten about the head and tossed into the backseat of a car. Terrified, Parker screamed for help the entire time. No one in the small town went to his aid.

Parker was taken in a procession of five cars to a bridge over the muddy, churning Pearl River. There he was shot twice in the chest with a .38–caliber pistol. His body was weighted down with chains and then tossed over the railing into the river. The men stood on the bridge and watched as the body sank out of sight, then they returned to their cars and drove off into the night.

Within hours of the abduction, the highway patrol, Governor Coleman, the FBI, and the White House were notified. The next day, news reporters from across the nation descended on Poplarville. Despite the high-profile nature of the case, no one was ever charged with Parker's murder.

Four years after the lynching, a Mississippi circuit judge was speaking to a civics club in Connecticut on behalf of the Sovereignty Commission when someone in the audience asked him if he thought Parker's killers would ever be brought to justice.

Without thinking, the judge responded that three of the killers had already died.

The Mack Charles Parker lynching wasn't the only event to make life difficult for the Commission. In March 1958, a full year before the lynching, there had been talk in the Mississippi legislature of abolishing the Commission. According to news reports, questions about the Commission's efficiency were raised during a debate on whether the legislature should investigate the NAACP.

Four senators—W.C. Lucas, Ellis Bodron, W.F. Rosenblatt, and Jewell Smith—introduced a bill to do away with the agency. "I don't think it's worth $250,000," Lucas told reporters. "I don't think it's any good." The bill was a product of the Legislative Tax Study Committee, chaired by Representative Hilton Waits of Washington County, a predominately black area that had a reputation for moderation in racial matters. Among the legislators there was talk of using the money spent on the Commission to finance activities of the Citizens' Councils.

In the end, it was decided that the General Legislative Investigating Committee, not the Commission, would undertake a probe of NAACP activities. The Commission was granted funds for another two years, even though it was clear that dissatisfaction with the secret agency was growing.

Internally, the Commission was struggling to carry out its mandate. Director Ney Gore had abruptly resigned in the latter part of 1957, and the agency was rudderless until well into 1958, at which time a caretaker administrator, Maurice Malone, was hired to oversee the agency. In September 1958, the Commission was jolted by a report issued by the state auditor that was highly critical of the Commission's financial dealings.

The report pointed out abuses in the travel expense accounts and said telephone calls that had "no connection with the commission's activities" were made at state expense. DeCell was devastated by the report. Up until that point, he had had the reputation of being a hardworking journalist. He was proud of the editorials he had written over the years calling lawmakers to task for their wasteful spending. Now the spending practices of the

Commission had been called into question. The experience would embitter him and eventually turn him against the Commission.

Not much is known about the Commission's activities during 1958 and 1959. Investigators continued to compile dossiers on anyone who had a reputation as a liberal, but public pronouncements were infrequent. DeCell, his pride injured by the state auditor's report, quietly faded into the woodwork.

The biggest crisis the Commission faced in 1958 occurred when a black man named Clyde Kennard attempted to enroll in the all-white Mississippi Southern College (now called the University of Southern Mississippi) in Hattiesburg. After his application was received, Kennard was called into a meeting with college president William McCain and Commission agent Van Landingham, who attempted to determine his reasons for wanting to enroll in the college. After he left the office, he was arrested on campus and charged with reckless driving and possession of five bottles of liquor, at that time a crime in "dry" Mississippi.

With the help of the NAACP, Kennard successfully fought the charges and pressed on with his efforts to enroll in the college, but he was again arrested, this time on charges he was an accomplice in the theft of chicken feed. He was convicted and sentenced to seven years at Parchman penitentiary. His alleged accomplice, who testified against him, received a suspended sentence.

When he heard the verdict, the NAACP's new field director in Mississippi, Medgar Evers, was outraged. He told a reporter the verdict was a "mockery of justice." For making that comment, Evers was arrested and charged with contempt of court. He was sentenced to thirty days in jail.

One day, while working in the cotton fields at the prison, Kennard complained of stomach pains. He was taken to the University of Mississippi Hospital in Jackson, where doctors diagnosed cancer. They operated and recommended that he be paroled because of the "extremely poor" prognosis. Prison officials would not hear of that, and Kennard was returned to Parchman, where he was expected to continue working in the cotton fields. He died before he could reapply for admission to the college.

One major success the Commission had in those years was the recruitment of a prominent black educator: B.L. Bell, longtime principal of the Cleveland Colored Consolidated School, agreed to become an informer.

Known to his friends as Professor Bell, he volunteered his services in a letter to Governor Coleman, which read, in part: "It is my greatest ambition to hold a job with the state Sovereignty Commission. Many white friends of mine here in this county know personally how that I have been able to get over to my people the best things for us."

Coleman sent the letter over to the Commission, which, after talking with Bell, reported that he was "a white man's Negro." By 1959, the Commission was paying Bell $100 a month for his efforts to establish a "secret underground organization of Negroes to assist in maintaining segregation in Mississippi."

Bell's assignment was to attend NAACP meetings, take names, and report back on what was said. Apparently, NAACP officials became suspicious of Bell's loyalty, because at one meeting he was openly accused of being a Commission spy. Bell was vociferous in his denials of an association with the Commission.

Encouraged by the success it had with Bell, the Commission extended its spy network to every county in the state.

CHAPTER 3

1960

It was December 1959 and Mississippi governor J.P. Coleman was in a foul mood. With only a few weeks left in his term of office (state law prohibited governors from running for a second consecutive term), he was a lame-duck administrator, severely limited in what he could accomplish.

The gubernatorial campaign that fall had been unusually vicious, even by Mississippi standards. All three candidates—Lieutenant Governor Carroll Gartin, who had Coleman's support; District Attorney Charles Sullivan; and Jackson attorney Ross Barnett—had waged racist campaigns that focused on preserving segregation, though Sullivan, a resident of the Delta, was the least rabid of the three. There was no other major issue in the campaign. From the outset, it was clear that the candidate who could spew the most venom and make the most promises about preserving the "Southern way of life" would win the election.

Ross Barnett won that contest hands down. His "Roll with Ross" campaign slogan struck just the right chord with the voters. Barnett's message was clear: his predecessor, Governor Coleman, had let the state down by knuckling under to the federal government. He vowed to be a stand-up governor who would not hesitate to use the power of his office to roll over anyone who got in his way, even the federal government.

Barnett's first public appearance after the election was at a dinner held to raise money for the Citizens' Council. In November, two months after the election, Barnett stoked the fires of hate by criticizing a federal government decision to reenter the Poplarville lynching case. He told reporters the federal government had no jurisdiction in the case and should allow local officials to conduct the investigation.

The lynching already had been on everyone's mind all year. After one of the suspects was questioned by the FBI, he was hospitalized for what his doctor called a "nervous breakdown." A second suspect was sent to the hospital for treatment of a cerebral hemorrhage after FBI agents spent several hours grilling him on his whereabouts the day of the lynching. The news media were pumping the story for all it was worth, and the focus shifted from the crime itself to the way the federal government was "abusing" the good citizens of Mississippi.

State Auditor Boyd Golding, who the year before had criticized the Sovereignty Commission for its travel expenses and sloppy record keeping, called on Coleman to run the FBI out of Mississippi. "I never thought I would live to witness the invitation of outsiders to come to the sovereign state of Mississippi to harass, browbeat and torture people to the brink of death," Golding said in a letter to Coleman. Golding told reporters the FBI was using "behind the iron curtain tactics" in its investigation of the lynching.

The FBI's role in the investigation was further criticized after the Associated Press reported that agents had been spotted burning four boxes of papers at an incinerator outside their offices. When reporters tried to see what the agents were burning, they were forced away from the incinerator. The implication was that they were burning important evidence.

The growing hysterics led Coleman to say that he thought race relations in the state had reached a new low. After a meeting with Representative Hilton Waits, Coleman decided to call a special session of the legislature that December for the purpose of "cleaning up some loose ends" of government. Since the legislature was already scheduled to convene in January under the leadership of Governor-elect Ross Barnett, many people were surprised at Coleman's announcement.

The session began with a temporary change in leadership of the House of Representatives. Speaker of the House Walter Sillers had been in Germany on a mission for the U.S. State Department when he suffered a heart attack. From his hospital bed, he designated Waits, a longtime friend and political ally, to be speaker pro tem of the House for the special session. Waits, whose grandfather, Steven Turner, had served on the delegation that wrote the Mississippi Constitution of 1890, had served in the legislature since 1931 and had received national attention as an author of one of the nation's first comprehensive sales tax packages. That August, he was defeated for reelection by DeLoach Cope, a gentleman farmer from near Hollandale whose claim to fame was that he had carried champagne in the cockpit of his fighter plane during service in World War II.

Whatever Coleman had envisioned for the legislature that session, the final product was certainly less than anticipated. For the longest time, no one could figure out why the session was held in the first place. The two most memorable actions taken by the lawmakers dealt with the Civil War and Miss America.

A bill was passed memorializing Walter Williams, who, as a former member of Quantrill's Raiders, had been the last surviving soldier of the Civil War. He had died on December 19, 1959, in a Houston, Texas, hospital. Gone was America's last living link to the bloodiest war in the nation's history. The lawmakers observed a moment of silence for the last soldier, then, with a war whoop that could be heard all the way down the street, turned their attention to more important business—getting a date with Miss America.

A couple of months before the start of that session, Linda Lea Meade had become Mississippi's second Miss America in as many years. The lawmakers were so in awe of her that they voted to invite her to address a joint session of the legislature. The way the lawmakers saw it, the judges for the Miss America contest had not only honored a native of Mississippi, they had endorsed the Southern way of life, which is to say the lawmakers saw it as a vote for segregation.

Thus, with a tip of the hat to veterans of the Civil War—and a wink to a pretty woman whose victory seemed to represent all the values for which they fought—the legislature closed the door on the administration of Governor J.P. Coleman. It wasn't exactly the way Coleman wanted to be remembered, but he must have felt it was better than nothing.

Causing Carlos Marcello the most trouble in New Orleans was a prosecutor named Aaron Kohn, who had taken it upon himself to build a case against the Dixie godfather. To his surprise, the FBI was not cooperative. Agents in the New Orleans bureau described Marcello as a "stupid little man" who did not have the capability to commit the crimes being investigated by Kohn. FBI agents assured Kohn that Marcello was a salesman for the Pelican Tomato Company, and nothing more.

Frustrated by the FBI's reluctance to help in the investigation, Kohn had shifted the focus of his attack to corrupt public officials, who, he said, were taking bribes from Marcello. He had better luck there and succeeded in obtaining indictments on several high-ranking officials in 1957 and 1958. But he refused to give up on Marcello.

In 1959, Senator John Kennedy's brother, Robert Kennedy, was appointed chief counsel of a senate committee investigating corruption in labor and management. Kennedy asked Kohn to come to Washington to personally brief him on Marcello's activities. At the end of that four-hour meeting, according to author John Davis, Kennedy told Kohn: "I can assure you that, sooner or later, we will do something about Mr. Marcello. We cannot permit this kind of corruption to exist in the United States."

At the time of Kennedy's meeting with Kohn, Marcello's deportation order was five years old. Since no nation would accept the native-born Sicilian, the United States could not force him to leave the country. Each time government officials thought they had finally found a country that would accept him, that nation's officials would mysteriously change their minds. Powerful as he was, Marcello was not the only force at work in Louisiana.

Leander Perez was still calling the shots on the political front.

In 1959, Perez could claim Citizens' Council organizations (with a total membership of 100,000) in thirty-four of the state's sixty-four parishes. His greatest political victory came in 1960 when Jimmie Davis succeeded Earl Long as governor. Perez had managed Davis's blatantly racist campaign, and, after Davis took office, Perez was allowed to personally draft a bill to create a Louisiana sovereignty commission. Perez used the Mississippi commission as a model and stepped up his attacks against integration, often reprinting and distributing race-baiting speeches delivered by his friend, Representative John Bell Williams of Mississippi. The AFL-CIO demanded, but did not get, a federal investigation of Perez's activities in support of right-wing groups, labeling them "neo Klan" organizations.

Toward the end of 1960, Perez advised a group of right-wing activists in Biloxi, Mississippi, on how to prevent blacks from using facilities on Gulf Coast beaches. He urged the gathering to follow the lead of Governor Ross Barnett. Before leaving Biloxi, he issued a warning to those in attendance: If they didn't prevent blacks from using the beaches, they "may as well close [their] shops and hotels, barricade [their] homes and keep [their] wives and daughters off the front porches."

Leander Perez was on a roll in Louisiana, but it was his longtime enemy, Earl Long, who had the last word. "Whatchya gonna do now, Leander?" Long asked in a taunting manner when it became obvious the schools would have to be desegregated. "The feds have got the atom bomb."

In Memphis, the heat was on in a different way. The problem there was not an investigation; no one had ever investigated the Memphis cartel—not in thirty years of operation. The problem was economic. After growing fat on government contracts during and after World War II, and then again during the Korean War, the Memphis cartel was fearful of losing its political grip during the latter part of the 1950s.

By the start of 1960, the political arm of the Federation for Constitutional Government—now mostly represented by Mississippi, Louisiana, and west Tennessee—was in disarray, with political leaders from most of the other Southern states falling by the wayside. But federation leaders were not disheartened, for they saw the makings of a new alliance with the most powerful wheeler-dealer in Congress, Senator Lyndon Johnson of Texas.

At the beginning of 1960, Johnson was at the height of his congressional power. There were two reasons for that: As Senate majority leader he had a bulldog's grip on all legislation entering and exiting the Senate, and as a close personal friend of his counterpart in the House of Representatives, Speaker Sam Rayburn of Texas, he was able to extend his influence to that body as well. Johnson and Rayburn were an unbeatable pair. Their combined power equaled that of the president.

As the new decade began, Johnson formed a strong dislike of Senator Kefauver, whom he saw as a threat to his presidential ambitions. When a vacancy opened up on the powerful Foreign Relations Committee, Johnson blocked the assignment to Kefauver, who was in line for it, and gave it to Senator John F. Kennedy. It was rumored, prophetically as it turned out, that Johnson was attempting to build an alliance with Kennedy for a possible presidential ticket. Johnson also aligned himself with Senator James Eastland.

In 1960, Abe Fortas was clearly the most significant Memphian in Washington, and his influence with Lyndon Johnson was growing. In early 1960 the hard-talking, flinty-eyed senator from Texas seemed like the Great White Hope, not just to racist politicians in the federation, but to those who had created an underground economy that sometimes teetered on the verge of collapse.

Ironically, Fortas's political ascendancy highlighted a long-simmering area of disagreement between the Memphis cartel and federation leaders. The Memphis cartel, which had the support of Jewish businessmen, was held at arm's length by the federation. Some members, such as Perez, were just as prejudiced against Jews as they were against African Americans. That anti-Semitic streak had been evident as far back as 1944, when Memphis political boss E.H. Crump wrote Senator McKellar a letter chastising him for using anti-Semitic comments. Crump reminded McKellar that Memphis Jews were on their team and suggested he "refrain from making it appear that [he was] attacking the Jewish people."

On January 10, 1960, Ross Barnett was sworn in as governor. It was a bitterly cold day, and Barnett, red-faced and bleary-eyed, scurried down the stairway on his way to the reviewing platform, almost bowling over a startled teenager who suddenly found himself in the governor-elect's path. Ross Barnett didn't stand aside for anyone—not in politics, not in real life. In his inaugural address, Barnett pledged that segregation would be maintained "at all costs." The only statement that received comparable applause from those gathered in the subfreezing cold at the capitol steps was his castigation of the "radical left-wing elements" of the National Democratic Party." He promised to do something about them as well. With his battle plan in place, he proceeded to launch the most vicious attack against blacks and white liberals in the state's history.

The new governor's first priority was to beef up the Sovereignty Commission. For the past eighteen months or so it had foundered on indecision as Coleman limited its activities to spying and the manufacture of dossiers on black and liberal residents. Exactly what was done with the dossiers is not known, but there is evidence they were passed among state lawmakers who could benefit politically or financially from the secret information they contained.

His first week in office, Barnett met with leaders of the Citizens' Council, which by that time claimed a statewide membership of more than 80,000. He also met with Council leaders from Little Rock, Arkansas, and he traveled to Columbia, South Carolina, to attend a fund-raising banquet for the Association of Citizens' Councils of South Carolina. One result of those meetings was a decision by Barnett to allow the Sovereignty Commission to make sizable donations to the Council war chest.

Since the fiscal year ran from July 1 to June 30, Barnett waited until June 1960 to reorganize the Commission. To head up the Commission, he chose Albert Jones, a former Hinds County sheriff. He was tough, had extensive contacts in law enforcement, and could be counted on to carry out orders without asking troublesome questions.

For public relations director, Barnett selected the man who had handled his publicity during the election campaign, Erle Johnston. His job was to keep the state's news media in line. Only two or three newspapers in the state had dared suggest that black residents should have equal rights, so it was not a difficult task, but it did involve a great deal of behind-the-scenes maneuvering to make sure that the media understood what they were to print and what they were not to print.

Johnston was well suited for the job. As publisher of the weekly *Scott County Times* at Forest, Mississippi, he had strong credentials as a journalist. He was on a first-name basis with most of the state's newspaper editors and publishers, and he knew how to apply pressure when it was needed. Even more important, Johnston had a flare for politics. He had proved himself during the campaign to be a skillful manipulator, not only of the media but of the white-male voting pool that decided the outcome of all statewide elections. Also hired were five investigators—Virgil Downing, Hugh Boren, Andrew Hopkins, Tom Scarbrough, and Robert Thomas—six secretaries, and a librarian.

Attending the first meeting, in addition to Governor Barnett, were Lieutenant Governor Paul B. Johnson, Attorney General Joe T. Patterson, Speaker of the House Walter Sillers, and several senators and representatives appointed to serve as commissioners. Barnett made it clear that he wanted the Commission to be aggressive in its defense of segregation.

For starters, he asked the Commission to approve a request from William J. Simmons of the Citizens' Council for a $20,000 grant and a monthly payment of $5,000 to help support Council activities. Later, when he announced the grant, Commission director Jones justified the financial assistance by pointing out the Councils' "record of solid accomplishment."

In addition, the Commission approved a suggestion by Johnston to send prominent Mississippians out on the road to give speeches in support of segregation. That plan was actually the brainchild of Senator James Eastland, who continued to be a powerful, behind-the-scenes player in Commission activities.

With a staff of six investigators, the Commission undertook covert actions against residents it felt were not loyal to the cause. Investigators interviewed friends and families of targets, photographed them at public meetings, and kept notes on gossip that suggested moral or ethical lapses.

One of the Commission's more ludicrous missions that year was to send an investigator to the Gulf Coast to spy on three hundred Jewish teenagers who had gathered from five states to attend a B'nai B'rith youth meeting. In his report, the investigator wrote: "These youths sang songs and a general party atmosphere prevailed. We observed them and listened to them, but we could observe nothing or hear nothing that indicated that they were advocating subversion, integration or anything of a communistic nature."

The reason for that assignment is rooted in an earlier incident that year on the Gulf Coast. On April 24 a riot broke out when four blacks went swimming in the Mississippi Sound near an all-white beach in Biloxi. Mobs of club-toting whites swarmed over the beach resort. Ten people were injured by gunfire during the fighting, and four others received wounds from hand-to-hand combat that took place on the beach.

In July, Governor Barnett, leading a delegation made up largely of Citizens' Council members, went to Los Angeles to attend the National

Democratic Convention. He was not optimistic the Democratic Party would embrace a states' rights philosophy. All summer, John Kennedy had been touted as the only candidate who could defeat Republican Richard Nixon. The other two most often mentioned as possible candidates were Senators Hubert Humphrey of Minnesota and Lyndon Johnson. As Kennedy traveled around the country, he called Johnson his "principal adversary."

Johnson seemed to think he was a serious contender for the nomination, though few, if any, political commentators thought he had a chance. Johnson's strategy was a mirror image of the Memphis plan that had proved successful for nearly half a century. Following the Crump–McKellar strategy of building a coalition of black and white voters, offering each their support on the basis of excluding the other, Johnson used his post as majority leader to pass a civil rights bill that year in the Senate.

At the time, commentators were baffled by Johnson's strategy, but that's because none understood the role Abe Fortas played as an advisor to Johnson. It is one of the great ironies of the era that a Memphis Jew was the political point man for a Texas politician who openly sought black political support. The Memphis cartel supported segregation because it was good business, and it sought the support of black voters because it kept them in business. Johnson adopted the same dual strategy.

In April 1960, three months before the Democratic convention, *The New Republic* gave Johnson a pat on the back for his support of the civil rights bill, but the magazine expressed confusion over his position. "Where did Johnson stand in the fight over civil rights?" the magazine asked in an editorial. "Certainly, he worked hard to over-ride Southerners who wanted no bill at all. But he also worked—and just as strenuously—to over-ride others who wanted a stronger bill." In the final analysis, concluded the magazine, Johnson had made so many enemies on both sides of the issue that he was left out on a political limb. "On the face of it, Johnson's remarkable performance would seem to have increased his stature as a Presidential candidate," said the magazine. "Curiously, it has worked the other way. Rather than dramatizing his position as a leader of his party, it has dramatized his isolation from the mainstreams of Democratic thought."

In his bid for the nomination, Johnson had made serious errors in judgment. Just because the race card won every hand in Memphis did not mean it would have the same results elsewhere. What Johnson had to figure out was how to maintain the support of the three states left in the federation, while building a political base broad enough to keep him in the game at the national level.

Governor Barnett gave a fire-and-brimstone states' rights speech at the convention that was carried on national television. When he finished speaking, the entire nation knew that white Mississippi opposed the civil rights platform adopted by the delegates and would never support a presidential candidate who endorsed it.

Kennedy's victory at the convention surprised no one. He had made the strongest showing in the primaries by convincing Democrats that he was the only candidate who could beat Nixon. What surprised everyone was his choice for vice president—Lyndon Johnson. Even Johnson was surprised.

Kennedy's strategy was simple. As president, he would need a strong supporter in the important post of Senate majority leader. Johnson was the last person he wanted in that position. His first goal was to "promote" him out of his current job. His second goal was to have a Southerner on the ticket, someone who could mitigate Nixon's support in the South. Kennedy had no personal affection for Johnson, but he was a pragmatist. If elected, he planned to bury Johnson for four years in the most obscure office the nation had to offer. Johnson had little choice but to accept the nomination.

Barnett returned to Jackson and complained about how "nauseating" the convention had made him feel about the political process, but when he was asked if Mississippians should vote for unpledged electors in protest, he said he wanted to see what the Republicans did at their convention before making up his mind. He complained that everyone was out "to get the Negro vote."

Perhaps because it was an election year, civil rights activity increased across the nation. In Montgomery, Alabama, blacks made news when they occupied the municipal library reading room. In Augusta, Georgia, blacks were arrested when they sat in the white section of a city bus. In Beaumont, Texas, there was a sit-in by Lamar Tech students at a downtown lunch counter. In Dallas, a black minister made news when he was served at three previously all-white lunch counters.

"We've known all along that Negroes swing a heavy economic club, especially in towns where they make up over half of the population," the *Wall Street Journal* quoted an Atlanta businessman as saying a few weeks after the sit-ins began. "If they learn how to use that power, they can do a good deal of damage."

Understanding that leverage all too well was Martin Luther King, who promoted sit-ins as an example of the direct, nonviolent action that could turn the tide in favor of the blacks. Official reaction across the South was to arrest anyone engaged in a sit-in.

During the presidential campaign, King was arrested in Atlanta for "parading without a permit" and sentenced to four months at hard labor. When he heard about the arrest, John Kennedy telephoned King's wife, Coretta, and offered his sympathy. He also reaffirmed his intention of eliminating all barriers to integration if elected.

That telephone call cemented Kennedy's already strong position with black voters, but it caused a tremor at FBI headquarters since it suggested that King, by that time J. Edgar Hoover's worst enemy, would have influence in a Kennedy White House. Unknown to Kennedy, Hoover had been conducting covert actions against King for almost two years. That meant the FBI was not only spying on civil rights leaders, it was inadvertently spying on any presidential candidates who contacted them. Although no evidence has yet been found that would indicate King's telephone was bugged on the day Kennedy called, the possibility that it might have been offers a chilling example of how the FBI could have had a negative impact on the political process.

As election day loomed, the tri-state federation saw it had no place to go. If anything, Kennedy stepped up his attack against segregation. At a speech in New York, he promised to integrate the nation's churches in an effort to provide "equal access" to blacks. Richard Nixon, who had fought a tough battle against Barry Goldwater's right-wing flirtations, was in no mood to be accommodating to extremists in the South. Barnett's solution, unpledged electors, had failed miserably four years earlier under the Dixiecrat banner led by Leander Perez and John Barr.

Following the guidelines set by the Sovereignty Commission, the Mississippi news media maintained a solid front behind Barnett, with a few exceptions. Hodding Carter III, who had replaced his father as editor of the *Delta Democrat-Times,* kept up the pressure, as did Oliver Emmerich, by then editor of the McComb *Enterprise-Journal* and the Jackson *State Times.* Emmerich had protested the Commission's funding of the Citizens' Councils, calling the decision a "grave error in judgment."

The Hederman media block was solidly behind Barnett. *The Clarion-Ledger* and the *Jackson Daily News* praised the governor's every move. That support also extended to television stations WJTV and WLBT. Thurgood Marshall, then a civil rights attorney, was being interviewed on the *Today Show,* which was broadcast over WLBT, when suddenly, in the middle of the black attorney's comments, television viewers saw their screens go blank. A logo that said "cable difficulty" appeared on the screen. Moments later, when the Marshall interview was concluded, the *Today Show* returned to the air.

Suspicious of the blackout, Hodding Carter called the NBC network and asked them if there had been transmission difficulties. They replied there had been none. Some time later, Fred Beard, the station manager, attended a Citizens' Council meeting at which he complained about how the networks had become mouthpieces for black propaganda. Then, to wild applause, he confessed that he himself had pulled the plug on the Thurgood Marshall interview.

As election day approached, the Commission grew bolder in its manipulations of public opinion. Erle Johnston called a friendly editor at a newspaper in Pipestone, Minnesota, and asked him to run an editorial he had
written about Mississippi. The editorial bore the headline, "Mississippi Is
Being Watched." It began: "The eyes of the nation will be watching Mississippi on November 8 because results of the election may indicate a new
viewpoint on segregation. . . . A Kennedy victory in Mississippi would indicate that segregation in that state is no longer a concern because Kennedy
says he will integrate life in Mississippi at all levels."

The editor balked at printing the editorial since he said his newspaper
normally didn't run editorials. Johnston asked as a favor, if he would run
off about a dozen newspapers with the editorial for use in Mississippi. The
editor agreed, and Johnston distributed the fake newspapers, advertising the
editorial as one written by a "Minnesota" editor.

Senator James Eastland had his hands full. Everyone, it seemed, wanted
a piece of his hide. Under pressure to support Mississippi's unpledged
elector slate, he had to retreat into his party affiliation. If he didn't support
the Democratic ticket, he explained, he would be stripped of his seniority
and would lose his chairmanship of the powerful Senate Judiciary Committee. That wouldn't do, not at all.

At a televised press conference, Eastland said he would support the
Kennedy–Johnson ticket, but he made it clear that his support did not ex-
tend to the party's platform, which he said was "out of step" with the
American people.

Time magazine labeled Eastland the "nation's most dangerous dema-
gogue." The *New York Times* gave Eastland credit for using his position on
the Judiciary Committee to bottle up 122 civil rights bills. In a 1965 profile
of Eastland for *The Nation* magazine, writer Robert Sherrill offered a description of the senator as a "good planter, a kind planter, who 'never whips
his niggers and would fire any white worker who did.' "

In the article, Sherrill expressed fascination at Eastland's ability to say
things that often flew in the face of reason—and truth—yet left him relatively unscathed. As an example, he pointed out how Eastland would say he
was "against any organization which indulges, which promotes, racial and
religious prejudice, hatred and bigotry," while at the same time supporting
"the John Birch society, the Citizens' Council and every major white-su-
premacy organization" in the South.

Sherrill quoted Eastland as saying, "I have never engaged in a filibuster.

Southern Senators have never filibustered but we have conducted campaigns of education," although the senator had "done service in every anti-civil rights filibuster that has taken place in the Senate in the last twenty-four years."

What Sherrill didn't understand was that in issues as emotionally charged as racial integration, words—or their relationship to the truth—had little meaning to true believers. To a man of Eastland's psychological construction, lying for a good cause was not lying; it was standing up for a higher cause.

"The private image of Eastland as a kindly paternal planter somehow keeps getting gobbled up by his carnivorous public image, however, and despite the best efforts of his friends and family it remains true that none of America's anti-Southern cults has more devotees than the one that directs its hatred at Senator James Eastland," concluded Sherrill. "He, more than any other extant politician, seems to symbolize what so many Negroes, liberals, laborers, intellectuals, seekers, mystics and mavericks are trying to remove from the world."

Eastland did not care what people north of the Mason-Dixon line said about him. Attacks in the media only served to solidify his base of support in Mississippi. By 1960, he was a millionaire many times over. He honestly cared more about a busted tractor on his plantation than he did about anything said about him in the *New York Times*.

When Eastland told Sherrill that Mississippi had "no voting qualifications based on race, none at all," the writer telephoned the NAACP for facts and figures on Eastland's home county. The NAACP pointed out that there were 13,524 blacks of voting age in the county, but only 164 were registered.

Although Eastland turned down a request for a tour of his plantation, Sherrill waited until dark, then got someone to take him onto the plantation over a circuitous route of back roads. Cotton choppers told him they were paid three dollars a day, but only had a four-month work year. Some workers told him they had never tasted beef. One woman told him she had eaten turkey twice: once when she received one as a gift from comedian Dick Gregory, then again when she bought one on an installment plan.

An excellent writer and researcher, Sherrill missed the point, through no fault of his own. Most likely Eastland knew exactly where Sherrill was when he was on the plantation. Those who knew him would not have been surprised if he had hand-picked the workers interviewed by Sherrill. Eastland knew that comments about low wages or beef- and turkey-poor families would help his image in the Magnolia State, not tarnish it.

The real story, the one Sherrill missed, was going on beneath the surface. Eastland's job was to take care of business—and he did that as well as anyone has ever done it. Racism of the sort expressed by Eastland was never about race. It was always about money—and political influence. Those were the real issues. If there was no money in being a racist, Eastland might never have been one.

Amid the hot-tempered racial rhetoric bandied about in 1960 were serious issues that impacted the tri-state federation. As chairman of the Judiciary Committee, Eastland had enormous power over who was nominated and confirmed for federal court positions. If the "right" people were in place on the federal bench, it afforded the federation backup protection should matters ever get out of hand on the home turf.

A good example of how that worked can be seen in correspondence in 1960 between Eastland and Judge John Martin, a Memphian who sat on the United States Circuit Court of Appeals for the Sixth Circuit, a territory that includes Tennessee, Ohio, Michigan, and Kentucky. Memphis put a lot of its hopes into John Martin. Along with Abe Fortas, he was the best prospect the city had for continued political influence. Martin was born in Memphis in 1883 and attended Memphis University School, where he was editor of the school newspaper and a football player. By 1919, he had obtained a law degree from the University of Virginia and become a close associate of E.H. Crump. Actually, he was more than an associate. He was Crump's cousin.

Martin worked diligently for the Crump machine. He was rewarded with an appointment to the Western Tennessee federal court bench, then later elevated to the Court of Appeals, a position he had held for twenty years by 1960.

When Crump had died in October 1954, Martin sent a telegram to his widow in which he expressed hope the memory of "Cousin Ed" would live on forever. Said Martin: "His constructive militant leadership in righteous causes assure the perpetuation of his memory on earth and his everlasting life in Heaven."

When Judge Potter Stewart, who served on the appeals court with Martin, was appointed to the Supreme Court—and a second judge on the court offered his retirement—Martin wrote Eastland a letter on Court of Appeals stationery in which he suggested a replacement for Stewart. Martin's choice was Judge Clifford O'Sullivan of Detroit, a man he described as an "excellent addition to our court."

Eastland responded the next day with a letter that acknowledged Martin's request. "I am glad to have your endorsement of Judge Clifford O'Sullivan and I will certainly be glad to do what I can to expedite his confirmation," wrote Eastland.

Other requests followed that year. On June 1, Martin wrote Eastland a letter in which he told the senator that his law clerk was leaving to practice law in Memphis. "As you know, I am very strong for Mississippians,"

Martin wrote. "And it has occurred to me that you might have in mind some worthy young law graduate (preferably a single man) . . . who might qualify as my law clerk. . . . I should be glad to appoint your nominee if you have some young man in mind."

Subsequently, in a telegram that suggested some urgency, Martin provided Eastland with his choice for yet another vacancy on the appeals court. The man he wanted this time was John Feikens of Detroit.

Eastland gave Martin half of what he wanted. He could not deliver O'Sullivan, but he did make sure that Feikens was confirmed for a position on the appeals court. Needless to say, federal appeals court judges are not supposed to be choosing their associates on the bench. Martin's indulgences with the legal system do provide a good indication of how Eastland and others were able to stack the legal deck in their favor over several decades. The good citizens of Detroit had no idea that the quality of their justice was being determined in dank offices in Tennessee and Mississippi.

Writers and liberal commentators could rail all they wanted about Eastland's racial politics; the real game was going on out of their view, and—despite their harsh words and insults—he was taking care of business.

When the ballots were counted on November 8, 1960, Mississippians, for the first time in history, went with an "unpledged" slate, as Governor Barnett had requested. Kennedy came in second with 108,362 votes; Nixon was third with 73,561 votes. Since it was a "winner take all" system, unpledged electors would be allowed to cast all eight of Mississippi's votes at the electoral college.

Election reports were so close that evening that television commentators were speculating there was a possibility that Mississippi's eight unpledged votes could decide the next president. That scenario was avoided only when Illinois's twenty-seven votes went to Kennedy and gave him the victory.

Ross Barnett was horrified at the thought of having John Kennedy as the next president, for Kennedy had made it clear he would be a strong advocate for civil rights. But Barnett could take comfort in the fact that his unpledged electors scheme almost worked. Had it not been for the miracle that occurred in the ballot boxes in Chicago, Barnett would have been in a position to hand-pick the next president of the United States.

CHAPTER 4

1961 – 1962

On February 10, 1961, Virgil Downing, an investigator for the Sovereignty Commission, went to Philadelphia, Mississippi, at the request of Commission director Albert Jones to compile a report on NAACP activity in Neshoba County.

Downing's primary target was a white man he had heard was engaging in "subversive" activities with the NAACP. The only real information he had on the man was that he had in 1958 challenged Jack Tannehill, editor of the *Neshoba Democrat,* to a duel. After arriving in town about noon, Downing went straight to the sheriff's office.

"I contacted Sheriff E.G. Barnett and his chief outside deputy, L.A. Rainey," Downing said in his report [Rainey, who was subsequently charged in the murders of three civil rights workers, ended up becoming an important contact for the Commission]. "They both stated they did not know of any trouble the NAACP was causing at this time. They were very cooperative and said they would notify the Sovereignty Commission if the NAACP caused them any trouble in the county."

Downing's report continued: "I talked to Sheriff Barnett . . . alone about [the man]. He stated in all of his life he has never seen a man like [him], that all he wanted was publicity and he would do anything to get it. He stated that [he] was very unreliable and that he personally would not trust him with anything. He said that he thought [he] might be weak in the head. . . . He said that he understood that [he] was studying law but he didn't think he would ever pass the bar examination. He stated that [he] has got his nose stuck in every bodies business and his friends are very very few. The sheriff said that [he] is the type man to let alone and to not to have any dealings with. He said if you did it would be trouble on the other end for you."

After completing his interview with Sheriff Barnett, Downing went to the newspaper office to talk to Tannehill, but was told the editor was out of town and would not return for several days. From there he went to the courthouse to talk to chancery clerk I.D. Darby. Said Downing: "I was informed by his daughter, Miss Elizabeth Darby, that her father would not be in the office all day. Miss Darby was very cooperative and stated she did not know of any trouble the NAACP was causing in Neshoba County at this time. She said she would give her father my card and tell the purpose of my visit. She stated she was sure her father would be glad to cooperate with the Sovereignty Commission in every way possible should the NAACP ever cause any trouble in the county."

Downing also dropped in on the circuit clerk, T.A. Sansing, but was informed by his wife that he was in court for the day. "She said that she did not know just how many Negroes were qualified to vote in Neshoba County but was sure it was only a few," he reported. Next he went to the office of the superintendent of education, A.D. Bassett, but as it turned out, he, too, was out of the office for the day.

Whether all the officials Downing tried to meet in that rural county of 20,000 were actually unavailable or had ducked into back rooms after being tipped off that the Commission car was in town—the cars were not marked with an insignia, but were recognizable by the iridescent, paste-on numbers attached to the doors—we may never know, but it should be remembered that the Commission was not universally loved by everyone in the white community, any more than it was universally hated by everyone in the black community.

Downing's report is important for the insight it offers into the Commission's covert operations and for evidence of early contact with Deputy Sheriff Rainey, but it is also important for the picture it offers of elected officials in small towns. Not all white Mississippians were racists. Many white elected officials were careful to keep their distance from the Commission.

Many Mississippians were having second thoughts about the Commission. About a month after Downing's trip, the *Jackson Daily News* published a story headlined, "Sparks of Dissension Dart Sovereignty Commission." The newspaper reported that there was a behind-the-scenes battle over the role the Commission should play in the affairs of the Citizens' Council. At issue were the $5,000–a-month payments being made to the Council.

"Gov. Ross Barnett, ex officio chairman of the Commission, said he disagreed with the $5,000 per month grant," reported the newspaper. "The governor is interested in learning where the Council's 'Forum' is heard. [The "Citizens' Council Forum" was a series of interviews that supposedly were being aired on television and radio stations around the country.] We don't know at this time where the programs are seen or heard," complained Barnett. "We've got to know where the money goes."

When he learned of the controversy, disgruntled ex-Commission member Hal DeCell offered a reward of one hundred dollars to anyone who could produce a list of radio and television stations outside the South who were airing the "Forum." Pressed to provide a list of stations to the new Commission director Erle Johnston, William Simmons refused on the grounds that such a list would subject the stations to "pressure and harassment." No one claimed the reward, and DeCell labeled the Council's claims of national influence a "farce."

Thirty-five years later, DeCell's oldest son, Hal Jr., told the author that he recalled, as a child, hearing his father discuss the Commission. "I remember him saying that the files never should have been done," he says. "I don't know what's in the files, but I know my father, and I know he would never do anything to hurt other folks." Hal Jr. works for the federal government today, and his brother, Ken, is a senior editor at *Washingtonian* magazine.

One of the Commission's more public attacks in 1961 was directed against Billy C. Barton, a twenty-year-old University of Mississippi senior. After spending the previous summer in Atlanta working as an intern for the *Atlanta Journal,* he had returned to the university, where he was the managing editor of the student newspaper, *The Mississippian.* In the spring of 1961 he announced his intention to run for editor, an elected position.

Unknown to Barton, the Commission had compiled a dossier on him. According to Johnston, who mentioned the episode in his memoirs, Barton was targeted after the Commission received reports the student had been involved in "sit-ins" in Atlanta. In reality, he was covering the sit-ins for the *Atlanta Journal,* but by the time the gossip reached the ears of Commission investigators, he had been caught red-handed expressing "subversive tendencies" of a most dangerous nature.

In an effort to sabotage Barton's election as editor (his only opponent was a student named Jimmy Robertson), the Commission sent the university a confidential report that said the student was a "left-winger" who had been planted on the campus by the NAACP. The report said that investigators considered Barton a "very dangerous" individual.

That campus election became a statewide news story, with the Hederman press pumping it for all it was worth. Tom Hederman's educational allegiance was to Mississippi College, the private, Baptist-supported institution near Jackson. The *Jackson State Times* rose to Barton's defense, first with a story that quoted his opponent as saying, "It will be a sad day for the University when state officials are allowed to dictate who will be student body officers," then by giving Barton a lie detector test, which he passed with flying colors. After that, the *Jackson Daily News* admitted that the Sovereignty Commission and the Citizens' Council had "pulled a boo-boo."

In the end, Barton lost the election. His opponent went on to become a justice of the Mississippi Supreme Court. Barton went to Vietnam, where he lost an eye in a "friendly fire" incident. He subsequently was killed in an automobile accident.

The debate over the Commission's links to the Citizens' Council continued into the summer. It was so intense that Governor Barnett called Johnston and told him he was postponing the scheduled June meeting to give everyone a cooling-off period. Although the spat between Johnston and the Council was a public one, the real reasons for the disagreement were hidden beneath the surface.

In his memoirs, *Mississippi's Defiant Years,* self-published nearly thirty-five years after the fact, Johnston depicted himself as a racial moderate, someone who was attempting to lessen the impact of the Councils' strident racism. However, there is no evidence this was ever the case. On the contrary, the Commission, under Governor Barnett's leadership, was secretly gearing up for a no-holds-barred attack against blacks and their white supporters, an attack unprecedented in American history.

The real issue was over how limited resources should be spent. The Council wanted to make radio and television shows depicting the "Southern way of life." The Commission wanted to use the money for covert operations.

Barnett eventually ended the dispute by reading a statement, which, unknown to him, had been written by Johnston: "Both Erle Johnston . . . and William J. Simmons, leader of the Citizens' Councils, are dedicated segregationists. Both in their respective fields have made invaluable contributions to the success of our cause. Mississippi needs the continued dedicated efforts of both men." The headline in the *Clarion-Ledger* said, "Johnston Retained Despite CC Blasts."

That bit of dirty laundry aired in public, the Commission focused more of its efforts on covert activities and less on public relations. The dispute was nothing more than a screen, but it was reflective of the feelings of many Commission and federation members that winning the battle against integrationists would require action, not the sort of incessant talk for which the Council was noted.

The lot of ex-governors in Mississippi is not enviable. Traditionally, they have had only two options: They could join a prestigious law firm, where they could utilize their business and political contacts, and settle gracefully into retirement, or they could run for a so-called higher office such as United States senator.

Governor Coleman didn't want to do either. He ran for—and he won—a seat in the lowly state House of Representatives. That was quite a leap, from chief executive to the House of Representatives, where he found himself in a freshman class of wet-behind-the-ears political neophytes. But Coleman had a plan. To implement that plan, all he had to do was bide his time—and keep a low profile.

Coleman's chief ally was William Winter, whom he had appointed tax collector in 1956 to serve out the term of an incumbent who had died in office. When he accepted the post, Winter said he would not run for reelection in 1959 because he wanted to see the legislature abolish the office and transfer its duties to the State Tax Commission.

The legislature did not accommodate him, and he ended up running for—and winning—the office when his appointed term ended. Winter was destined to serve eight years in an ex officio status on the Sovereignty Commission, but at this point his political career was most notable for his unswerving devotion to Coleman, a man who had been his hero since high school.

By 1961, the political front of the federation movement in Mississippi, Tennessee, and Louisiana had undergone significant changes. The dispute between the Citizens' Council and the Commission is a good example of how politics was changing in the South. John Kennedy's election loosened the federation's hold on the electorate, causing political leaders such as Leander Perez and John U. Barr to lose favor in the public eye.

The Citizens' Council was particularly concerned about recent events in Memphis, where elected officials, facing a potential majority black electorate, backpedaled on their earlier pronouncements of "never." In October, the Council's magazine, *The Citizen,* ran an editorial that blasted Memphis officials for "an outright betrayal of public trust" for the manner in which they had "surrendered" on the issue of desegregation.

In November, the Council sent a delegation of Mississippians to Memphis for a meeting at the Hotel King Cotton. Midway through the meeting, which attracted about two hundred people, Council officials spotted newspaper reporters in the audience and ordered them to leave the room. One of the reporters, John Spence of the *Memphis Press-Scimitar,* was there long enough to get a story for the next day's edition. Spence reported that William Simmons, leader of the Jackson Citizens' Council, gave a speech that offered advice on how to influence court proceedings involving civil rights activists.

"Pack the courtroom two hours before the trial," Simmons told the crowd. "Think of the effect on witnesses."

Packing the courtrooms in a different manner was Senator Eastland. That fall, Thurgood Marshall, then a counsel for the NAACP, was nominated to the Second Circuit Court of Appeals. To get there, he had to pass through Eastland's committee. Realizing that he could delay—but not block—the nomination, Eastland offered a horse trade to the president. According to author Robert Sherrill, Eastland made the offer to Attorney General Robert Kennedy after meeting him by chance in the corridor outside the committee room. "Tell your brother that if he will give me Harold Cox I will give him the nigger [meaning Marshall]," Eastland reportedly told Kennedy.

Harold Cox was Eastland's old college roommate, and he wanted to see him appointed to the Fifth Circuit. As a result of that horse trade, Marshall was confirmed for the appeals court, and Cox, who in court once referred to a black civil rights defendant as a "chimpanzee," was confirmed for the Fifth Circuit.

Newspapers across the country did a good job of reporting the facts as they saw them at the time. What they saw was a changing political climate and they reported it as such, at least the honest ones did. The dishonest newspapers—and they were the majority in Mississippi—reported what they were told to report.

What was not understood at the time was that while the tri-state federation was crumbling on one level, it was restructuring on another as an underground movement with a more menacing agenda. History shows us that the further it was pushed underground, the more closely aligned it became with organized crime and the more determined it became to infiltrate the government, especially the court system, where financial fortunes were made or lost on the decisions of a single judge.

~~~~~

Almost from the day he was elected, there was loose talk in Mississippi, Louisiana, and Tennessee of killing President John F. Kennedy. During the presidential race, Carlos Marcello invested $500,000 in Richard Nixon's campaign, according to author John H. Davis, and was not happy when his candidate lost. To Marcello and others in the tri-state federation, Kennedy was a threat to their vast business interests.

Kennedy was not the only target. If Kennedy was feared for what he could do to disrupt the financial base of underworld operations, Martin Luther King was feared for what he could do to disrupt the social order.

In the fall of 1961, a prominent member of the Ku Klux Klan, William Hugh Morris of New Orleans—according to FBI intelligence reports—told a Klan gathering that the South's racial problems could only be solved by the murder of Dr. King. According to those reports, he told the gathering he had a New Orleans underworld contact who would "kill anyone for a price." Morris subsequently denied making those statements when called before a congressional committee. The committee accepted his denial and the matter was closed to further inquiry.

As 1961 faded into 1962, talk of violence escalated. Always the same three names arose: John Kennedy, Robert Kennedy, Martin Luther King. In July and August of 1962, according to author Walter Sheridan, James Hoffa, head of the Teamsters Union, told Edward Partin, who headed Teamsters Local No. 5 in Baton Rouge, that "that son of a bitch" Bobby Kennedy "has got to go."

Hoffa told Partin about the layout at Robert Kennedy's home and informed him of Kennedy's penchant for riding in an open convertible. He said he would be an easy target for an assassin equipped with a .270–caliber rifle. The key to killing Kennedy, Hoffa said, was to do it in the South, where it could be blamed on rabid segregationists.

That same month, according to the *Washington Post,* Florida Mafia boss Santos Trafficante Jr., told a wealthy Cuban exile named Jose Aleman Jr., that Jack Kennedy was "in trouble" and would "get what is coming to him." Aleman predicted that Kennedy would not get reelected. Trafficante replied, "No, Jose, he is going to be hit."

Aleman told *Washington Post* reporter George Crile III in a 1976 interview that he passed that information along to the FBI in 1962 and 1963. He gave Crile the names of the agents he contacted, but when the reporter tracked them down and asked about Aleman's story they refused to deny or confirm the contact without approval from FBI headquarters—and, of course, that approval was never given.

If Aleman's story is true, it is significant because J. Edgar Hoover never informed the Kennedys of any threats made by Trafficante. As a result of that newspaper story, Trafficante and Aleman were called before the House Select Committee on Assassinations in 1978 and asked about the report. Aleman said he may have misunderstood Trafficante, that he may have meant the president would be hit by "a lot of votes from the Republican Party or something like that." Trafficante denied making any threats against the president.

Down on the Gulf, Marcello met that same month with two of his associates, Edward Becker and Carl Roppolo, at his 3,000–acre plantation outside New Orleans. According to author John Davis, Marcello exploded when Becker said he thought Bobby Kennedy was giving him "a rough time": *"Livarsi na petra di la scarpa!"* Marcello said, ". . . Take the stone out of my shoe!" Marcello followed this old Sicilian curse with, "Don't worry about that little Bobby son of a bitch. He's going to be taken care of."

While all the talk about killing the Kennedys and King was circulating throughout the tri-state federation, Hoover escalated his private war against King. In May 1962, Hoover ordered that King be labeled "Communist" in the bureau's secret file of people slated to be arrested and held during a national emergency. Hoover knew that he could hurt King more with a behind-the-scenes whispering campaign than he ever could in a frontal assault. He wanted to raise doubts about King with his bosses, the Kennedys.

Memphis crime families were undergoing significant changes in the early 1960s, as were crime families all across the country, according to the Justice Department and the author's sources. The Kennedys, with their troublesome stands on civil rights and organized crime, were considered a threat.

Over the years, the Cosa Nostra was able to bribe small-time officials on a consistent basis, but it was never able to get to the top figures, as the Memphis cartel had proved it could do for several decades. Besides its ability to deliver political favors, the Memphis cartel had demonstrated its ability to pack the court system with judges of its choosing. Other than the racial turmoil enveloping the city in the early 1960s, Memphis power-brokers were concerned with two primary issues: the ascent of Abe Fortas into the inner sanctum of government, and the defeat of that archenemy of the Memphis cartel, Senator Kefauver.

In June 1961, the *New York Times* reported that President Kennedy was considering Kefauver as a replacement for aging Southerner Hugo Black on the Supreme Court. Crump and McKellar had earmarked appeals court judge John Martin for that slot, but in 1961 his age—at seventy-eight—was not to his advantage (he died the following year). Apparently, Kefauver's name was launched as a trial balloon. Kennedy knew Eastland would never let the Tennessee senator past his Judiciary Committee.

In 1961, Memphis had a new reason for despising Kefauver. For more than a year, the senator had been using the Senate Antitrust and Monopoly Subcommittee, which he chaired, as a vehicle to investigate price fixing in the drug industry. It may have been a coincidence that Memphis's most promising growth industry was Plough, Inc., a patent medicine company that sold products such as St. Joseph Aspirin and St. Joseph Liver Regulator, but, coincidence or not, Kefauver's investigative probes were making Memphians increasingly nervous. There is no evidence Plough was affiliated with the Memphis cartel in any way, but as one of the city's most promising new growth industries it would have attracted the attention of the cartel, which was becoming increasingly protective of the city's industries.

Kefauver's hearings on the drug industry, which ran from July 1961 to February 1962, were his finest hour as a public servant. The picture of the drug industry that emerged from those hearings revealed an industry engaged in lawless price fixing and frenzied levels of competition that prevented citizens from obtaining needed drugs at reasonable prices. The result was landmark legislation that gave American consumers, for the first time, protection against unscrupulous drug companies.

When the legislation passed both Houses in 1962, the *New York Times* singled out Kefauver as "the hero of this victory." If Kefauver had lived— he died suddenly and unexpectedly in 1963—he undoubtedly would have posed new threats to the Memphis cartel. His untimely death stilled a voice that has yet to be replaced.

In April 1961, Abe Fortas returned to Memphis to address the Rotarians. He was introduced by Jack Goldsmith, with whom he was acquainted because of his work for Federated Department Stores. During the past several years, Fortas had been recruiting projects for his Washington law firm, Arnold, Fortas and Porter. Increasingly, those projects were taking him out of the country on trips to Europe and the Caribbean. One of his new clients was the Commonwealth of Puerto Rico.

In Memphis, Fortas spoke glowingly of the Kennedy administration. Instinctively, he knew what his audience wanted to hear—that more money was headed their way. Said Fortas: "What I like about the domestic programs the President has thus far announced—extension of unemployment compensation, medical aid to the aged, increased housing, acceleration of road building—is the basic principle—the willingness of the federal government to put more money into the economy than it takes out, or as its foes call it, willingness to unbalance the budget."

What Fortas did not tell the Rotarians was how much of his time was being spent running interference between his friend Lyndon Johnson and the Kennedys. Johnson couldn't bear to talk to the Kennedys. When he needed to communicate with a Kennedy, he called on Abe, who dutifully hastened to the White House to represent his friend.

On March 27, 1961, nine black students were arrested after they entered the Jackson Municipal Library to research material for school work. They called it a "read-in." Most of the students were enrolled at Tougaloo College, an all-black institution located just outside the city. Police hustled the students into squad cars and took them to jail.

A few weeks earlier, Jackson residents were shaken when newspapers reported that St. Andrews Episcopal Church had begun having integrated meetings. Never in history had a Mississippi church allowed African Americans to participate as equals. Bowing to public pressure, the church board called an emergency meeting and voted to remove the minister responsible.

By May 1961, busloads of civil rights activists, later dubbed "Freedom Riders," began to arrive from points outside the South. Their goal was to pressure the federal government into enforcing Supreme Court rulings that affirmed the unconstitutionality of state laws requiring segregated seating on interstate buses.

Reaction in Mississippi was predictable. Governor Barnett instructed the highway patrol to escort the Freedom Riders "non-stop" across the state. Attorney General Joe Patterson told reporters the Freedom Riders would be arrested and jailed if they violated state segregation laws. Senator Eastland rushed to the floor of the Senate and proclaimed the Freedom Rider project "part of the Communist movement."

When the first Freedom Rider buses arrived in Mississippi, they were escorted to Jackson by nine highway patrol and National Guard vehicles. Hundreds of National Guard troops were stationed along the route. Once they arrived at the Jackson bus station, the Freedom Riders entered waiting rooms labeled "whites only" and were arrested and taken off to jail. Some were arrested when they entered the "whites only" cafeteria.

That scenario continued into the summer, with each busload of Freedom Riders attracting more and more attention from the national media. One of the most celebrated Freedom Riders arrested was the Reverend Robert Pierson, the son-in-law of New York governor Nelson Rockefeller. Another activist who later achieved fame was Harold Ickes, whose father served as Interior Secretary—and was Abe Fortas's boss—during the Roosevelt administration. Ickes went on to become deputy White House chief of staff in President Bill Clinton's administration. Pierson and Ickes were both targeted for dossiers.

The Sovereignty Commission stepped up its covert activities during this time and recruited students to spy on other students on the state's college campuses. Special attention was given to the University of Mississippi, which the Commission felt was at greatest risk as a target for desegregation.

The phrase "masters of deceit" was used in the 1950s by J. Edgar Hoover to describe the activities of communist agents during the Cold War, but, as a descriptive phrase, it was just as applicable to the Commission. In 1961, four members of the Commission's board also served on the board of directors of the Citizens' Council. Three others, including Governor Barnett, were Council members.

The trend throughout the tri-state federation for pro-segregation organizations was to go underground. They were losing the battle on the public relations front. Their best hope for victory lay in covert activities. The celebrated "spat" between the Commission and the Citizens' Council appeared to be nothing more than a charade to mask that shift in emphasis.

Erle Johnston, still at that point Commission public relations director, started making speeches urging moderation. "The only way we can retain our segregated school system is through the cooperation of the colored race," he told white students in Grenada in a commencement address. "I have often thought that if the extremists at both ends of this racial situation would quit wildly wagging their tongues, and suspiciously pointing their fingers, we could restore some racial harmony in Mississippi and make better progress."

Johnston said there were certain individuals on the "opposite side" who thought they could solve the state's problems with "threats and intimidation." They "mean well," he said, but "there is some question as to whether this attitude is a help, a hindrance, or merely creates hysteria."

In his public comments, Johnston utilized a "good cop/bad cop" theme, in which he depicted himself as the "good cop." The Commission had decided to play hardball with its enemies. The time for talk was past. Johnston's so-called voice of reason would have been more believable if the Commission had not been secretly gearing up for a covert, all-out war.

By the fall of 1961, the Freedom Rides had fizzled, countered by an offer from the New Orleans Citizens' Council to provide free transportation—one way, of course—and spending money to any African American families in the South who wanted to move to Hyannis Port, Massachusetts, home of the Kennedy family. After a sudden rash of newspaper publicity over the invitation, the offer was quickly rescinded. Whether there was a multitude of takers—or no takers at all—is not known.

Although Mississippi newspapers were as adoring of the Commission as ever—*Jackson Daily News* editor Jimmy Ward continued to lead the attack against those advocating integration—the gadflies were becoming bolder in their criticisms. Interestingly, none of the state's liberal newspaper editors was actually in favor of integration. What they did favor was a peaceful transition in which the rights of everyone involved were protected under the law.

Hazel Brannon Smith, editor of the Lexington *Advertiser* and the Durant *News,* blasted the "spy activities" and "character assassination" tactics of the Commission on a regular basis, while maintaining her support of segregation and the Southern way of life.

Greenville novelist Josephine Haxton, who writes under the name of Ellen Douglas, once said of her friend *Delta Democrat-Times* editor Hodding Carter: "He really was a very conservative man. He just didn't think people ought to lynch each other."

By 1962, Carter, called "Big" Hodding by his friends, had had enough strident politics to last him a lifetime. He accepted a position as writer in residence at Tulane University in New Orleans—by that time he had penned more than a dozen books—and turned over the reins of the newspaper to his oldest son, Hodding Carter III, a summa cum laude graduate of Princeton.

At twenty-seven, "Little" Hodding was one of the youngest newspaper editors in the state. He was more liberal and more political than his father, but he was an astute businessman who was careful not to push his Delta readership further than it felt comfortable going in the direction of moderation.

On January 21, 1961, the day after the inauguration of President John F. Kennedy, James Meredith, a twenty-eight-year-old black United States Air Force veteran with nine years' service to his country, wrote the registrar at the University of Mississippi to request an application for admission.

Five days later, the university sent Meredith the requested application forms, along with a letter expressing pleasure in his interest "in becoming a member of our student body." After receiving the application forms, Meredith, who lived in Jackson where he had been attending the all-black Jackson State College, went to see Medgar Evers, the director of the NAACP field office in Mississippi.

Evers saw that Meredith was determined to pursue the matter, so he suggested that he contact Thurgood Marshall, then director of the NAACP Legal Defense Fund. In his letter to Marshall, Meredith said he anticipated "encountering some type of difficulty."

With the guidance of the NAACP, Meredith submitted his application by registered mail to the University of Mississippi. He identified himself as "an American-Mississippi-Negro citizen." He said that he could not comply with the application requirement that he submit the names of six Ole Miss graduates as references since "they are all white."

Meredith was denied admission for a variety of reasons, all procedural, but each was calculated to prevent black students from enrolling at the university. For four months, Meredith corresponded with the university and attempted to negotiate his enrollment. Eventually the matter ended up with the Mississippi Board of Trustees for Institutions of Higher Learning, commonly referred to as the Mississippi college board, which supervised and set policy for all the state's institutions of higher learning.

The college board president was a lawyer named Tom Tubb. An appointee of Governor Coleman, he had decided to vote in favor of Meredith's acceptance, but on the day the board was scheduled to vote Governor Barnett gave a speech in which he said there was a legal way to keep Meredith out. Hearing that, the board delayed its vote one day, so that members could meet with the governor. A persuasive speaker, Barnett convinced the board members, some of whom he had appointed, that victory was at hand.

As a result, the college board voted to deny Meredith admission to the university. Tom Tubb, having decided that the law was the law, stuck with his original decision to vote to admit. He would never regret that decision.

Meredith appealed to the federal courts. The legal skirmishes continued for the remainder of the year and then spilled over into 1962. In June, the matter went before the Fifth Circuit Court of Appeals in New Orleans. Inside the courtroom, the situation was tense. Appeals court hearings are usually devoid of passion, but not on this day.

At one end of the table were lawyers representing the Mississippi college board, and at the other were NAACP lawyers representing James Meredith. The NAACP lawyers argued, quite convincingly according to those present, that the court should jail the state college board for contempt and appoint its own board. At that point, the court took a short recess and each side retreated to private rooms.

Years later, Tom Tubb told journalist and author David Halberstam what had happened behind closed doors. "We went in one of those conference rooms, and one of Barnett's people came over to me and said, 'Tom, you're a lawyer and I'm not, and I don't hear so good. But I do understand that nigger woman from the NAACP to say that if we don't let Meredith in, then *I'm* going to jail and *he's* going to the *University,*' Tubb said. I said that was an exceptionally accurate summation of our position.

" 'Well, goddam,' he said, 'vote me to admit the nigger.'

"That ended it."

On June 25, 1962, the Fifth Circuit Court of Appeals in a 3–2 vote, ruled that Meredith should be admitted to the University of Mississippi. Legal wrangling continued through the summer and it was not until September 13, after the Supreme Court refused to hear an appeal, that the appeals court ordered University of Mississippi officials to admit Meredith. Barnett was horrified.

Meredith had become a matter of honor for Barnett. He had promised white Mississippi that the "nigger" would never sully the Ole Miss campus, and he had no intention of giving up without a fight. "Schools will not be closed if this can possibly be avoided, but they will not be integrated," Barnett said. "Therefore in obedience to legislative and constitutional sanction, I interpose the rights of the sovereign state of Mississippi to enforce its laws and to regulate its own internal affairs without interference on the part of the federal government."

Barnett's position was given a vote of confidence by most of the state's elected officials, including Senator Eastland and Lieutenant Governor Paul Johnson.

Mississippi was electrified in a way it had not been since the Civil War. In effect, Barnett was telling the federal government that it would have to shoot its way into Mississippi if it wanted Meredith in the university. That was fine with most of the state's white citizens, who quietly went about the business of oiling their shotguns and stocking their pantries with groceries for a shoot-out they felt was inevitable.

You would have to live through it to understand the depth of passion involved. The only situation comparable, by today's standards, would be the incidents at the Davidian compound at Waco, Texas, and the shoot-out at Ruby Ridge, Idaho, in which federal authorities used force to implement federal authority over civil disobedience. In 1962, the entire state of Mississippi was preparing for a shoot-out with the federal government.

Madness was in the air.

As Barnett positioned Mississippi for a rendezvous with destiny that was illuminated by his own distorted apocalyptic vision, federal officials decided that Meredith would be registered at the college board's offices in Jackson. Before that could happen, Barnett issued an executive order calling for the arrest of any federal official who attempted to prevent a state official from carrying out his duties.

Meredith arrived at the college board offices escorted by Department of Justice attorney John Doar. Barnett stood in the doorway and blocked their entry into the office. Playing to the assembled press corps—and to a greater degree to the people of Mississippi—Barnett glared at Doar, obviously a white male, and at Meredith, the only black male in the building—and asked a question that made the crowd roar with laughter.

"Which one of you gentlemen is James Meredith?" Barnett asked.

Doar was not amused. Meredith, being above all else a native Mississippian, cracked a smile at Barnett's home-spun bravado. When the laughter subsided, Doar, showing no hint of amusement, tried to hand the governor a court order. He suggested they get on with the registration.

Barnett wouldn't accept the court order. Instead, he read a statement that said, in part, "I do, hereby, finally deny you admission to the University of Mississippi." With that, Doar and Meredith, flanked by Commissioner T.B.

Birdsong, director of the state highway patrol, and several patrolmen, hurried from the building.

The following day, Doar, bolstered by a large force of U.S. marshals, escorted Meredith to the University of Mississippi campus at Oxford. Barnett and Lieutenant Governor Paul Johnson had planned to be there to block Meredith's entry, but Barnett did not show up (he later blamed his absence on bad weather that grounded his airplane).

It was Johnson's job to stand up for Mississippi.

Johnson was a wiry, hawk-faced man who perpetually wore a grimace. Like Barnett, he was born with that peculiar lack of grace familiar to fans of William Faulkner's villainous Snopeses. When James McShane, the U.S. marshal accompanying Meredith, tried to hand Johnson a court order, Johnson refused to take it. McShane touched the papers against Johnson and let them fall to the ground.

Johnson, flanked by dozens of Mississippi highway patrolmen, doubled up his fist and drew back his arm as if to strike someone. McShane doubled up his fists and stepped forward. "You understand that we have got to break through," said the marshal.

"You can't," answered Johnson. "If there is any violence, then you and Meredith are responsible."

Doar, McShane, Meredith, and the U.S. marshals retreated and left the campus. Shortly after they left, Governor Barnett arrived and apologized for being late. He commended Johnson for "standing tall" for Mississippi. The Court of Appeals was not amused. It already had issued a contempt order against Governor Barnett. Now it issued one against Lieutenant Governor Johnson.

By then, President Kennedy had had enough.

Over the next several days, President Kennedy and his brother, Attorney General Robert Kennedy, engaged in a series of telephone conversations with Governor Barnett in an attempt to bring a peaceful resolution to the conflict. Barnett was not informed that the conversations were being recorded. The existence of the secret tapes would not be acknowledged until 1983, when transcripts of the conversations were released. The tapes are now on file in the archives of the John F. Kennedy Memorial Library, where they are available to researchers.

After days of tense conversations, Barnett and President Kennedy agreed that Meredith would be enrolled on September 27. Barnett was told that Meredith would be accompanied by about thirty armed U.S. marshals. In a conversation with Robert Kennedy, Barnett asked if it would be possible for the marshals to draw their pistols.

"We'll have a big crowd here and if we all turn away because of one gun, it would be embarrassing," said Barnett. "When you draw the guns, I will then tell the people. In other words, we will step aside and you can walk in."

"I don't think that will be very pleasant, Governor," said Robert Kennedy. "I think you are making a mistake handling it in that fashion. . . . I think it is silly going through this whole facade of your standing there; our people drawing guns; your stepping aside; to me, it is dangerous and I think this has gone beyond the stage of politics, and you have a responsibility to the people of the state and to the people of the United States. This is a real disservice."

"I am not interested in politics personally," said Barnett. "I have said so many times—we couldn't have integration and I have got to do something. I can't just walk back."

As the negotiations for Meredith's enrollment continued to dwell on matters such as who would draw guns and who would not, John and Robert Kennedy became increasingly irritated. When the Justice Department suggested that Meredith be secretly enrolled in Jackson while all the media attention was focused on the Oxford campus, both President Kennedy and the governor agreed to that solution.

Then, as support continued to build within the state for Barnett—and word got out that thousands of armed men were arriving in Mississippi from neighboring states such as Alabama—he backed away from the agreement to enroll Meredith in Jackson. When Robert Kennedy learned of that, he called Barnett and told him the president was going on national television that night to say that Barnett had gone back on his word.

"That won't do at all," said Barnett.

"You broke your word to him," said Robert Kennedy.

"You don't mean the president is going to say that tonight?" said Barnett.

"Of course, he is. You broke your word."

Jack and Robert Kennedy could see the pressure Barnett was under. They also could see signs that he was cracking under the strain. They returned to their original plan to escort Meredith to the Oxford campus. With him would be armed U.S. marshals. Barnett was advised to call out the National Guard as a backup to the highway patrol.

At 2:30 P.M. on September 30, the day Meredith was scheduled to arrive, President Kennedy and Governor Barnett had another telephone conversation. The night before, Barnett had attended an Ole Miss–Kentucky football game at Veterans Memorial Stadium in Jackson. The crowd had cheered wildly when he was introduced. Barnett was more than the governor, he was everyone's hero.

"Mr. President, let me say this—they are calling me and others from all over the state wanting to send 1,000, 500 and 200 and all such as that," said Barnett.

"I know," said the president.

"We don't want such as that," said Barnett.

"I know, well we don't want to have, don't want to have people getting hurt or killed down there," said the president.

Then, in a comment indicative of Barnett's deteriorating mental state, the governor thanked the president, adding this unusual afterthought: "Appreciate your interest in our poultry program and all those things. Thank you so much."

Later that afternoon, at about 4 P.M., trucks containing U.S. marshals began arriving on the Ole Miss campus. The marshals, wearing white helmets, were outfitted with tear gas guns, gas masks, arm bands, and pistols. Also arriving on campus were Deputy Attorney General Nicholas Katzenbach and others from the Department of Justice, who flew into the small airport aboard an Air Force plane. They were escorted to the campus by Commissioner Birdsong and a group of highway patrolmen.

As the convoy made its way along the two-mile route to the campus, it was greeted by jeers of "nigger lover" by crowds that were becoming increasingly vocal and hostile.

Meredith arrived at the airport at 5:30 aboard a border patrol plane. He was escorted to the campus, where he was taken to Baxter Hall, a men's dormitory located on a hill that was one of the highest points on the campus. As crowds continued to form on the campus, Meredith tried to get settled into the dorm.

"I had been assigned two bedrooms, a living room, and a bathroom," he wrote in his memoir *Three Years in Mississippi*. "The first thing that I did was to make my bed. When the trouble started, I could not see or hear very much of it. Most of the events occurred on the other end of the campus, and I did not look out the window. I think I read a newspaper and went to bed around ten o'clock. I was awakened several times in the night by the noise and shooting outside, but it was not near the hall, and I had no way of knowing what was going on."

The "shooting" that Meredith referred to was a full-scale riot. Cars were overturned and set ablaze. Snipers fired out of the darkness at the marshals. Molotov cocktails exploded all over the campus. Roving mobs of men threw stones and slabs of concrete at the marshals. It was a war zone.

At 8:14, President Kennedy and Barnett had an urgent conversation. Kennedy wanted Commissioner Birdsong to move his patrolmen into place to aid the marshals who were engaged in a pitched battle. Barnett told the president that there were 150 patrolmen on their way to the scene.

"I see," said the president. "Now you can get them so we can stop this rifle shooting. That is what we have to stop."

"He says he is doing all he can," said Barnett of Birdsong's efforts. "He said there are strangers in. . . ."

"Yeah, I know, that's what we hear."

"And . . . uh . . . he understands it. He's doing all he can."

"I think this is very important, Governor, aside from this issue, we don't want a lot of people killed just because they . . . evidently two or three guardsmen have been shot—our marshals and then, of course, that state trooper."

Barnett told him the state had two hundred law enforcement officers in place.

"We got to get this situation under control—that is more important than anything else. Let me talk to my people—let me find out what the situation is—they called me a few minutes ago and said they had some high-powered rifles there, so we don't want to start moving anybody around."

"People are wiring me and calling me and saying, now you have given up," said Barnett. "I had to say 'No, I'm not giving up. I'm not giving up any fight.' I'll never give up, I have courage and faith and we will win this fight, you understand. That's just [for] the Mississippi people."

"Yeah, I don't think any of the Mississippi people or anyone else wants a lot of people killed."

"Oh, no, no," said Barnett.

Kennedy didn't know Mississippi radio stations were giving play-by-play reporting on the riot, treating it as if it were a football game. All across the state, static-riddled radios hummed with news about the riot. White male Mississippians began arming themselves and loading their trucks and cars with ammunition and supplies for a prolonged war.

The fighting raged all night. Many people were injured, but no reliable numbers are available since most of those seeking medical attention at local clinics and hospitals did not identify themselves as rioters. By the time the sun rose the next morning, order had been restored and the campus had been cleared of troublemakers. Tear gas fumes lingered like draped confetti across the campus, which bore a striking resemblance to photos of cities in war-torn Europe during World War II.

Two men died in the fighting. Paul Guihard was a thirty-one-year-old reporter with Agence France Presse. Sent to Ole Miss from his bureau office in New York, he was on the campus only a couple of hours when he was shot at close range, about twelve inches, and left to die. The second victim was Walter Ray Gunter, a twenty-three-year-old jukebox serviceman from Oxford, who was shot in the forehead.

As of 1998, both murders were still unsolved.

Early the following morning, as Meredith was escorted to the administration building to register for classes, he was overheard to remark upon looking out across the battle-scarred campus: "This is not a happy occasion."

That afternoon Barnett telephoned Robert Kennedy. He was told the attorney general had stayed up all night monitoring activities on the campus and had gone home to get some sleep. Instead, Barnett spoke to Assistant Attorney General Burke Marshall.

"Why don't you encourage the attorney general to take Meredith off campus," said Barnett. "He's already registered."

"He's entitled to stay there," said Marshall. "The attorney general has nothing to do with that. His duty is to enforce the court order. He doesn't have anything to do with that. . . ."

"Marshall, we have a plan in Mississippi where I think—I am not sure—but I think we could pay [Meredith's] expenses in another state, in another school, and if he will agree to go to school somewhere else and our law permits it, we can do that, you see. He would be happier, everybody would be happy, and the whole problem would be solved."

The following Saturday, the Ole Miss Rebels played Houston University at Memorial Stadium in Jackson and defeated them by a score of 40–7. Debris from the riot had been cleared away on the campus, but damaged egos still festered.

Ole Miss went on to win the Sugar Bowl that year, giving the football team its best record (10–0) in school history. Both the Associated Press writers poll and the United Press International's coaches poll ranked the 1962 Ole Miss team number three in the nation behind Wisconsin and national champion Southern California.

CHAPTER 5

1963 – 1964

As Ross Barnett entered his final year in office, Mississippi was still reeling from the Ole Miss riot and the realization that it had no *legal* means by which to combat the federal government. But Mississippi wasn't alone; the other states in the Federation for Constitutional Government were undergoing the same trauma.

President Kennedy and Attorney General Robert Kennedy were blamed for all the "trouble" taking place in the South. Mississippi's senators and five congressmen issued a statement attacking the president for his "invasion" of the state.

But opposition to the Kennedys was not universal.

Tennessee senator Estes Kefauver defended the president's actions at Ole Miss and was critical of Barnett's handling of the situation. In a telegram to the president, Kefauver said: "I want to congratulate you upon the calm, fair and yet positive way you have handled the tragic situation in Mississippi." Of Barnett, he said: "The authority of the United States Government has got to prevail in this kind of situation. If Barnett had realized that, the sad and disgraceful situation could have been avoided."

Despite the still-raging public debate over his admission to the university, James Meredith settled into a routine that was remarkable for its lack of drama. Although he was conspicuous on the campus because of the U.S. marshals who accompanied him wherever he went, he was not jeered, hooted, or threatened by the students, who, with few exceptions, largely ignored his presence.

A championship football team and the emergence of a new wave of popular music coming out of Stax studios in Memphis were the main focus of student attention.

In June 1963, Meredith was joined on campus by a second African American student. Unlike Meredith, who entered the undergraduate program, Cleve McDowell enrolled in the law school. He arrived on campus with a team of U.S. marshals and there were no incidents. There were still about 150 federal troops on the campus, and many of them maintained positions on the roofs of campus buildings, where they could be spotted communicating with each other by two-way radio. It was an eerie sight.

McDowell, at twenty-one, was several years younger than Meredith. He told Charles Brown, a reporter with the *Memphis Press-Scimitar,* that he felt "just like any other student." Notified of McDowell's peaceful enrollment, Attorney General Kennedy said, "I wish it could have happened that way the first time." When Brown asked Meredith about McDowell's uneventful reception, he answered, "Maybe it's just me they don't like."

Governor Barnett had the good sense to stay away from the campus during McDowell's enrollment, but he couldn't resist issuing a statement of protest. "The State of Mississippi cannot cope with the United States Army," he said. "We have done everything in our power to prevent the enrollment of Cleve McDowell in the university law school. His entry is in violation of the laws of the state."

About two weeks after McDowell's enrollment, five African Americans were sprayed with shotgun pellets in Canton, a suburb of Jackson, as they walked along a street in the vicinity of a voter registration meeting. United Press International quoted Police Chief Dan Thompson as saying the incident "did not appear to be racially motivated." The news story did not identify the victims by name or sex, only as "Negroes."

⌒⌀⁓

Dennis Hale felt far removed from the violence associated with the civil rights movement. As pastor of Harmony Baptist Church, he watched over a small congregation in a rural community near Picayune, Mississippi. There weren't many blacks in the sandy, scrub-pine communities around Picayune, but Hale and his wife felt compelled to speak out on the issue of equal rights. They didn't like what was happening to blacks in Mississippi.

Hale wrote a letter to Senator Eastland expressing his views, then resumed his pastoral duties, forgetting about the letter. One day, sometime later, two investigators with the Mississippi Sovereignty Commission showed up unannounced at Hale's house. They flashed their badges and informed the startled couple that someone had been signing their names to letters and sending them to members of Congress.

Hale said he didn't know anything about that, but, in fact, he had written letters to Senator Eastland and others. When the investigators asked to see copies of the letters, Hale refused on the grounds it violated his first amendment rights.

With that, the visit became confrontational. When the investigators asked the couple if they wanted their children to marry "niggers," Hale became angry and asked them to leave his house. The Hales were perplexed by the incident. They had no way of knowing that Senator Eastland was working closely with the Commission and providing them with tips on a regular basis. He had forwarded their heartfelt plea for moderation to the Commission, thus labeling them as subversives.

The Commission was conducting investigations all over the state, but it was especially interested in what was happening in Philadelphia. In April, investigator Andy Hopkins made another trip to the city to look into the activities of the white male the Commission suspected of having ties to the NAACP.

Hopkins's first stop was at an Amoco service station owned by an informant named W.H. Holland. He told Hopkins he had obtained information about the NAACP from his cook, an elderly black woman. Holland gave the investigator the names of four black men suspected of being members of the NAACP. Two of the men worked as janitors at the local bank, one worked for the *Neshoba Democrat,* and the fourth worked at a wholesale grocery. It was the fourth man who troubled Holland the most, perhaps because he had heard the man had once gotten into a fight with a white man.

To the investigator's disappointment, Holland said the only thing he knew about the suspected NAACP sympathizer was that he had recently purchased a new blue Volkswagen and had been observed visiting the post office several times a day. When the investigator asked if he could question his cook, Holland said no, that he felt the investigator's questions would get her too "excited," and he was concerned about the effect that would have on her at her age.

As the investigator went door to door, questioning people about the people named by Holland, he was gently rebuffed by almost everyone except Sheriff Barnett, who had proved himself to be a reliable supporter of the Commission. With the sheriff's help, the investigator continued to question people about the man.

Finally, he found someone who would talk to him. The man informed him that a friend of his, a retired FBI agent, had seen a secret file on the man and had concluded that he could "kill a man and get away with it." The investigator obtained the man's car-tag number and returned to Jackson, where he filed a report in which he said he had been unable to find anything incriminating on the man or any of the black males named as possible supporters of the NAACP.

"All of the Negroes listed . . . are employed by prominent white people who seem to have them well under control as far as attempting to register and vote, demonstrating, parading, etc.," he said. "If you deem it wise to do so, I will return to Philadelphia and make a further investigation regarding the suspected NAACP members by contacting members of the school board and others who may have information regarding these subjects."

In April 1963, the Commission underwent a significant shakeup as Director Albert Jones was replaced by former public relations director Erle Johnston, a master manipulator who reveled in his image as a crusading, small-town newspaper editor. Beneath that facade was a different person. Under his leadership, the Commission stepped up covert activities and plunged into dark areas previously unentered.

As investigators continued to compile dossiers on residents, black and white, the Commission met on July 19, 1963, to chart a more secretive course of action. Presiding over the meeting was Governor Barnett, who had grown increasingly bitter over his humiliating and very public defeats at the University of Mississippi.

Commission director Erle Johnston said he had approved a mail-out of 7,000 pamphlets that criticized a recent Supreme Court decision that voided a 1775 public accommodation law. He also told board members that a propaganda film produced by the Commission, *Oxford, U.S.A.*, was being aired in Iowa, Illinois, and Ohio.

Once the routine business was taken care of, the Commission turned its attention to the most pressing issue at hand: the proposed civil rights act of 1963. If passed, it would have a devastating effect on the state's ability to regulate civil rights litigation.

Johnston introduced John C. Satterfield to the board. Satterfield was a prominent attorney from Yazoo City, a former president of the American Bar Association. He had a national reputation, not just for his legal expertise but for his devotion to right-wing causes such as the Citizens' Council. He was a hard-core racist in every respect.

Satterfield told the board that individuals from the other Southern states were using private money to establish an office in Washington, D.C., to fight the proposed civil rights act. He said the individuals contributing the money preferred not to be identified, but he asked the board for a donation of $10,000 for the fund, which he said was projected to exceed $200,000. Additional contributions, he said, would be made by national trade groups. The board approved the $10,000 donation and a $25–an-hour fee to Satterfield for his legal services, then adjourned with little apparent recognition that it had propelled the Commission into deep and dangerous waters.

In the early morning hours of June 12, 1963, shortly after midnight, Medgar Evers, the Mississippi field secretary for the NAACP, pulled into the driveway of his Jackson home. Inside the house, his wife, Myrlie, and two of their three children were watching television, struggling to stay awake at that late hour.

Wearing a white shirt, Evers got out of his blue Oldsmobile and gathered up an armload of papers and a bundle of NAACP T-shirts. Earlier in the evening he had attended a rally at a church, where he had a private meeting with Tougaloo College chaplain Ed King. As Evers slammed the car door shut, a gunshot shattered the night stillness. A .30–06 slug penetrated his right shoulder blade, then ripped through his body and crashed into a window of the house, landing finally with a thud on the kitchen counter.

Leaving a trail of blood, Evers crawled up the driveway to the back door of the house, then collapsed, face down, still clutching his car keys. That is what Myrlie saw when she threw open the back door. That—and the memory of her children's screams—is what has stuck with her all these years. On the way to the hospital, Evers regained consciousness and tried to sit up in the ambulance, but the damage done to his chest by the .30–06 slug was too severe and he died fifty minutes later at the hospital.

Police found a 1917, .30–06 Enfield rifle, equipped with a telescopic sight, hidden in a honeysuckle patch behind a tree across the street from Evers's house. The large-caliber rifle was popular with the military and with big-game hunters across the South. The killer—or killers—had vanished.

Considering the high level of surveillance the Sovereignty Commission maintained on Evers, it is odd that one of its investigators was not there to witness the assassination. As far back as December 1961, former Commission director Albert Jones had personally participated in surveillance activities against Evers.

On one occasion, Jones reported that he and one of his investigators had peered in the windows of a Lynch Street address and witnessed Evers in conversation with Hazel B. Smith, the white editor of the Lexington and Durant newspapers. As the leader of the Mississippi branch of the NAACP, Evers was one of the Commission's primary targets.

The hatred against Evers had soared a few weeks before his death when he was given seventeen minutes of air time on television station WLBT to respond to comments made by Jackson mayor Allen Thompson. WLBT did not want to give Evers the air time; the television station was ordered to do so by the Federal Communications Commission under its fairness doctrine.

The response of white viewers was predictable. They wanted Evers off the air—immediately. One caller angrily said: "You don't have to put these black jungle bunnies on TV." Another caller said: "I'd just like to call in and tell you that I think that's very horrible, this nigra on TV with all his lies. . . ."

By July, the FBI had a suspect in the murder.

Fingerprints lifted from the rifle matched those of a forty-two-year-old ex-Marine from Greenwood, a rabid segregationist named Byron De La Beckwith. Upon his arrest the *Clarion-Ledger* offered the following head-line: "Californian Is Charged With Murder of Evers," a reference to the fact that the suspect had not been born in Mississippi.

As Charles Evers, the slain leader's brother, took over management of the NAACP field office, the murder trial went forward under the direction of District Attorney William L. Waller, known to his family and friends as "Bill." Since serving as district attorney was a part-time job at best, Waller, a graduate of the Ole Miss law school, continued to maintain his private law accounts with his partner John Fox, a practice that was neither uncommon nor illegal in Mississippi at the time.

At the trial, which was held in February 1964, Beckwith said he was innocent. He admitted that the rifle had belonged to him, but he said it was stolen shortly before the murder took place. He produced witnesses who testified that he was in Greenwood when the murder was committed. When the all-male, all-white jury was unable to reach a verdict, a mistrial was declared and a second trial date was set for April.

As Waller prepared for the second trial, investigators with the Sovereignty Commission secretly intervened on Beckwith's behalf. It is not known to what extent the Commission aided Beckwith in his first trial, but it is known that investigators played a significant role in the second trial.

Records show that Commission investigator Andy Hopkins, the same investigator who had earlier focused so much of his efforts in Philadelphia, obtained a list of prospective jurors in the Beckwith case and investigated their backgrounds. That information, which contained comments such as "believed to be Jewish" or "fair and impartial" scrawled out beside individual names, was provided to Beckwith's lawyers.

One of the jurors was a member of the Citizens' Council, which had held a fund-raiser for Beckwith to help with his legal expenses. Another juror was a distant cousin of Hopkins. The full extent to which the Commission intervened, whether individual jurors were contacted or information was relayed to them, is unknown, but the results of Hopkins's work were certainly favorable to Beckwith: For a second time, an all-male, all-white jury was unable reach a verdict.

Again, a mistrial was declared and Beckwith was released from jail.

Twenty-five years later, Jerry Mitchell, a reporter with the *Clarion-Ledger,* asked Waller if he thought the hung jury resulted from Commission contact. "I don't think so, but that's a judgment call," Waller said.

~~~~

On August 15, 1963, three days before James Meredith was scheduled to graduate from the University of Mississippi, Commission director Johnston received a midmorning telephone call from E.R. Jobe, the executive secretary of the state college board. Jobe told Johnston that the college board was going to have a meeting in thirty minutes to discuss a new development in the Meredith case. He asked Johnston to send a representative to the meeting.

At issue were statements made earlier in the summer by Meredith, statements some members of the college board considered "inflammatory." Meredith had been disciplined by the university for making the statements, but the university was now prepared to issue Meredith his graduation diploma.

Some board members wanted to know if they could somehow use those statements to prevent Meredith from receiving his diploma. By a 6 to 5 vote, reason prevailed and the college board adjourned without beating Meredith out of his diploma. Johnston was asked to tell the Commission that the college board had tried its best.

A week before his graduation, during an interview with a newspaper reporter, Meredith was asked if he felt he had made gains in the direction of equal rights. "You can't make gains," he responded. "There's no in-between. Either a citizen has equal protection or he doesn't. If a man is innocent but unfairly sentenced to one hundred years in jail, you can't say it would represent a gain if he had been unfairly sentenced to only ten years."

On his last day of classes Meredith wore the same clothes he had worn on the day he enrolled—a dark suit, white shirt, red necktie, and black shoes. But there was one difference, as he noted in his memoirs: "I put on (upside down) one of the 'Never, Never' buttons that Barnett had made so popular on the campus and many students had worn during the first few weeks after I enrolled. I am a Mississippian in all respects, even the bad ones."

That August, James Meredith became the first African American to receive a degree from the University of Mississippi. The excitement over that milestone was short-lived, however, because the following month Cleve McDowell was expelled from the university for carrying a pistol on campus. Earlier that summer, when he learned the federal government was going to withdraw the guards assigned to Meredith, he called the U.S. marshal's office from Meredith's dormitory room and asked for permission to carry a firearm. That request was denied.

McDowell had reason to be afraid, although aside from an occasional catcall he had little to fear from the other students. He was more concerned about the Sovereignty Commission investigators who had visited his family and teachers upon his enrollment at the university. He was more concerned about the hotheads who perpetually patrolled the back roads of the state with loaded guns and Lord knows what else.

McDowell was expelled after appearing before the five-member student judicial council. The council was chaired by a law student named Champ Terney. McDowell probably didn't know it at the time, but Terney was the son-in-law of Senator Eastland and his chances of getting past Terney were zilch.

There wasn't much celebration on campus when McDowell left. The university was once again lily-white, but something important had been taken from the students. They weren't sure exactly what, but they felt it. There were no parades proclaiming victory. When one of the white students who had seen McDowell drop the pistol on the steps of the law school was asked about it by a reporter, he seemed sympathetic to McDowell's plight. "I just wish I hadn't been there," said the student.

The summer of 1963 was a rough one for President Kennedy. Not only did he have to deal with Medgar Evers's assassination, opposition to the civil rights bill, and continuing fallout from the Cuban missile crisis, he had to oversee his brother's unrelenting pursuit of teamster Jimmy Hoffa.

Three times Attorney General Robert Kennedy thought he had Hoffa—and three times the union official slipped out of his grasp. Kennedy was convinced the Teamsters were controlled by organized crime and felt that if he kept after Hoffa he would nail him, on jury tampering charges if nothing else.

Tennessee seemed the ideal place to set a trap for Hoffa. Kennedy had many reasons for picking the "Volunteer State"—John Seigenthaler, with whom he co-wrote his best-selling book about the Teamsters, *The Enemy Within,* had returned to be editor of the Nashville *Tennessean* early in 1962—but one of the strongest reasons was that it was the political base from which Senator Kefauver had launched his very successful attack against organized crime.

Hoffa was charged with a violation of the Taft–Hartley Act, which prohibits union officials from receiving payments other than wages from their unions. The trial proceeded all fall and into the winter of 1962 (actually the Kennedys had monitored the Hoffa case and the Ole Miss riots at the same time), but when the jury reported two days before Christmas, as Hoffa had expected, that it was hopelessly deadlocked, the judge declared a mistrial. Hoffa wished the jurors a happy Christmas and took the next flight to Detroit.

Unknown to Hoffa, Robert Kennedy had laid a trap. In January, the federal government presented evidence to a Nashville grand jury that Hoffa had engaged in jury tampering during the trial. By April, Kennedy had new indictments.

The second trial, scheduled to begin in November, was moved to Chattanooga on a change of venue request. That was just as well for the federal government. With the sudden death in August of Senator Kefauver, Nashville had lost some of its luster.

Throughout the traumas of the summer, politics droned on in Mississippi with a vapid predictability as voters listlessly prepared to choose a new governor. The three candidates for the Democratic nomination were Lieutenant Governor Paul B. Johnson, former governor J.P. Coleman (now state representative), and Charles Sullivan, a former district attorney. Since Governor Barnett had commended Johnson for "standing tall" during the Ole Miss crisis, Johnson adopted the phrase, "stand tall with Paul," as his campaign slogan.

The campaign was a vicious one, even to Mississippi tastes. Johnson went so far to the right that he was able to successfully depict Coleman as a flaming liberal. Johnson easily defeated Coleman and went on to defeat Rubel Phillips, the lackluster Republican candidate, in the general election in November.

On Friday, November 22, 1963, the Ole Miss campus was relatively quiet. The Ole Miss Rebels had the weekend off to prepare for the season finale the following week against the Mississippi State Bulldogs. With Ole Miss ranked number three in the nation and Mississippi State ranked thirteenth, everyone was expecting a real battle.

It had been two months since Cleve McDowell had been expelled, but few students continued to talk about it. Ole Miss was again a segregated institution. Life went on somehow, with emphasis again shifting to issues such as football and weekend parties. Politics and social issues seemed far removed from the reality of getting an education.

That afternoon the sky was deep blue. The temperature was in the fifties, crisp and cold for Mississippians. As the noise began, students were subjected to blasts of icy air when they opened their windows to peer out into the street. Car horns echoed across the campus. Cars sped up and down the narrow streets, as students hung out the car windows, their arms outstretched. Rebel yells filled the air.

"He's dead!" someone screamed. "The son of a bitch is dead!"

A large Rebel flag the size of a bed sheet was unfurled from a dormitory window. Bug-eyed students, their faces flushed with excitement, rushed out into the street.

"Kennedy's been shot!"

Someone began a cheer. "Hotty toddy, God a'mighty, who in the hell are we?" went the cheer, then ended with, "Ole Miss, by damn!"

As students at Ole Miss danced in the streets—and while an entire nation was paralyzed by shock—news of the assassination of President John F. Kennedy filtered out across the country. Not since 1901, when William McKinley was gunned down, had an American president been assassinated.

That Friday, at 3:38 P.M., a little more than two hours after the shooting, Vice President Lyndon Johnson was sworn in as president aboard *Air Force One*. On the trip from Dallas to Washington, the jet's flight path took it directly over Memphis. At 4:35 P.M., *Air Force One* pilots noted that darkness had fallen on Memphis. One of the first people the new president called after taking office was his old friend Abe Fortas.

~~~~~~

Four to six weeks before the assassination, an Ole Miss student had hitchhiked home from school. The journey from the red clay hills of Oxford to the black gumbo of the Delta usually took about two and a half hours.

In 1963 it was still customary for upperclassmen to shave the heads of freshmen students in a public ceremony outside the student union. This student had been no exception. To cover his still-fuzzy head he wore an Ole Miss beanie. Not only did it keep his head from getting sunburned, it identified him as an Ole Miss student and increased the odds he would be picked up by a motorist with ties to the university.

Just outside Greenwood, the student was given a ride by a short, stocky, middle-aged man in a dark green or black car. The man was driving west on Highway 80. He asked the student rapid-fire questions about Ole Miss, especially about James Meredith and Cleve McDowell, but he didn't seem very interested in the football team.

When they reached Indianola, the driver pulled over at a roadside cafe.

The man had a gruff demeanor and didn't smile often, but he impressed the student as a nice guy, if not somewhat mysterious. Over coffee, he told the student he had driven up from Louisiana to check on some of his business investments. When the student asked him what business he was in, he said he owned a few pinball machines.

About twenty miles down the road the man dropped the student off at the crossroads where Highways 80 and 61 intersect. Before continuing on to Greenville, the man admonished the student to "stay out of trouble" and "get a good education." When the student arrived home, he told friends he had thumbed a ride with a gangster. "Yeah, sure," they had said. It was some time later that the student saw a photograph of the man and identified him as Carlos Marcello.

In retrospect, the fall of 1963 was a turning point not just for race relations but for organized crime in America. It was during this time (eight weeks before the assassination of the president) that Joseph Valachi, a thirty-year veteran of Cosa Nostra and the Genovese crime family, testified before a U.S. Senate subcommittee and exposed the Cosa Nostra as a national conspiracy, whose power was derived from racketeering, gambling, loansharking, narcotics, and the corruption of public officials.

With Valachi squealing, Jimmy Hoffa backed against the wall, and Carlos Marcello earmarked for a government takedown, Attorney General Robert Kennedy twisted the screws on organized crime even tighter. Publicity is anathema to the mob. The Cosa Nostra was quickly becoming an embarrassment to non-Mafia crime families, especially in Memphis, where the public follies of their "dago" crime partners were perceived as a threat to the cartel's stability.

Valachi was the wedge that was driven between the Memphis cartel and the Dixie Mafia. The two organizations continued doing business, because what choice did they really have? But for the Memphis cartel, the publicity over the Cosa Nostra only served to highlight the differences between the two organizations. The Dixie Mafia saw its future, as it always had, as one based on whores, drugs, pinball machines, and whatever new vices the American public wanted to embrace. The Memphis cartel wanted no part of a whore and pinball economy. It wanted government contracts, for that was where the real money was. In time, it would set its sights on the multimillion dollar defense industry, but, for now, according to sources, road and bridge contracts, and funds diverted for FHA and VHA projects pumped millions into its coffers.

After the assassination of President Kennedy, Abe Fortas was easily the second most powerful man in Washington. Even before his friend Lyndon Johnson was elevated to power, he had built his law firm of Arnold, Fortas, and Porter into a Washington powerhouse. Fortas had a brilliant legal mind; however, the source of his power resided not in his knowledge of the law but in his relationships with people in high places—and his willingness to bend, twist, or otherwise distort the law in a manner that best served the interests of his clients.

An example of that can be found in the way he manipulated legislation in 1955 that was considered important to one of his clients, the Commonwealth of Puerto Rico. There was a bill before a Senate subcommittee that would have increased the minimum wage by twenty-five cents per hour. The Puerto Rican government, under pressure from local businesses to kill the measure, was opposed to it.

Fortas was asked to block the increase.

To accomplish that, Fortas had made a call to Walter Jenkins, chief aide to then Senate Majority Leader Lyndon Johnson, to suggest an amendment, one that would exempt Puerto Rico from the wage increase. Fortas followed up the call with a letter that contained language for the amendment.

"You know how sorry I am to bother you," he said in the letter, "but this is a matter that I think is important to the nation and is very dear to my heart."

When the legislation was enacted the following month, it contained Fortas's amendment. Fortas sent a note to Jenkins: "The wage and hour bill passed in form that is satisfactory to the Commonwealth of Puerto Rico. Thanks for your interest and help."

After the assassination, Lyndon Johnson's biggest dilemma, aside from maintaining national security in the midst of the Cold War, was what to do about the murder. It was not a violation of federal law to kill a sitting president. By law, the prosecution of the president's alleged killer, Lee Harvey Oswald, was a local matter to be handled by the Dallas police department.

Johnson asked Fortas what he should do.

Four weeks earlier, he had asked Fortas to get his former Senate aide, Bobby Baker, out of hot water after he was targeted for a congressional investigation because of his associations with more than twenty vending machine and insurance companies. There were rumors of organized crime involvement. As vice president, Johnson could be tainted by a scandal involving Baker. He asked Fortas to neutralize the investigation. With little effort, Fortas was successful in getting Baker off the hook, thus averting disaster for Johnson. For the second time he had saved his friend's political career.

Now Johnson needed Fortas to take care of the assassination investigation. Fortas agreed with Johnson that the investigation should remain in Texas. They decided to set up a Texas commission, with all non-Texans, including federal officials, excluded from the investigation. When acting Attorney General Nick Katzenbach, who temporarily had replaced Robert Kennedy, heard about the Texas scheme, he blew his top. According to William Manchester, author of *The Death of a President,* he stormed over to Abe Fortas's office and told him the idea was a "ghastly mistake."

Johnson and Fortas fought against establishing a federal commission to investigate the assassination, but public pressure was so intense they had no alternative. Once Johnson realized a commission was inevitable, he put Fortas in charge of selecting the individuals who would serve. The seven-member body would become known as the Warren Commission.

To represent the interests of the FBI, which had hastily issued a report concluding that Oswald was the lone assassin, Fortas chose Representative Gerald Ford. When FBI director J. Edgar Hoover learned of Ford's appointment, he made a notation on an internal memo that Ford could be counted on to "look after" the FBI.

To represent the interests of Oswald's home state of Louisiana, Fortas chose Representative Hale Boggs. According to author John H. Davis, Boggs's chief financial backer and behind-the-scenes advisor was Carlos Marcello. To represent the interests of the segregationist South, Fortas chose, in addition to Boggs, Senators Richard Russell of Georgia and John Sherman Cooper of Kentucky.

To round out the commission, Fortas chose ex-CIA director Allen Dulles, a man who could keep secrets if there ever was one; Supreme Court Chief Justice Earl Warren; and John J. McCloy, an international banker with ties to the military-industrial complex.

Johnson's first major address was the State of the Union. Early drafts of his speech show that he intended to take a strong stand against cigarette advertising. The Federal Trade Commission had announced plans to put health warnings on cigarette packages. When it learned of Johnson's position, the Philip Morris Company, one of the world's largest manufacturers of tobacco products, hired Fortas's law firm to represent its interests. By the time Johnson delivered his State of the Union address, all references to cigarettes had been deleted from the speech.

In its final report, issued in September 1964, the Warren Commission concluded that Oswald had acted alone. Further, it said there was no evidence of a conspiracy. Probably the only surprise encountered by Fortas was Senator Russell, who refused to accept the commission's verdict of no conspiracy. Russell asked Warren to list him as a dissenter, but Warren refused. Boggs later expressed skepticism about the reports submitted to the commission by the FBI.

With that bit of dirty work out of the way, Fortas turned his attention to a more important matter: Lyndon Johnson's presidential campaign. It was, after all, an election year. One of Fortas's first suggestions to the president was that he go to Memphis, Tennessee, to deliver a speech to the Tennessee Valley Authority.

～～～

Mississippi governor Paul B. Johnson was sworn in on January 22, 1964. One of his first acts as governor was to send one of the Commission's top-secret investigators to the Gulf Coast to compile a report on the Dixie Mafia. As chief executive of a state whose underworld assets were equally divided between the Dixie and Memphis Mafiosi, Johnson felt he needed more information.

Two weeks later, the investigator, Rex Armistead, submitted a report to the governor stamped "Confidential." The purpose of the investigation, he said, "was to determine the gambling, prostitution and narcotic activities taking place on the Mississippi Gulf coast."

In the eight-page report, Armistead listed the names of fifteen nightclubs he had visited as an undercover operative. He described the structure of each building, noting whether it was of concrete block or "white stone" construction, and he listed the number of slot machines and gambling tables in each club. He reported on the availability of illegal drugs and prostitutes. He listed the owners of each club, their relationship with the New Orleans "syndicate," and the criminal records of the employees.

For example, he pointed out that one club, the Shangri-La, had a black-jack table and two electric slots, and employed four or five strippers who performed in continuous shows. "These girls double as 'B' drinkers and prostitutes," he reported. "The cost of a date at this particular place starts at $75. It is a well-known hangout for shills and hoods during the early part of the evening." He listed the names of two strippers who had records with the New Orleans police department, complete with case numbers.

Armistead said a club named Sa-When had one dice table, one blackjack table, and two slot machines. It had no strippers, but allowed employees to turn tricks with customers. "The dice are not straight and the card game at the bar is capped," he said. "Three men in front of the place carry a revolver at all times. This establishment, in recent weeks, has been the scene of several attempted take-overs."

A club named the Hide-a-Way was a good place to buy illegal drugs. "Pep pills such as Dexedrine, Benzedrine and Dexamil, to name a few, are frequently passed around, and may be bought across the counter. The average price for pep pills is fifty cents." Although barbiturates and amphetamines were the most popular drugs on the coast, he said, marijuana was also available.

Most of the prostitutes were from the New Orleans–Jefferson Parish area. They worked a circuit that extended from Houston, Texas, to Galveston, through New Orleans and the Mississippi coast, over to Pensacola, then down to Fort Lauderdale and Miami. The women often were brought to the Mississippi coast by boat under the supervision of Tommy Murrello, "a well-known procurer with the syndicate."

Armistead's report reveals Governor Johnson's desire to better understand the business operations of the Dixie Mafia. He had no intention of prosecuting any of the individuals named in the report. He just wanted to know what kind of people he was dealing with. The fact that he asked Armistead, who had no authority to make arrests, to conduct the investigation shows that he had more confidence in the Sovereignty Commission than he did in the highway patrol or other law enforcement agencies. It also offers insight into how the governor used the Commission as a private police agency, a Southern-drawl Gestapo.

That same month, Armistead was sent to the University of Mississippi to conduct covert surveillance of television news commentator Howard K. Smith, who had been invited to speak to students at Fulton Chapel, the main campus auditorium. Armistead shadowed Smith's every move, noting his precise times of movement, but, in the end, he reported that he observed no "subversive" activities by the newsman.

While keeping an eye on Smith, he witnessed an incident that occurred when five blacks showed up at the auditorium to hear Smith's speech. "At the alcove inside the main door, one of the Negroes was stopped by a student . . . [who] advised him that he was not wanted there and that this was a meeting for white people and [he] was asked to leave," reported Armistead.

"The Negro attempted to walk over to the student, at which time the student grabbed him and carried him outside and proceeded to give him a good whipping. Chief Tatum [head of campus security] immediately grabbed the white student and without attempting to find the cause of the disturbance, began to beat the student across the ears and face and then pushed him down a flight of stairs where other campus police were waiting. At this time Chief Tatum advised the student that he was under arrest and was to be placed in the county jail."

When the student was transported to the jail, the county sheriff refused to incarcerate him. Instead, he took the student home with him and allowed him to spend the night. Armistead said there was general agreement among law enforcement officers that Chief Tatum should be removed from office.

"By doing so, eighty percent of the campus trouble would be dissolved," he concluded.

Howard K. Smith was not the only national television personality to come under scrutiny that month. Dossiers were prepared on three of the stars of a popular NBC television show, *Bonanza*, after the men refused to appear as scheduled for an advertised event in Jackson.

The three men, Lorne Green, Michael Landon, and Dan Blocker, canceled their appearance after they learned it was for a segregated audience. To punish the actors, Erle Johnston pressured General Motors, the sponsor of the show, and television station WLBT, the NBC affiliate in Jackson, to drop the top-rated program. Both the television station and the automaker refused to bow to the Commission's demands.

The Commission found Ole Miss fertile ground for the cultivation of informants. One group of students, which named itself, "The Knights of the Great Forest," spied on professors and turned in the names of those they thought supported racial integration. On another occasion, the Commission persuaded two Ole Miss students to infiltrate the Congress of Federated Organizations (COFO) office in Jackson. It was the most hated of all the civil rights organizations in the state. "We were able to convince them we were integrationists," the students reported. "May God never let this be true."

One of the most bizarre escapades conducted by Commission investigators occurred at the end of March. The Commission sent investigator Tom Scarbrough to Grenada to investigate reports that a white woman had given birth to a racially mixed child. After meeting with his initial source, who informed him that the thirty-eight-year-old woman had been having an affair with a thirty-one-year-old black motel employee, Scarbrough met with the local sheriff, who expressed relief at seeing him in town.

"[He said] that people in Grenada were very much disturbed about the rumors going about pertaining to [the woman]," Scarbrough reported. "The sheriff further stated the reason why so much talk was going on concerning this matter was that [the woman's ex-husband] came from a prominent family and the [woman] came from a fairly good family."

Scarbrough decided the easiest way to solve the dilemma would be for him to examine the baby to determine if it had had a black father. The sheriff agreed. He called the woman and got her to stop by his office. She denied having an affair with a black man, but admitted having an affair with a white man who worked at the motel.

"I told her I knew for a fact that [the sheriff] had expressed himself as being in sympathy with her and that if the child were not a Negro the sheriff could go a long way toward squelching this vicious talk going around about her having given birth to a half Negro," Scarbrough said in his report. "And further, I believed it would be to her advantage to let the sheriff take someone with him and look at the child. She stated she had no objection to the sheriff or anyone else seeing the baby, as she had not been trying to conceal it."

After arranging a time for the visit, Scarbrough went to the motel to interview the black man mentioned as the father. He asked him point blank if he had ever had sex with the white woman.

"No sir," he answered.

The next morning, the sheriff went to view the baby. When he returned to his office, where Scarbrough was waiting, he said he had seen the baby, but wasn't sure about the child's parentage. He asked Scarbrough if he would mind taking a look at the baby.

The men returned to the woman's apartment.

"We both looked at the baby again and I was looking at the child's fingernails and the end of its fingers very closely when she remarked, 'I know what you're thinking, but that baby is not part Negro. Its father is an Italian,' " Scarbrough said in his report. "After viewing the child I had a weak feeling in the pit of my stomach and the sheriff expressed he felt likewise. We both agreed we were not qualified to say it was a part Negro child, but we could say it was not 100 percent Caucasian."

Scarbrough returned to the motel and told the black man's employer what he had concluded. "He stated there was nothing left for him to do except to dismiss [the black man] from his employ," he said in the report. "What disposition will be made of [the black man] is yet to be seen."

As Governor Johnson began his second month in office, the Commission identified three main areas of concern: reports of weapons shipments entering the state, ostensibly for use by militants; an administration viewed as out of control at Tougaloo College; and increased civil rights activity, particularly in Meridian and Philadelphia.

That March, State Representative Betty Jane Long of Meridian wrote Governor Johnson to request an investigation of a white couple in her district, Michael and Rita Schwerner, who ran the CORE office in Meridian. After getting the referral from Johnson, Commission director Erle Johnston assigned an investigator to the case.

A dossier was compiled on the couple, along with reports of their daily activities and their schedules, and that information was passed on to Representative Long in a series of reports. (Long later served on the Commission from 1968 to 1972.) Included in the report were a description of the 1963 station wagon the couple drove and the vehicle's license number—H25 503 (Hinds County).

The Commission had a particular hatred for the Schwerners because they were white. Blacks who participated in the civil rights movement were despised, but, at least, their actions were understandable, even by the rawest redneck. Whites who helped them were traitors, not just to the state of Mississippi but to the white race.

As surveillance of the Schwerners intensified, the Commission sent an undercover agent—identified only as "Investigator #51" (but probably Armistead)—to Selma, Alabama, to make an arms purchase.

"We authorized the investigator to buy two .38–caliber pistols and bring them back to the Sovereignty Commission," Johnston said in a report to the governor. "These revolvers are being sold by the dealer for only $11 each and are very similar to the pistols which were shipped into Walthall County by a dealer in California. These pistols are now in a cabinet in the Sovereignty Commission office. The dealer had on hand about 1,500 rifles and several cases of weapons still unopened."

In his report, the investigator said that after he picked out the pistols, the dealer took out a note pad and asked the investigator for his name. "I gave the name as Douglas Graves, Route 1, Brandon, Mississippi," the investigator said, indicating he had lied. As the dealer finished his paperwork, the investigator cased the room.

"A negro helper was engaged in taking rifles from cases and stacking them in a storeroom next to the shop," he said. "These were .30–caliber, bolt-action rifles packed about 50 to the crate. The crates were marked from International Arms Corporation, Alexandria, Virginia . . . A survey of the area revealed that there are no windows in the shop or storerooms, and each door has a large padlock on it, in addition to the regular Yale door locks. This area is just behind [the dealer's] house and any forced entry could easily be seen from the house."

The Commission viewed Tougaloo College as a threat because it was a private institution over which the state had only limited control. By 1964, the college was considered a focal point for organizers of the civil rights movement. Most of the students were black (nine white students were enrolled), but the chaplain, the Reverend Edwin King, was white, and so were half the members of the faculty.

In a report to the governor dated March 10, 1964, Johnston explained the Commission's plan to revoke the college's charter and destroy the school's accreditation. As evidence of the college's subversive activities, Johnston offered the name of Dr. Otto Nathan of New York. He pointed out that Nathan, who recently had been invited to speak at the college, had appeared before the House Committee on Un-American Activities in 1956 and had refused to answer whether he was a member of the Communist Party.

"In a statement to the press, Dr. A.D. Beittel, president of Tougaloo, said he was aware of Dr. Nathan's identity with 'subversive organizations,' but said Dr. Nathan would be welcome to return to Tougaloo at any time," said Johnston. "In his talk at Tougaloo, Dr. Nathan bitterly attacked the Un-American Activities Committee and the Committee on Internal Security headed by Senator Jim Eastland."

Johnston listed other individuals identified as undesirable, including Dr. Ernst Borinski, chairman of the sociology department, whom Johnston identified as a "German Jew." Johnston also mentioned the Reverend Edwin King, but said information about him would be forthcoming in a separate report.

Johnston had something special in mind for King. On March 13, Johnston drove to Memphis for a secret meeting with King's mother. With him he took a former FBI agent, John Sullivan, who owned a private investigator's service in Vicksburg (King's hometown). Johnston's report doesn't provide information about the substance of the meeting, but it says that King's mother did "furnish a few leads." In Johnston's opinion, King's mother was "ashamed of her son's activities, but wants to retain his affection."

The Commission had plenty of weapons in its arsenal as it launched its 1964 offensive against desegregation, but, by far, the most significant was the secret committee that had been formed in 1963 with the help of lawyer John Satterfield. Funded with money provided by the Sovereignty Commission and private donations, the committee—named the Coordinating Committee for Fundamental American Freedoms—was formed to combat the civil rights act being debated in Congress.

From its offices in Washington, D.C., the Coordinating Committee for Fundamental American Freedoms lobbied against civil rights legislation and bought full-page newspaper ads proclaiming that the legislation would lead to racial quotas, influence teacher hirings, and dictate job seniority. Majority whip Senator Hubert Humphrey denounced the ads and the committee for their "outright lies."

When an audit of Washington lobbyists was released in 1963, it was disclosed that the Coordinating Committee for Fundamental American Freedoms had spent $141,785.88 in its effort to influence Congress. That made it the third largest spender for the year. The only lobbies laying out more were the United Federation of Postal Clerks ($202,996.97) and the AFL-CIO ($145,635.97).

The Coordinating Committee for Fundamental American Freedoms was nothing more than a front for the tri-state federation. When the Civil Rights Act of 1964 was passed by Congress, the committee was dissolved and the tri-state federation looked for new ways of exerting influence. In June, less than a month before the Civil Rights Act went into effect, Erle Johnston informed the governor of an anonymous donation of $50,000. He said it was to fund a new organization meant to replace the committee.

Johnston deposited the money in a private account at the First National Bank in Jackson, although by the time the deposit slip was filled out the amount had decreased to $49,561.23. The money went into account number 00–481–21. Johnston said the money had been received from "anonymous donors" in the East who had agreed to furnish an additional $200,000 if Mississippi contributed matching funds.

Like every state agency, the Sovereignty Commission was required to submit vouchers for all its expenditures to the state auditor, who wrote the actual checks. Unlike other agencies, the Commission was allowed to accept private donations and deposit them in a private account beyond the watchful eyes of the state auditor.

Thirty-three years later, the source of that private funding is still secret, although it was almost certainly channeled through one of the tri-state federation's many front organizations.

Less than six months into the new governor's term, the Commission had a private bank account and the ability to launder money from private benefactors, two .38–caliber pistols purchased under a fake name, and a membership dedicated to doing whatever it took to win a victory against the enemies of segregation.

On Sunday, June 21, 1964, three civil rights workers, Michael Schwerner and Andrew Goodman of New York, and James Chaney of Meridian, set out from Meridian to investigate the burning of the Mount Zion Methodist Church in the eastern part of Neshoba County.

All three men had been under surveillance by the Commission for several months, but surviving records show that Schwerner and his blue 1964 station wagon—license number H25 503—had been targeted as early as March. As they passed through Philadelphia, the Neshoba County seat, they were stopped for speeding by Deputy Sheriff Cecil Price. Chaney was behind the wheel.

After he pulled them over, Price asked Chaney, who was black, and Schwerner and Goodman, who were white, what they were doing in Neshoba County. They said they had come to investigate a church burning. Price gave Chaney a ticket for speeding, and told them he was going to have to take them in for questioning about the church burning. As they were talking, one of the station wagon's tires went flat. Price radioed for backup from the highway patrol and then helped the men change the tire.

Two highway patrolmen, one named Wiggs and the other named Poe, arrived while they were changing the tire and escorted the deputy sheriff and the men in the station wagon to the Neshoba County jail. The three prisoners were fed a big country dinner, held until 10:30 that night, then released after they paid a twenty-dollar bond set by the justice of the peace. As they were leaving, Price asked them where they were headed. They said they were returning to Meridian. Price stood outside the courthouse and watched them drive onto Highway 45 and head toward Meridian.

When the three men failed to return to Meridian that night, their families and friends notified authorities. By the next morning, word had spread like wildfire throughout Philadelphia that something bad had happened to the men after their release. Buford Posey, a Neshoba County resident who had been under surveillance by the Commission for voicing pro-NAACP opinions, received two telephone calls the next morning, one from the jailer's wife, the other from his daughter. Both women expressed concern that something bad had happened to the men.

Posey notified the FBI. Then, fearful for his safety, he fled to Tennessee to stay with his sister at Oak Ridge. Subsequently, he expressed a belief to interviewers that Sheriff Rainey was a member of the Ku Klux Klan.

On Tuesday, June 23, an anonymous caller notified the FBI of the whereabouts of the station wagon the men had been driving. With little trouble, FBI agents located the vehicle on a narrow country road near the Bogue Chitto swamp. It had been doused with gasoline and burned. There was no sign of the civil rights workers.

As news of the discovery made headlines across the nation, law enforcement officers from Madison County, Yazoo County, Hinds County, the highway patrol, the Sovereignty Commission and others descended upon Philadelphia. Attorney General Robert Kennedy ordered an FBI investigation and President Lyndon Johnson ordered two hundred sailors from the naval base in Meridian to assist in the search for the missing men.

On Wednesday, June 24, former CIA director Allen Dulles walked into the offices of the Sovereignty Commission for a meeting with Erle Johnston. Dulles had been sent by President Johnson to compile a report on the activities of two organizations: the White Knights of the Ku Klux Klan and the Americans for the Preservation of the White Race. When Dulles returned to Washington, he met with the president, then issued a statement in which he said Mississippi had a "very real" law enforcement problem.

Johnston was stunned by Dulles's comments. The Commission had used the CIA as a model for its organizational structure. He was not used to other government agencies being critical of his operations. While Dulles was not technically a member of the government, he was—as everyone knew—one of the nation's top former spies.

Because of the controversy, Johnston felt the need to send a memo to the governor explaining his meeting with Dulles. "They asked me if it were true that the APWR [Americans for the Preservation of the White Race] was responsible for five deaths in southwest Mississippi," he said. "I informed them that the Sovereignty Commission had a few files on both of these organizations and some of their literature, but we had no cause for any concern or policies toward these groups so long as the groups and their members observed Governor Johnson's policies of law and order. I told him that we had no knowledge of any connection between APWR as an organization and any violence in southwest Mississippi."

On the day after Johnston's meeting with Dulles, the parents of Goodman and Schwerner went on national television in New York to talk about their missing sons. Chaney's mother joined them from Mississippi via a telephone hookup.

During a speech in St. Augustine, Florida, Martin Luther King was critical of the "climate of lawlessness" in Mississippi. "If we have no satisfaction from the federal government we will have to offer our bodies as sacrifice," he said.

America may have been outraged by the inability of law enforcement officials to locate the missing civil rights workers, but for the Commission it was business as usual that week. On June 26, Johnston sent a memo to the highway patrol requesting an escort for a paid informant who was traveling back to Mississippi from Oxford, Ohio, where he had participated in a Congress of Racial Equality (CORE) training program for civil rights workers. The informant was identified only as a black male.

Johnston informed the highway patrol that the CORE informant would be traveling in a 1957 green-and-beige Cadillac that bore Mississippi license plate number HD8 942. He said the informant would be accompanied by his wife and a white male. They would travel on Highway 45 to Corinth, then go to Tupelo, where they would take the Natchez Trace for the remainder of the trip to Jackson.

"It is very important that you understand that the white male does not know about the informant's connection with the Sovereignty Commission," Johnston said in the memo. "Subject has been advised that if the car is stopped for any traffic violation, etc., that whatever fines are imposed be paid without question."

When the informant arrived in Jackson, he submitted a report to the Commission. He reported that John Doar, the U.S. Justice Department official who had assisted James Meredith at Ole Miss, was a guest speaker at the training session. He detailed some of the group's activities, then told John-ston what he wanted to hear: "It might be noted that during the eleven days I have been in Oxford I have noticed a good deal of drinking going on among the students. . . . Further the white girls have been going around with the negro boys and negro girls going with the white boys. I have seen these integrated couples going into the dorms together for extended periods of time."

The informant concluded his report with an observation about the high-way patrol escort he had received into Jackson. "The other occupants of my car were impressed by this and thought it was a good thing for the state to be doing," he said tongue-in-cheek.

At the very moment that concerned citizens, FBI agents, sailors from the naval base, and CORE volunteers searched through the unfriendly Neshoba County countryside for the missing civil rights workers, the Sovereignty Commission was providing a CORE informant with safe passage through the state. There could be no doubt that CORE—and those who worked for the organization—were at the top of the Commission's hit list.

By the summer of 1964, Charles Evers had become the most visible black leader in Mississippi. He felt an inner rage over the state's inabil-ity—or downright refusal—to punish his brother's killer. Years later, he revealed in his memoirs that he fantasized about going on killing sprees to take out all the white peckerwoods in Mississippi. But that's all they were—fantasies.

Despite his less than saintly background—he had once operated a num-bers racket and a prostitution ring in Chicago—he was able to find a niche for himself in the civil rights movement. He and Medgar had been close. As the new field secretary of the NAACP office in Mississippi, Charles was determined to live his life in a manner that would bring credit to his slain brother.

On July 2, Erle Johnston notified the governor that Charles Evers was planning a test of public accommodations in Jackson on July 4, the day the civil rights bill was scheduled to be signed into law by President Johnson.

"The NAACP has adequate funds to provide bail money for arrested demonstrators, however [it] does not have the manpower," said Johnston. "Evers has tried to get COFO [Council of Federated Organizations] to furnish personnel for demonstrations in return for guaranteed bail money if COFO participants are arrested. . . .

"Evers also is trying to revive a strong boycott of Capitol Street stores. He has urged the outside students working for COFO not to patronize any stores on the boycott list. He is organizing some 'goon squads' to watch these establishments and harass any Negroes who do any trading there."

Pressured by Attorney General Robert Kennedy to solve the case involving the missing civil rights workers, FBI director J. Edgar Hoover traveled to Jackson in early July to open a bureau field office. While there, he met with Governor Paul Johnson and Attorney General Joe Patterson. One result of that meeting was Hoover's acceptance of five Mississippi highway patrol officers into the next session of the FBI National Academy. He also agreed to allow the agency to participate in police training activities in Mississippi.

The FBI National Academy, founded in 1935 as the FBI Police Training School, had become an important tool for the bureau in establishing relationships with law enforcement officials at the state level. Typically, candidates were given a twelve-week training course, then presented with a diploma and membership in a special alumni association. Once the graduates returned home, special agents at the academy stayed in contact with them, telephoning every sixty days or so.

The academy's goal was not so much to upgrade the training of police officers as to give the bureau contacts in local police departments. In that sense, it was a covert operation aimed at the police departments. One of the early directors of the academy was Special Agent W. Webb Burke, an Ole Miss graduate who took on many sensitive assignments in his long career with the FBI.

When he returned to Washington, Hoover wrote a letter to Colonel T.B. Birdsong, head of the Mississippi highway patrol, thanking him for his hospitality. Birdsong responded with a letter that expressed approval of a "close association" with the bureau. "Be assured of our abiding friendship and desire to cooperate with your department," he said.

Those were assurances that had been understood for quite some time by the Sovereignty Commission, which had been receiving help from former agents on a regular basis since 1956. But there was some confusion at the Commission over just how far it should go in cooperating with the FBI.

Later in the year, after a series of bombings in McComb, Erle Johnston wrote a memo to Governor Johnson in which he said the FBI had asked the Commission to share the information in its files. Johnston was disturbed by the request.

"Prior to the arrests at McComb for bombings, we would have politely declined to furnish the FBI with any information," said Johnston. "However, in view of the publicly announced cooperation between the state highway patrol and the FBI on the McComb cases, we would like to know from you whether the Sovereignty Commission also should cooperate with the FBI and, if so, to what extent."

Several weeks earlier, Special Agent Roy Moore, head of the new FBI field office in Jackson, had provided the governor with a list of law enforcement officials in the state suspected of membership in the Ku Klux Klan. The list included names of highway patrol officers, game wardens, city marshals, town constables, and county sheriffs.

"If you intend taking any action against the above-named individuals, their Klan membership should be established by separate investigation as this Bureau would be unable to produce any individuals to testify at any necessary hearings," said Moore. Was Moore, who once had made national headlines after solving an airplane bombing case, sincere in his efforts to share information? Or was he simply letting the Commission know he had the names of police officers who were members of the KKK?

Governor Johnson passed the letter on to Colonel Birdsong, who replied to the agent in a letter dated August 24. "I deeply appreciate this information," said Birdsong. "Steps have now been taken to eliminate this situation, *in part.*"

Sovereignty Commission investigator Andy Hopkins returned to Neshoba County on June 29 to continue surveillance of the FBI. The investigation into the disappearance of the three civil rights workers was entering its eighth day.

Hopkins met with Sheriff Lawrence Rainey and Deputy Sheriff Cecil Price. Rainey told Hopkins that he, Price, and Hale Singletary, an investigator with the Mississippi Fire Marshal's office, were at the burned church when they received word that the station wagon driven by the civil rights workers had been found. Together, they rushed over to the swamp, where they found twelve FBI agents at the crime scene.

"The sheriff stated that an FBI agent at the scene told him not to go near the car and that he did not go near the car until later when FBI agent John Procter of Meridian told him that he could approach it," said Hopkins. "Sheriff Rainey stated that he asked Agent Procter who found the car and who they reported it to. Procter told him that someone reported it to him at his office in Meridian, but he could not tell him who it was."

From the details contained in his report, it was obvious that Hopkins knew as much—or perhaps more—about the crime as the FBI. "The results of my investigation indicate that the automobile was parked and burned on the log road between 11:00 A.M. and 1:30 P.M., Monday, June 22," he said in his report.

"I reached this conclusion because a witness was working on a log truck within 200 feet of the spot where the car burned. . . . The condition of the car, the washed out tire and footprints indicated that the car and terrain was rained on after the car was burned. I was in the Philadelphia area at this time and the only rain in this area between 11:00 A.M. Monday and Tuesday afternoon when the car was found, occurred between 1:30 P.M. and 3:00 P.M. Monday, June 22."

Sheriff Rainey told Hopkins he "resented" the way the FBI had treated his wife. She was in the hospital convalescing after surgery, he said, when she was questioned by FBI agents about his whereabouts on the evening the civil rights workers disappeared.

"Sheriff Rainey is a suspect in the church burning and the alleged whipping of several Negroes and possibly the disappearance of the three civil rights workers," said Hopkins in his report. "FBI agents questioned him for a period of approximately three hours Tuesday afternoon, June 30, and indicated by their questions that he was a suspect and knew more than he was telling about the case.

"The sheriff stated that near the end of the interview, an agent said to him: 'Now come on sheriff and tell us what you did with those people.' One agent asked the sheriff if he was a member of the KKK and, of course, the sheriff denied being a member of the Klan as he has repeatedly denied it to me since the beginning of this investigation. At one point, the sheriff stated that an agent pointed his finger at him and said: 'Don't you defy the federal government!' "

Hopkins asked the FBI who had reported the location of the station wagon, but agents refused to share that information with him. Hopkins poked around on his own and found out that the car was discovered by a Choctaw Indian, who reported it to the Bureau of Indian Affairs, which, in turn, contacted the FBI.

"At this point in the investigation, Sheriff Rainey and his deputy, Cecil Price, and Richard Willis, a night policeman of Philadelphia, are the prime suspects in this case as Deputy Price and Richard Willis were the last two persons to have seen the missing individuals and Sheriff Rainey is reported to have been in the group that whipped or beat the Negroes the night that the church burned," Hopkins said. "Sheriff Rainey advised me today, Thursday, July 2, that he expected to be arrested by the FBI at any time. In fact, he has already called Attorney General Joe Patterson to ascertain the procedure in making bond after he is arrested."

As the FBI dug for more information about the missing civil rights workers, Hopkins continued his surveillance of the FBI. He noted that they had set up headquarters in room 18 at the Delphia Motel in Philadelphia, "where they have a radio and straight-line telephones installed." On July 1, he observed the FBI installing a radio antenna on top of the city water tower "in an effort to contact Meridian direct by radio and to better receive communications from their mobile units." Hopkins returned to Jackson that weekend.

About one month later, on Tuesday, August 4, the FBI discovered the bodies of the civil rights workers buried deep within an earthen dam just outside Philadelphia. When he heard the news late that afternoon, Hopkins rushed back to Neshoba County, arriving at 9:45 that evening. His first stop was the sheriff's office, where he spoke to Mrs. Frankie Chisolm, an office deputy. She had heard rumors the day before that the FBI was preparing to uncover the bodies and planned to arrest Deputy Sheriff Cecil Price and charge him with the murders.

Mrs. Chisolm told Hopkins that Sheriff Rainey was vacationing in Biloxi with his wife and two sons when the bodies were discovered, but was expected to arrive back in town shortly before midnight. After talking to Mrs. Chisolm, Hopkins drove out to the crime scene, a distance of about six miles from the courthouse.

A half-mile from the earthen dam, Hopkins encountered a roadblock manned by two Mississippi highway patrolmen. They told him the bodies had been removed and were en route to the University Hospital in Jackson, where an autopsy would be performed. Because it was late, Hopkins decided to wait until daylight to inspect the crime scene.

The tone of his report—and the type of details offered—indicate Hopkins was considerably more interested in finding out who had tipped off the FBI about the location of the bodies than he was in identifying their killers. He notified his superiors that he had learned that the FBI had offered Deputy Sheriff Price one million dollars for evidence that would solve the case. Noted Hopkins: "The agents told Price that he could 'leave Mississippi with that kind of money and buy a cattle ranch in Wyoming.' "

Hopkins concluded that the FBI informant must have been someone who was there when the civil rights workers were killed "since the bodies were found in the section where very little searching had been done." He said he felt the informant was Olen Burrage, the man who owned the property where the bodies were found.

"My informant did not know whether Mr. Burrage accompanied the agents to the grave, whether he gave them oral instructions as to how to find it, or whether he drew a map or directed them in some other manner," Hopkins said in his report. "The informant stated that Mr. Burrage received $30,000 from the FBI for this information. He did not know whether Mr. Burrage had been promised exoneration or lenience if he, himself, was involved in the murder of these subjects."

Hopkins also was interested in finding out if the FBI knew the caliber of the gun that was used to shoot the three men. The highway patrol informed him that there was one bullet in Schwerner's body, one bullet in Goodman's body, and three bullets in Chaney's body, but the caliber of the bullets or whether they were all fired from the same gun was still unknown. Hopkins told his superiors that he was sharing the results of his information with the highway patrol, but not with the FBI, because, as he explained, "they already have most of it."

When Hopkins arrived at the crime scene, he encountered Sheriff Rainey and Deputy Price, who were inspecting the area with a coroner's jury. Rainey told him the FBI had made "threats" if he did not tell them what he knew about the crime. By "threats," he explained they had told him they had information linking him to a bootlegging operation. If that information was turned over to the IRS, the agents allegedly told him, he would owe several thousand dollars in back taxes. If he would cooperate with them, the agents said, they would keep quiet about the bootlegging.

Hopkins remained in Philadelphia through August 6, then returned to Jackson. In his report, he said that the FBI informant would be in "danger" if his identity was ever revealed. "Several people, including trouble-makers, have expressed their dissatisfaction that someone informed to the FBI and have made remarks that they would hate to be in his shoes when people find out who he is," he said. "The fact that the information furnished by the informant was so accurate indicates that he was a witness to the burial and most likely knows the names of others involved and was very probably involved himself."

Less than a week after the bodies of the three civil rights workers were discovered, President Lyndon Johnson signed the Gulf of Tonkin resolution, which was passed by Congress after reports that American ships had been attacked by North Vietnamese torpedo boats. Johnson had requested the resolution in support of his "fight if we must" policy in Southeast Asia. The event was noted by the media and duly reported, but little emphasis was given to its ultimate significance.

The Democratic Party convention later that month was meant to be a coronation for Johnson. Everyone had agreed in advance that no other names would be placed in nomination and no major platform fights would be tolerated. Unfortunately for Democratic Party regulars, no one bothered to explain that to the Mississippi Freedom Democratic Party (FDP), a delegation of black activists and white liberals who traveled to Atlantic City to challenge the credentials of the sitting Mississippi delegation.

Johnson saw the FDP as a threat to his reelection effort. If the convention turned back the FDP delegation, it would hurt him with black voters. If the convention seated the FDP delegation, it would hurt him with white voters in the South, a voting block he had no intention of tossing to the Republican Party.

Johnson turned to Abe Fortas for help. With the assistance of presidential advisors Clark Clifford and Walter Jenkins, Fortas devised a plan in which Senator Hubert Humphrey, a respected liberal with strong civil rights credentials, would act as a broker. If he was successful, he would become Johnson's choice for vice president. If he failed . . . well, Minnesota was pleasant enough that time of the year.

The Mississippi challenge was the top news story of the convention. The more attention the challenge received, the more Johnson retreated from public view. Johnson wanted it fixed, dammit—and quick.

Just when it appeared the issue would be resolved, an entirely new issue arose. The FDP newsletter published a letter to the editor calling on draft-age blacks in Mississippi to refuse induction for service in Vietnam. "Negro boys should not honor the draft here in Mississippi," said the letter. "Mothers should encourage their sons not to go."

Although the antidraft sentiments were expressed in a letter, not an editorial, enemies of the FDP used it to cause dissent among the FDP delegates in Atlantic City. Some of the more conservative members of the FDP were appalled. One of the more active white members of the FDP, *Delta Democrat-Times* editor Hodding Carter III, himself a former U.S. Marine, called the antiwar statement "close to treason."

For the first time, opposition to the war in Vietnam was associated with the civil rights movement. When Fortas received word that Puerto Rico was going to support the FDP position, he scurried over to the delegation and brought it back into line.

All-out war on the floor of the convention was averted when Johnson offered a compromise: Two of the FDP delegates—black civil rights leader Aaron Henry and Tougaloo College chaplain Ed King— would be seated as "at-large" delegates, with the remaining FDP delegates welcomed as "honored guests."

Only those members of the regular Mississippi delegation would be seated who signed a loyalty oath pledging to support the party's nominees in the November election. Additionally, the Democratic Party agreed to create a committee to examine and resolve the conflict before the 1968 convention.

That issue resolved, Lyndon Johnson and his vice presidential running mate, Senator Hubert Humphrey, accepted the Democratic Party's nominations. Their GOP opponents would be Senator Barry Goldwater of Arizona and Representative William Miller of New York.

Most Southern governors remained loyal to the Democratic Party and endorsed the Johnson–Humphrey ticket. The major exceptions were Governor George Wallace of Alabama and Mississippi governor Paul Johnson, who broke with tradition and endorsed Goldwater, who had voted against the Civil Rights Act of 1964.

When the votes were counted, Johnson had won by a landslide, with 43 million votes to Goldwater's 27 million. Mississippi and Alabama gave Goldwater his largest margins of victory, with Mississippians casting over 350,000 votes for the Arizona senator and only 52,000 votes for Johnson. Goldwater won in Louisiana, but he lost in Tennessee by more than 100,000 votes. The election signaled a potentially devastating fissure in the tri-state federation.

The Commission observed the delegate fight with great interest. It now had a new enemy—the Mississippi Freedom Democratic Party. As it began compiling dossiers on the organization's membership, it stepped up covert activities against a broad range of "enemies." One new enemy was the National Lawyers Guild.

In September, a lawyer named Benjamin Smith moved to Jackson to oversee work at the guild's new office on North Farish Street. Unknown to Smith, the Commission had planted a spy among his office staff.

Erle Johnston detailed the covert operation in a memo dated September 25, 1964: "We learned [Smith] has called an employment service for temporary stenographic help. Through the cooperation of the employment service, a steno was sent to Smith who has agreed to give us copies of all office correspondence and other memos which will add to our file on this subject and his associates. We have agreed to match the hourly rate paid the steno in return for this service. Because we dealt through other parties, the steno, herself, does not know the extra compensation is coming from the Sovereignty Commission."

On the morning of December 4, 1964, Mrs. Frankie Chisolm of the Neshoba County sheriff's office turned on her radio and heard that the FBI was making arrests in the murder case involving the civil rights workers. Her worst suspicions were soon confirmed. Her boss, Sheriff Lawrence Rainey, and his chief deputy, Cecil Price, had been arrested, along with nineteen other citizens of Philadelphia and Meridian.

One of the first people Mrs. Chisolm called was Commission investigator Andy Hopkins, who rushed to Neshoba County as soon as he got the news. When he arrived he learned that all twenty-one men had been carried before a federal commissioner in Meridian and charged with violating the civil rights of the murdered men. They were being held at the naval base in Meridian and were not being allowed visitors. Among those arrested was Olen Burrage, the man Hopkins had identified as the informant.

"Strictly from the standpoint of deduction, it appears that the FBI does not have as strong a case against those arrested as they have stated they have, as they are still allegedly attempting to get Price and Rainey to confess or tell what they know about the case," Hopkins said.

"The FBI evidently believes that the plot to kill Schwerner was formulated over a period of several weeks and that Chaney and Goodman just happened to be along when he was murdered. Their theory seems to be that some of those involved observed the civil rights workers when they left Meridian and then notified others in the Philadelphia area who were in on the plot.

"They evidently believe that these subjects were followed out of Philadelphia for several miles where they were stopped by several carloads of white men who blocked the highway (four cars). From that point, the FBI evidently believes that the victims were taken to a deserted spot in rural Neshoba County where they were executed. The bureau also seems to believe that a site for hiding the bodies already had been selected."

On December 8, 1964, U.S. Commissioner Esther Carter dropped charges against nineteen of the men. Carter, a grandmotherly woman in her sixties, was not a lawyer and had requested that a law clerk sit at her side during the proceedings.

Federal prosecutors were stunned by her decision.

A second commissioner in Biloxi then released a twentieth defendant. The two remaining defendants were held in jails in Gulfport, Mississippi, and in Louisiana for a while longer, then charges against them also were dropped.

The Sovereignty Commission ended the year by notifying the State Board of Health that a white woman who had been working with COFO workers in McComb was a carrier of venereal disease. "Subject is said to wear black stockings to conceal sores," Erle Johnston said in the report. "She reportedly has been afraid she will be picked up by a public health officer. . . . We notified Dr. Blakey of the state board of health. Dr. Blakey said they would pick up the subject for an examination and notify the Sovereignty Commission if the tests were positive. . . . Any further steps regarding above subject will be determined after a report from the state health department."

CHAPTER 6

1965 – 1966

The 1965 inauguration of Lyndon Johnson was pivotal. The tri-state federation was falling apart as a political entity. The Citizens' Councils were on their last legs. The public expression of racism by elected officials was quickly diminishing. And city after city in the South joined the desegregation bandwagon and opened up schools and libraries to citizens of all races.

Liberal publications such as the *New Republic* and *Harper's* embraced the new president with all the editorial enthusiasm they could muster. "Johnson is the one original New Dealer still prominent in American political life," wrote Peter F. Drucker in *Harper's.* "In the year since he succeeded himself to the Presidency, Mr. Johnson has proven himself effective, shrewd, energetic, and self-confident. And in Hubert Humphrey he has a Vice President of rare sensitivity to the new issues and to the needs and values of the new generation. . . . No one—neither Johnson nor Goldwater—will be able to push this country back onto the old, pre-1964 slope of the political watershed we crossed last fall."

More to the point was the teaser for Drucker's piece: "We are about to enter a time of political upheaval—how it will be dominated by a new power center and a new set of issues—and why the Republicans may have a rare opportunity to mold a new majority." The headline writer was right, but for the wrong reasons.

There *was* a new power center in America.

That the power center was built on a consensus of fair-minded, liberal thinkers who would put the country back on a course of New Deal idealism was but a myth. The reality was something altogether different.

The collapse of the political arm of the tri-state federation meant that power shifted to its underworld benefactors, the Dixie Mafia and the Memphis cartel. Since the two organizations had different concepts of political opportunism—the Dixie Mafia was vehemently antiblack; the Memphis cartel saw black voting strength as a means of accomplishing economic goals—it resulted in a tug-of-war for the soul of Lyndon Johnson.

At the center of Johnson's presidency was Abe Fortas. No other individual had so much power to shape domestic and international policy. No other individual had so much power to define the presidency itself. There is not much mystery about where Fortas obtained his blueprint for the Johnson presidency: it is a carbon copy of the one used so successfully by Boss Crump in Memphis.

As the new year began, the Mississippi Sovereignty Commission added a new weapon to its arsenal: eighty-two draft boards, one for each county in the state. The boards were composed of appointees of the president and had the power to decide who was drafted into the Army—and who was not.

In January, Erle Johnston received a letter from a frantic mother who said her white teenage daughter was having an affair with a man she thought might be part Negro. Johnston assigned the case to an investigator and ordered him to determine the man's racial heritage. Then, anticipating the worst, he proposed a solution. "If subject is at least twenty-two years old, it is possible we could arrange that he be drafted."

As early as 1964, the Vietnam War was showing signs of becoming a divisive issue in the civil rights movement. It caused a major rift in the Mississippi Freedom Democratic Party, alienating white supporters and nudging them to the right. At issue was whether black men who had been disenfranchised politically should be subjected to the draft. Most civil rights leaders said no.

In 1965—and for years to come—Mississippi draft boards were composed entirely of white males. Many board members also held membership in the Ku Klux Klan. When the Sovereignty Commission requested that targeted individuals be drafted, they were sent induction notices, no questions asked. Next to outright murder, it was the preferred method of removing civil rights troublemakers—male ones, anyway—from the state.

Vietnam was not the only issue dividing the movement. By late 1964, tensions between white civil rights workers and black political activists were obvious. "Operator 79," a Commission informant with the Council of Federated Organizations (COFO), identified the source of those tensions in a memo to the Commission: "There are racial conflicts within COFO. Most of our staff personnel are whites. The white personnel are in almost complete control. Issues are decided without the help of the Negroes."

Charles Evers, the state field secretary for the NAACP, later confirmed those tensions to *Clarion-Ledger* reporter Leesha Cooper. The COFO workers, most of whom were from the North, wanted to be in charge, said Evers. "They were too extreme," he said. "What we wanted was justice in Mississippi without violence."

Whether it was the racial tension described by Evers or the murder of the three civil rights workers in Neshoba County, most of the white Northerners working in COFO had left the state by the end of 1965. From that point, the civil rights movement in Mississippi relied on black leadership. When whites were allowed into the organizational framework, they were almost always native-born Mississippians.

That shakeup in the civil rights movement was only one result of the Neshoba County murders. It was generally accepted that the black victim, James Chaney, was not a primary target. He had been in the wrong place at the wrong time. It led many black leaders to conclude that white civil rights workers from the North hurt the cause more than they helped. They were lightning rods for trouble.

The other result could be seen in the impact those murders had on the FBI. Attorney General Robert Kennedy had insisted that President Johnson take drastic action to apprehend the killers. In turn, Johnson laid the problem squarely on the desk of J. Edgar Hoover, who was not in favor of federal intervention in the case.

As he did whenever forced into things he did not want to do, Hoover used it as an excuse to expand the power base of the bureau. The Ku Klux Klan was an easy target. It was easy to plant informants inside the Klan hierarchy and it was easy to anticipate the Klan's targets. It was like shooting fish in a barrel.

Declaring all-out war against the Klan was not comparable to declaring war against the mob, nor did it offer the same risks. In Mississippi, the Klan had never been much more than a training school for wannabes and gofers. It was never a source of real power, at least not since Reconstruction.

At times, the Klan's lack of savvy bordered on the ludicrous. On March 30, 1965, E.L. McDaniel, Grand Dragon of the United Klans of America, sent a letter to Sheriff Jack Cauthran of Madison County—a suburb of Jackson—informing him that klansmen wanted to pass out literature in his county. "We come as law-abiding, God-fearing men and respect the law in the highest," McDaniel said in his letter. "If there is a city ordinance prohibiting passing out literature in your city, please advise me immediately in order for me to get permission to do so. You will be notified in advance of the time as we do not want to create any hardships on our law-enforcement officers. . . . We commend you for the fine job you are doing."

Cauthran responded to the Grand Dragon by return mail, informing him that there was indeed a city ordinance prohibiting passing out literature. "I wish to advise you that we do not solicit nor welcome any outside radical elements and further advise that it is the opinion of the writer that this community will fare well without your presence," said the sheriff, who "cc'ed" the letter to Governor Johnson, the FBI, the Mississippi highway patrol, and to a judge with offices in the Hinds County courthouse. "We are enforcing all laws and making every effort to maintain the peace and dignity of our community and advise that anyone entering this county or city must be 'law abiding, God fearing men and respect the law,' as is recited in your letter."

The Neshoba County murders provided Hoover with an excuse to implement the bureau's first Cointelpro operation against a domestic target. Prior to the Neshoba County murders, the only Cointelpro operations carried out by the FBI had been against the Communist Party. Hoover authorized his agents to go after the Klan, using any means necessary.

More than a month after federal prosecutors were dealt a stunning defeat in the Neshoba County murder case, they were successful in obtaining indictments from a federal grand jury in Jackson on 18 of the 21 men originally charged.

The trial would be held in the courtroom of Judge Harold Cox, the race-baiting jurist Senator James Eastland had won in a trade for Supreme Court Justice Thurgood Marshall. Upon passage of the Civil Rights Act of 1964, Cox had editorialized in open court that he didn't "know anybody down here who [didn't] oppose it."

Eastland knew Cox would do the right thing.

Cox didn't disappoint.

His first judicial act in the Neshoba County murder case was to dismiss all the felony indictments. He ruled the defendants could only be charged with misdemeanors. This one decision alone, Senator Eastland could argue with pride, justified the horse trade that put a black man on the Supreme Court.

Disturbed by the indictments, the Sovereignty Commission sent investigator Andy Hopkins back to Neshoba County. In his report, Hopkins gave a detailed description of the murders, details, he said, that were obtained from a reliable source.

"I was informed that the civil rights workers were shot and killed in the following order," he wrote. "Michael Schwerner was shot one time and killed and was the first victim. Andrew Goodman was the second victim and was also shot one time and killed. James Chaney, the colored member of this group, is alleged to have broke from the group of men that were holding them captive. Shortly after he made the break, he was shot several times by several different people but was struck by only three bullets each of which was alleged to have been fired from a different firearm."

Hopkins said similar information was contained in confessions allegedly given to the FBI by two of the defendants. After the FBI arrested one of the men, he was taken to a local motel and forced to sit in a chair for ten hours without water. He was permitted to go to the bathroom only three times.

"I was further informed that on at least two occasions, the FBI gave this subject substantial sums of money for his confession or cooperation and offered him more money if he would go to Dallas, Texas, and remain there until the trial," he said.

Hopkins concluded with the ominous admission that "the defense attorneys already have this information and probably will handle it in the manner it should be handled."

By that time, the FBI had determined the type of weapon used in the murders. One bullet had been removed from the left lung of Michael Schwerner. One bullet had been removed from "near the chest" of Andrew Goodman. And three bullets had been removed from the body of James Chaney.

Ballistic experts concluded that four of the five bullets were fired from the same type weapon—a .38–caliber pistol. All four of the .38–caliber bullets were identified as "reloads," indicating they had been hand-loaded and not purchased in a store.

The pistol or pistols used in the murder were never found, according to FBI agent Joe Sullivan, who was sent to Mississippi from Washington to supervise the search for the missing civil rights activists. Interviewed by the author in 1997, Sullivan, who is now retired and living in New York, said the bureau was not aware of the two .38–caliber pistols purchased by an undercover agent for the Sovereignty Commission.

The pistols were never listed as office inventory by the Commission. If the FBI had known about the two .38–caliber pistols purchased by the Sovereignty Commission in 1965, and had asked to examine them, they might have found the pistols had mysteriously disappeared.

While Hopkins was in Neshoba County, Commission director Erle Johnston dealt with another matter of importance to the state of Mississippi. Dr.
Stephen Taller, of Berkeley, California, had written a letter to the Jackson
Chamber of Commerce advising that he had rejected two frozen chickens in
a market because they had been produced in Mississippi. The letter was
passed on to Johnston, who opened a file on Dr. Taller and sent him a letter
of his own.

"It so happens that I live in Scott County where more chickens are raised
and processed than any other county in Mississippi," Johnston said in his
bizarre rejoinder. "I happen to know, from personal observation, that Mississippi chickens are the most scientifically produced of any in the nation.
The breeder flocks are the most of the best strains. . . .

"We recommend broiled Mississippi chicken for breakfast, golden fried
Mississippi chicken for lunch, and appetizing baked Mississippi chicken for
dinner. . . . Maybe one of these days you will set aside your emotions and
again enjoy Mississippi chicken on your table."

There is no record of whether the doctor was persuaded to try another
Mississippi chicken.

As national attention focused again on Mississippi in the case of the
murdered civil rights workers, Governor Paul Johnson instructed Commission director Erle Johnston to search the agency's files for possible incriminatory information.

"It is necessary that we remove from the files any reports of investigators
which might in any way be construed to mean that the Sovereignty Commission has interfered in any way with voter registration drives or demonstrations," Johnston instructed his investigators in a written memo. All
future reports, he said, should refer to the targets of investigations as "subversives" and not put undue emphasis on their race.

In a memo to the governor, dated February 16, Johnston notified him that
"the files we considered incriminatory have been pulled and are now on the
big table in the large office. We await your further instructions." What those
instructions were is unknown, but there is evidence that the files pulled
were eventually destroyed.

Surveillance was stepped up by the Commission in 1965. In March,
Johnston received a request from the state tax commission, to which he
responded by letter: "In response to your request for a hidden tape recorder

to take statements from the sister of Fannie Lou Hamer [noted black civil rights activist], this is to advise we now have a recorder available. You may pick it up at the Sovereignty Commission office at any time."

The records don't show why the tax commission wanted to target the sister of Fannie Lou Hamer, but it is a matter of record that she had filed a federal lawsuit to block elections in Ruleville because of voter registration irregularities.

Wendell Paris, an activist who worked at that time with Hamer at the Student Nonviolent Coordinating Committee (SNCC), now lives in Jackson and said the real issue was land ownership. "Some of the folks involved with the Commission were the ones who did the most to take away black land ownership in the South," he said. "We owned twenty-two million acres at the turn of the century. . . . From the 1960s to the 1990s we have lost all but three million acres. . . . It was ironic. On the one hand, they granted civil rights, but on the other they took back our economic rights."

Increased activity at the Commission corresponded with similar activity at the FBI, where the hottest topic, behind closed doors, continued to be the secret Martin Luther King tapes, which purported to incriminate the civil rights leader in a variety of sexual indiscretions. King had heard rumors of the tapes for months. When he went to Sweden in December to accept the Nobel Prize for peace, he referred in his acceptance speech to an expectation of persecution.

Unknown to King, the FBI had mailed him an anonymous letter in November. The letter suggested that he commit suicide as a way out of the dilemma that faced him over the tapes. The letter, along with a copy of the tape, had been mailed to the Southern Christian Leadership Conference offices in Atlanta, but had not yet reached King.

It was early January when King's wife, Coretta Scott King, discovered the package containing the letter and the tape. Since it was her custom to open the mail addressed to her husband, she was the first to read the letter and to hear the tape. The letter, in part, read: "You are no clergyman and you know it. I repeat you are a colossal fraud and an evil, vicious one at that. . . . King, there is only one thing left for you to do. You know what it is. You have just thirty-four days in which to do this. . . . You better take it before your filthy, abnormal fraudulent self is bared to the nation."

When he read the letter and listened to the tape, King immediately knew who had sent them—the FBI. To Hoover's delight, King was overheard on a wiretap saying, "They are out to break me."

If there was a single issue that brought the Sovereignty Commission and the FBI together, it was a common hatred of Martin Luther King. He was for both agencies public enemy number one, a primary target of surveillance and dirty tricks.

Not only did the Commission at this point have a staff of three full-time investigators, it used a network of private detective agencies, most of which had ties to the FBI. It's not clear what, but something happened early in 1965 that spooked Governor Johnson on the Commission's use of private investigators. It may have had something to do with the Neshoba County case. Or it may have had something to do with the cozy relationship the Commission was developing with the FBI. Whatever the reason, Governor Johnson sent Erle Johnston a curt memo: "Please do not engage or employ any outside investigating agencies until further notice."

In his reply, Johnston said he would suspend use of private agencies until further notice. He listed the agencies the Commission had used—Rick Detective Agency, Harrison Detectives, Day Detectives, Delta Detective Agency, and Pendleton Detective Agency—and said he only used them when he had to. He then pointed out that one of the Commission's investigators, Virgil Downing, had died two weeks earlier, and a second, Andy Hopkins, had been out sick for more than six weeks.

Johnston also mentioned, for the first time, that one of his top-secret agents—code named "Operator X"—was being handled by Day Detectives. He assumed the governor would want him to continue to use the agency for that purpose.

That April, Senator Eastland was driving through Spartanburg, South Carolina, on his way back to Washington, when he stopped to chat with one of the commanders in the South Carolina highway patrol. Eastland learned that a car containing two black men and a white woman had been stopped for speeding in South Carolina.

When Eastland reached Washington, he telephoned the Mississippi highway patrol to give them a description of the car and its tag number, since he feared it might be headed for Mississippi. He said he didn't have the white girl's name, but he did have the names and addresses of the black men. That important information was duly passed on to highway patrol commanders and, of course, to the governor.

Such sharing of information was common practice. In March, FBI agent M.E. McCloughan telephoned the Mississippi highway patrol to alert them that baseball great Jackie Robinson was headed for a speaking engagement in Mississippi. McCloughan spoke to a secretary named Jennie. He gave her details of Robinson's trip, along with the location and times of his speeches.

"Mr. McCloughan stated he did not know how Jackie Robinson would be traveling," Jennie said in her report. "This was all the information he had."

Whether the FBI agent was calling to assist the highway patrol in protecting Jackie Robinson—or to cause problems for the baseball player during his visit—is not clear.

Sometimes unsolicited information arrived from law enforcement agencies in other states. In one instance, the Dallas police chief sent a letter to the Tippah County sheriff informing him that a twenty-four-year-old man who was on the teaching faculty at Blue Mountain College had recently been arrested in Dallas on a morals charge.

"He was arrested in a public restroom as he performed the act of masturbation on himself in full view of the arresting officers," said the Dallas police chief. "Upon being questioned by the arresting officers, this individual admitted being a homosexual for approximately three years."

It is not known what happened to the teacher, but the Dallas police chief's letter, which identified the man by name, ended up in the files of the Sovereignty Commission.

Sometimes investigators found out more than they wanted to know.

On a trip to Holly Springs to look for subversives (there were none), investigator Andy Hopkins was told by the sheriff that a white man from Memphis, a candy salesman, had been luring black girls, aged eight to thirteen, into his car on the pretense of taking them to a COFO meeting, and then driving them to a deserted part of the county where he proceeded to "whip them on their naked posteriors." Other than that, the sheriff said, there had been "no incidents concerning racial matters" in the county.

⌇⌇⌇

A few weeks after Judge Harold Cox dismissed the felony indictments in the Neshoba County civil rights case, Commission investigator Andy Hopkins returned to Philadelphia to check out rumors that a man he had been looking for had returned to the area. The man had been suspected by the Commission of collaborating with the federal government ever since an investigator for the Mississippi highway patrol arrived for an interview and found the man's father talking to an attorney for Michael Schwerner's family.

After the attorney left, the father had told the investigator that he and his son lived in fear of their lives. "[He] showed [me] three loaded shotguns and stated that he and [his son] had a signal worked out whereby they would not be taken at night," the investigator said. "[He] states that he has never done anything bad wrong in his life . . . and at this point, he broke down and began crying telling [me] that he and [his son] had planned to kill the Sheriff [Rainey] if he came to arrest [him].

"[The father] states that in the event the sheriff came to arrest [his son] that [he] would answer the door and upon seeing the sheriff would fall to the floor whereupon [his son] would shoot the sheriff from inside the house." The father went on to tell the investigator that he, too, thought Sheriff Rainey was a member of the Klan.

Andy Hopkins found a waitress who said the man had returned to town and a taxi driver who said he had not returned to town. "The situation in Philadelphia and Neshoba County has been extremely quiet lately," he said in his report. "A short time ago, COFO moved its headquarters out of Philadelphia and at the same time, the FBI agents that were stationed there were also moved."

Hopkins left without confirming whether the man had actually returned to town, but he was careful, per Erle Johnston's instructions, to use the words "subversive" and "Communist" in his report whenever possible.

By the first of June, Governor Johnson was again uneasy about the Sovereignty Commission. The Neshoba County murders, with the 150 or so FBI agents they had brought into the state, continued to make everyone jumpy. Johnson had his assistant, Herman Glazier, send a letter to Erle Johnston ordering him—once again—to stop using the services of private detective agencies: "Any service being utilized at the present time must be discontinued. No requisitions will be signed or approved by the Governor for any future services of this nature."

On June 15, Erle Johnston sent a memorandum to the governor in which he suggested the name of the agency be changed. Johnston may or may not have wanted the name changed, but the language of the memo was such that it is apparent it was sent as a "cover" for the agency's increasingly illegal clandestine activities.

Johnston understood the value of leaving a false "paper trail" that was favorable to the Commission. The memo obviously fell in that category. As a reason for the proposed name change, Johnston pointed out that the Commission was "shifting more and more" into public relations. "Since Governor Johnson has brought about a change of image, and we believe we are on the verge of a great public relations program with business, industry, and government participating, it would also seem that a new name for the state agency would be in order," he said.

One week later, on June 21, Johnston sent the governor a report from his top-secret agent "Operator X." The report had been submitted "gratis," he said, and "we have been notified this is the last we will hear of 'X' unless we can resume adequate compensation."

The report stated that agent "X" had risen to a position in which he was now "second in command" at both the Student Nonviolent Coordinating Committee and the Council of Federated Organizations, and was privy to all the private strategy meetings taking place in Jackson. As an example of the type of material "X" was able to provide, the report said that there would be a meeting in three days in which Ralph Abernathy, Martin Luther King's top assistant, would be present to meet with local ministers for the purpose of organizing demonstrations.

Johnston said that if the governor objected to making out checks to a private detective to pay for those services, the Commission could make other arrangements, presumably from its private banking account. "If the Sovereignty Commission is to continue to stay on top of the news from within these outside groups, I don't see how we can do without such services," he said.

Johnston did not mention the status of operator "Z," who was working in a different area. "Z's" main target was a man identified only as "Mack." It was Johnston's belief that "Mack" was a "Castroite" from Havana, Cuba. "Such information will be worthy of exploiting if we can prove he is an agent of Communist Cuba," he said in a report.

As Governor Johnson pondered the Commission director's request, another report was prepared and circulated concerning a civil rights march being organized in Louise, Mississippi. An informant told the Commission that the marchers had a "heated argument" over remarks made by Martin Luther King that he would not support the "black power" program advocated by Stokely Carmichael.

One marcher said the movement needed guns to create a black power structure in Mississippi. Another marcher said he was certain King would withdraw his support if the movement resorted to violence.

With that bit of political news out of the way, the informant then turned to a topic that always attracted attention in the Commission's inner circle. "Guards are being used to patrol the camp sites at night," said the informant. "One of the things they are on the lookout for are incidents which could be picked up by the press that would cast an unfavorable light on the march.

"Particularly they are watching for couples performing indecent acts. On this date, at night, the guards found a nude white girl and a nude colored male sitting in an automobile. They were kissing at the time. The guards pulled them apart."

Three days later, Governor Johnson changed his mind and authorized the Commission to continue paying for the services of operator "X." Once he received the approval, Johnston dictated a memo setting out the terms of "X's" employment. "We are authorized to pay a flat amount of $500 per month for these services," he said. "This will be increased proportionally if out-of-town trips or special expenses are necessary. Operator 'X' has been notified."

Guns, interracial sex, Communism—it was money in the bank.

As the Justice Department appealed Judge Cox's decision to the United States Supreme Court, prosecutors agreed with a defense motion in September to throw out the indictments on the grounds the grand jury was improperly drawn. At that point, despite the appeal, many people assumed the issue was closed.

Senator Eastland knew better. In July, he recommended to President Johnson that he appoint former Mississippi governor J.P. Coleman to a vacancy on the Fifth Circuit Court of Appeals in New Orleans. Johnson made the appointment on July 26, thus putting the founder of the Sovereignty Commission in a position to rule on all cases appealed from Mississippi, including those from the courtroom of Judge Harold Cox.

If Governor Johnson thought the Neshoba County case was closed, he must have been shocked to receive a sixteen-page letter later that month from Roy Moore, agent in charge of the Jackson FBI bureau. The letter, stamped "secret," provided the governor with the names of known KKK members in Mississippi.

Not only did the letter identify Sheriff Lawrence Rainey and two of his deputies, Cecil Price and Hop Barnett, as members of the Neshoba County Klavern of the White Knights of the Ku Klux Klan of Mississippi (WKKKKOM), it listed the names of sheriffs, constables, and highway patrolmen all across the state. In addition, the FBI letter listed the leadership of the statewide organizations of the United Klans of America, the Mississippi Ku Klux Klan, and the White Knights. Also included was a county-by-county breakdown, with the names of each Klan member listed in alphabetical order.

The FBI was particularly interested in Klan involvement among law enforcement officers. Earlier in the summer, the Klan had held a large rally at Delta City, a small community not far from Greenville, to swear in twenty-nine new members. Twenty-seven of the new members attended the ceremony. The two who did not were employees of the Mississippi highway patrol.

As the FBI targeted the KKK, the Sovereignty Commission stepped up its activities against antiwar demonstrators. Investigator Tom Scarbrough went to Sunflower County—Senator Eastland's home turf—to gather information on the Mississippi Freedom Democratic Party's involvement in the antiwar movement. When he attempted to update his dossier on Linda Seese, an FDP member who had traveled to Washington, D.C., to protest the government's policy in Vietnam, he was told by the sheriff the information already had been sent to Andy Hopkins.

Exactly why the Commission became obsessed with the antiwar movement in September is a mystery, but it is clear from Commission records
that U.S. Representative John Bell Williams and Senator Eastland were
exchanging information with the Commission on the identities of antiwar
demonstrators.

At Williams's request, Tom Scarbrough went to the Gulf Coast to gather
information on a man identified as an opponent of the war. To obtain that
information, he went to see Sheriff Cecil Byrd, one of the men identified in
the confidential FBI report as a member of the KKK. Byrd was out of the
office at the time, but his chief deputy, a man named Matthews, offered to
help Scarbrough get what he needed. Matthews told him that the man he
was interested in—and his brother—previously had been arrested in
Pascagoula for civil rights activity.

To Scarbrough's delight, Matthews produced a list of names that had
been found on the men when they were arrested. The list identified fifteen
people who had planned to go to Washington to protest the war. "All
persons listed in this report are Negroes and all have been active in all types
of civil rights activity, which goes along hand-in-glove with the Mississippi
Freedom Democratic Party," said Scarbrough.

When Johnston passed that information along to Williams, he referred in
his letter to another list of names the congressman had provided to the
Commission. He was unable to obtain information on nine of the people on
Williams's list, but was successful in compiling dossiers on ten others.

One of the individuals on the list, Max Sandin of Baltimore, was notable
because of his age—he was seventy-four—and because he had picketed the
White House in 1961 with a group demonstrating against nerve gas and
germ warfare. Some were cited for their work with civil rights organizations; others were identified as "Freedom Riders" who had invaded Mississippi in 1961.

Whenever possible, Commission investigators tried to link antiwar and
civil rights activists to the Freedom Democratic Party. Sometimes they
engaged in outright smear tactics, as when they disseminated information
that "39.2 percent" of the FDP membership had been diagnosed with venereal disease. "We have also been informed that some of the doctors and
nurses imported to treat these people have resigned in disgust and returned
to their respective homes in the north and east," Johnston said in a memo.

Responding to the Commission's strong prowar stance, the Ole Miss
Senate adopted a resolution in October supporting President Johnson's
Vietnam policy. In a page-one story, *The Mississippian* reported that "the
action was aimed at groups across the nation which have recently demonstrated in protest [of] American intervention in Southeast Asia."

Of the state's eight public universities and colleges, Ole Miss was the most fertile ground for informants. Students may have dropped the ball on integration, but they would make up for that by showing strong support of the government's Vietnam policy. Whatever the Commission needed, the students delivered on demand.

Toward the end of 1965, it became increasingly clear that the Commission had formed a special relationship with the FBI. It was a relationship that was probably helped along by the Commission's strident prowar stance.

In a memo to the governor, Erle Johnston referred to a speech scheduled for delivery in Pontotoc. "Confidentially, the FBI has not only cleared but approved the remarks," he said. "They agree with us that the Justice Department should publicize its findings in all those cases where there is no evidence to justify charges."

That was a startling admission for Johnston to make, for it indicated the Commission and the FBI were more intimately involved than either agency had ever admitted. It was a harbinger of even more sinister connections to come.

On November 18, Johnston met with ex-FBI agent John Sullivan of Vicksburg to discuss ways of dealing with the "subversives" that were flooding Mississippi. "He said in his opinion it will be more important than ever to keep an eye on their movements and even find ways of harassment to make them ineffective," Johnston wrote in a memo. "It is his suggestion that the Sovereignty Commission develop a broader and more comprehensive program for investigating subversives and filing information."

By the start of 1966, Carlos Marcello was on his way to becoming the wealthiest and most powerful Mafia leader in the United States, according to biographer John H. Davis. "His criminal organization was now generating an estimated annual income of nearly $2 billion, making it by far the largest industry in Louisiana," said Davis. "As the leader of the oldest Mafia family in the United States—'the first family of the Mafia,' as it was known in mob circles—Marcello enjoyed extraordinary privileges within the national syndicate."

One of the reasons for those "privileges" was his victory in 1965 over federal prosecutors and, by default, Robert Kennedy, who had resigned as attorney general to run for a New York senate seat.

Marcello had been indicted by a federal grand jury in 1964 on charges he conspired "to obstruct justice by fixing a juror and [sought] the murder of a government witness." Kennedy's replacement, Attorney General Nicholas

Katzenbach, was unable to obtain a conviction, and Marcello walked out of the courtroom a free man. His acquittal meant that after years of legal wrangling he was free of a series of federal charges that stemmed from his defiance of Robert Kennedy's Justice Department. He was free—at last—to pursue the American Dream. For years, rumors circulated that Marcello was involved in the Kennedy assassination, but he vehemently denied any connection to the murder.

Not enjoying the same gift of freedom was Teamster boss James Hoffa, who had been convicted in 1964 of jury tampering. He was sentenced to eight years in prison and fined ten thousand dollars. On the day Hoffa was sentenced, a letter was sent to Robert Kennedy from Frank Chavez, secretary-treasurer of Teamster Local 901 (ironically, the telephone area code of Memphis) in Puerto Rico.

The letter read: "The undersigned is going to solicit from the membership of our union that each one donate whatever they can afford to maintain, clean, beautify and supply with flowers the grave of Lee Harvey Oswald. You can rest assured contributions will be unanimous."

Abe Fortas's Puerto Rican connections were highlighted in April 1965 when he sent a letter to John Macy, who was serving both as President Johnson's chief personnel officer and chairman of the Civil Service Commission, asking that Admiral John Harllee be appointed to the Federal Maritime Commission.

"We represent, as you know, the Commonwealth of Puerto Rico with respect to maritime matters," Fortas said in his letter. "Since our viewpoint has been that of the Commonwealth of Puerto Rico, rather than that of a private shipper or carrier, I think we have had a unique opportunity to observe [Harllee's] work in terms of the public interest."

In response, Macy said he was pleased to have Fortas's observations. "The point of view from Puerto Rico was particularly helpful in gaining an assessment of reactions to [Harllee's] leadership," said Macy. "I will make certain that the President is aware of your interests on this appointment."

Fortas hardly needed anyone to intercede with Johnson on his behalf. In early 1965, he was probably seeing the president as often as his own family did. Fortas's letter to Macy was part of the charade he carried out in dealing with Johnson on sensitive matters. That charade would continue for the remainder of his life.

Fortas was second only to the president in his ability to set policy for the new administration. He had called the shots during the 1964 campaign and he continued to call the shots when it came to presidential appointments— and pardons, for Johnson had put him in charge of that as well.

It was during the first year-and-a-half of the Johnson administration that

Fortas built up a reputation as a thinking man's liberal among idealistic journalists, who viewed his support of civil rights as proof of his progressive ideas. In typical Memphis fashion, Fortas used the media—and the issue of civil rights—to conceal his true agenda.

The common criticism of Fortas was that he was too secretive, a fact later confirmed by the discovery that he destroyed documents and letters on a regular basis. Anthony Lewis, who had reported on the Federation for Constitutional Government for the *New York Times*, had a distinguished career as a journalist during the early days of the civil rights movement, but in a profile of Fortas for the *New York Times Magazine*, he fell into the trap encountered by other, less talented writers. He gushed and fawned over Fortas with the enthusiasm of a schoolboy attending his first professional baseball game. Unlike some of the other journalists, Lewis did seem concerned by Fortas's secretive nature. One of his sources admitted that he had known Fortas for years, "and I share his views—and I don't know him at all."

On July 28, 1965, President Johnson sent a nomination to the Senate that surprised no one. He nominated Abe Fortas to be an associate justice of the Supreme Court. At fifty-five, Fortas would fill the "Jewish seat" occupied by Justice Arthur Goldberg, who was pressured into resigning to become U.S. ambassador to the United Nations.

Three weeks before the nomination was announced, Fortas was made a vice president at Federated Department Stores, the Cincinnati-based company that had merged with Memphis's largest department store chain. By then, Fortas was serving on the boards of Texas-based Braniff International, Great America Corporation, the Sucrest Corporation, Franklin Life Insurance Company, and the Madison National Bank of Washington. He also served as a trustee of the John F. Kennedy Center for the Performing Arts, a position that endeared him to supporters of the arts.

There was little criticism of Johnson's choice of Fortas. In an editorial, the *Washington Post* said that whether Fortas is judged by "his intellectual capacity, his legal experience or his deep concern over civil liberties and civil rights," he is "admirably equipped to take his place on the Court, and there is every reason to believe that he will serve it with great distinction." Most newspapers applauded the choice.

Taking a more critical look was Louis Kohlmeir, a reporter for the *Wall Street Journal*. His story—headlined, "Johnson Names Abe Fortas to High Court; Their Close Friendship May Spur Criticism"—pointed out that although Fortas "is regarded as a top-flight lawyer, this reputation is far over-shadowed by his close relationship with the President."

Kohlmeir examined that relationship in greater detail than had been attempted by other journalists. "They speak to each other by telephone daily, and probably no one but the two know all the tasks Mr. Fortas has performed for his friend," he wrote. "Although the relationship may change, what Mr. Fortas won't necessarily give up when he dons the judicial robes is his position of influence with the president—a position in which he has been consulted by Mr. Johnson more than [any] other White House outsider."

Kohlmeir's intuitive reporting was prophetic.

In the two months that elapsed between his nomination, his senate approval, and his subsequent swearing in, Fortas remained in constant touch with the White House. He continued to send names to John Macy for appointments, especially for the courts. Hodding Carter III was probably never aware of it, but Fortas once submitted the Mississippian's name as a potential job candidate. As Kohlmeir predicted, that practice continued, even after Fortas took his seat on the high court.

In November, using a Supreme Court letterhead, Fortas sent John Macy a letter marked "personal," in which he recommended a Portland lawyer, Allan Hart, for a vacancy on the U.S. District Court in Portland. In response, Macy informed Fortas that although the Justice Department had the primary responsibility for recommending individuals for court appointments, it was his intention to extend that responsibility to individuals outside the legal circle. "I look forward to future association with you in developing candidates for the President's consideration in his continuing efforts to strengthen the judiciary," said Macy.

Since it was unprecedented for a Supreme Court justice to advise the president on matters of policy—technically it was a breach of the separation of powers doctrine—Fortas's continuing partnership with Johnson was hidden from public view.

Also kept secret was Fortas's role in developing war policy in Vietnam. From his chambers in the Supreme Court building, Fortas not only picked appointees for high positions in the administration, he advised the president on how the war in Vietnam should be conducted. He was a hawk, but not for the reasons others supported the war.

Shortly after Fortas donned his judicial robes, Johnson autographed a photograph of himself for his friend. "For Abe," Johnson wrote across the photograph, "The Isaac Stern of the Supreme Court. My first string man."

By 1966, the Ku Klux Klan had been infiltrated by so many FBI agents, psychos, and down-home hotheads, that its leadership was in disarray. Up until that time, the various organizations that made up the Mississippi Klan had been composed of a highly volatile mixture of gentleman-farmer types and hard-core rednecks who worked together to look after the interests of their white neighbors.

The FBI's Cointelpro program against the Klan was effective because the informants it put in place were successful in creating confusion and doubt among the klansmen. The working relationship that had existed for generations among the wealthy landowners and the sharecroppers and field workers in the Klan fell apart as each group began to suspect the other of deceit and collusion.

In January, Colonel T.B. Birdsong, head of the Mississippi highway patrol, received a report from one of his top officers, Charles Snodgrass, who had been contacted by the Grand Titan of Province Two of the United Klans of America. The klansman, who was a supervisor in Sharkey County (Hal DeCell's home base), told Snodgrass he felt that he and all other klansmen were "being used" and he suspected that their money was being mishandled by the Klan.

"His conscience is bothering him," Snodgrass said in his report. "He has been lied to and has lied to many people, whom he feels responsible to for having persuaded them to become Klan members. . . . [He] stated that Robert Shelton [the Imperial Wizard of the United Klans of America] sent word by an imperial order that the United Klansmen of Mississippi were expected to raise six thousand dollars to help cover expenses incurred at the House Un-American Activities Committee. Most of the klansmen in north Mississippi are disgruntled at having to continuously contribute and not being told to what use their money is being put."

The county supervisor supplied the highway patrol with the names of three Klan leaders who, like himself, wanted to pull out of the organization. Snodgrass told Birdsong he thought the county supervisor was sincere, but he doubted that he and his friends, working alone, would be able to disrupt the Klan.

What the county supervisor apparently didn't know was that the highway patrol itself was well represented in the Klan; or if he did know, he may have suspected the patrolmen were all informants (they were not). It is a good example of how the FBI, with Cointelpro, was able cause confusion.

What the FBI did not understand—or if it understood, it chose to disregard out of self-interest—was that the Mississippi Klan was not the primary source of the violence taking place in the state. The klansmen were only the fall guys.

The tri-state federation, the Commission, the political leadership of the state, all used the Klan as a convenient foil to divert attention from their own activities. Violence occurred for a reason—and it was seldom racism. The bottom line was usually financial.

As the highway patrol pondered the best way to deal with the Klan—and
its newest enemy, antiwar demonstrators—a new crisis arose: Robert Kennedy, the newly elected United States senator from New York, announced
that he would accept an invitation to visit Ole Miss in March.

Mississippi was stunned.

The Ole Miss newspaper, *The Mississippian,* was critical of the decision
to invite the senator, saying it was a matter of "great concern." Mary Cain,
editor of the *Summit Sun* and president of the Women for Constitutional
Government, condemned the visit. At her request, the WCG passed a resolution saying the organization "can neither forgive nor forget" the role
Kennedy played in the desegregation of Ole Miss.

To the disappointment of some, Governor Paul Johnson, who had physically blocked James Meredith's entry into the university, said he would
"stay out of it" this time.

In the days leading up to the senator's visit, the campus buzzed with
gossip. There were rumors of a potential riot. Professors paused during their
lectures to comment on the visit. Newspapers quoted right-wing activists
and Klan leaders as promising a strong presence on the campus. It had been
four years since Meredith's enrollment, and, except for a few panty raids
that got out of hand, most of the students had never witnessed anything
close to a full-blown race riot.

When Kennedy arrived on campus with his wife, Ethel, it was nothing
like what he had expected. The campus was calm and disarmingly charm-
ing. There were no mass demonstrations. He spoke in the coliseum, a new
basketball and concert arena that still smelled of fresh paint, to a carefully
screened audience—non-students were not allowed in the building.

Kennedy, wearing a pin-striped suit with a white handkerchief tucked
into his top front pocket, received a polite round of applause when he
walked onto the stage, flanked by a solemn procession of university officials and student leaders. To the surprise of some, he seemed shy and
hesitant in front of the student audience. He paced the stage with his hands
behind his back.

Kennedy began by saying he was told by friends in New York that his
visit to Ole Miss would be like a fox stepping into a chicken coop. That's
not the way it turned out, he told the students. Instead, he felt more like "a
chicken in a fox coop."

The students laughed, and Kennedy made new friends.

During a question-and-answer session following his speech, a student
asked who he felt was responsible for the 1962 riot. Kennedy declined to
place blame on any one individual, but he discussed his telephone conversation with Governor Ross Barnett, the one in which Barnett had asked if it

This photo was taken during the 1959 special session of the Mississippi Legislature. On the right is Mississippi Governor J.P. Coleman; on the left is state Representative Hilton Waits. Photo courtesy of the Mississippi Valley Collection, University of Memphis, University Libraries.

Abe Fortas (c. 1930s). Photo courtesy of the Mississippi Valley Collection, University of Memphis, University Libraries.

Assistant U.S. Attorney General Nicholas Katzenbach (left) and U.S. Marshall James McShane (right). This photo was taken at the University of Mississippi in 1962 during the registration of James Meredith. Photo courtesy of the Mississippi Valley Collection, University of Memphis, University Libraries.

James Meredith during his graduation from the University of Mississippi. Photo courtesy of the Mississippi Valley Collection, University of Memphis, University Libraries.

This photo was taken by *Jackson Daily News* editor Jimmy Ward during the inaugural parade of Mississippi Governor Paul Johnson (backseat on the right); on the left is former Mississippi Governor Hugh White. Photo courtesy of the Mississippi Valley Collection, University of Memphis, University Libraries.

Memphis policemen spraying Mace on black demonstrators after the King assassination. Photo courtesy of the Mississippi Valley Collection, University of Memphis, University Libraries.

The aftermath of the King assassination in Memphis. This demonstration was taking place on Beale Street. Photo courtesy of the Mississippi Valley Collection, University of Memphis, University Libraries.

Mourners view the body of Martin Luther King Jr. in 1968. Photo courtesy of the Mississippi Valley Collection, University of Memphis, University Libraries.

would be possible for the marshals to draw their guns. "I thought maybe he could just step aside when he saw the marshals," Kennedy said.

Not too enthusiastic about Kennedy's speech was Ross Barnett. The next day he issued a statement attacking Kennedy's "twisted" and "willful" misrepresentation of the facts. "It ill becomes a man who never tried a lawsuit in his life, but who occupied the high position of United States attorney general and who was responsible for using 30,000 troops and spent approximately six million dollars to put one unqualified student in Ole Miss to return to the scene of this crime and discuss any phase of this infamous affair," Barnett said. Kennedy was a "very sick and dangerous American."

Had Barnett known his telephone conversations with Robert Kennedy and President Kennedy had been secretly recorded, and would one day be released to the public, he probably would have been more restrained in his comments.

For some Mississippians, James Meredith was a nightmare that would not end. Less than three months after Kennedy's visit—and perhaps because of it—Meredith returned to public view with a voting rights march. It was scheduled to begin in Memphis and continue down the interstate to Jackson, a distance of about two hundred miles.

Just outside Memphis, about one mile south of Hernando, Meredith and a group of marchers walked past a white man standing beside the highway. The moment was captured by newspaper photographers stationed across the road. Just over the hill was a carload of FBI agents. About two hundred yards past them was the county sheriff.

After Meredith passed, the man called out: "Which one of you is James Meredith?" With that, the group scattered. The man's voice had that scary, redneck-in-a-woodpile sound to it. They had all heard it many times before. As they dived for cover, they heard three blasts from a 16–gauge, automatic shotgun.

Meredith was the only one struck by the buckshot.

The shooter, later identified as Memphian Aubrey Norvell, made no attempt to escape. After Meredith fell to the ground, wounded and bleeding, Norvell stayed where he was, looking awkwardly out of place as he waited for the police to arrive.

Meredith was taken to a Memphis hospital, where it was determined that his wounds were not serious, though troublesome enough to prevent him from rejoining the march. The nation reacted with outrage. Civil rights leaders such as Martin Luther King and rising star Stokely Carmichael rushed to Mississippi to lead the march on to Jackson. Amid the uproar, the Mississippi Sovereignty Commission dispatched investigators to the scene.

In a report labeled "Confidential—Not for the files," Tom Scarbrough detailed his investigation of the incident. It was his gut feeling that the shooting had been planned by civil rights activists to draw attention to the march.

When Scarbrough arrived at the sheriff's office, he found the lawman talking to one of Norvell's two attorneys. He called the sheriff aside for a private conversation. He asked the sheriff if he thought either of the lawyers was interested in "bringing the truth to light."

The sheriff said he already had talked to one of the lawyers about the possibility that Norvell had been hired to shoot Meredith. It was the lawyer's view, according to the sheriff, that if it was a shooting-for-hire, the lawyer would get "far more out of it in a monetary way than he could possibly get out of defending Norvell."

Scarbrough told the sheriff he was certain the courts would be lenient with Norvell if he provided the names of the people who hired him. Did the sheriff know the lawyers well enough to pass a message along to them? The sheriff did.

"I asked him if he would talk to [one of the lawyers] on his own and advise him that he would give him a sizable sum of money to get the truth out of Norvell concerning the shooting," Scarbrough said. The sheriff was told to start with an offer of $5,000. "I told the sheriff I personally would guarantee this amount if it could be shown that the shooting was a planned deal. I further told the sheriff that the proposition I was making him was on my own and did not involve the state in any shape, form or fashion, but he could rest assured in making the proposition to [the lawyer] that the money would be available when proof is shown that Norvell was hired to do the shooting. . . . I further told him if he could bring the truth out and expose this bunch of agitators as having hired someone to shoot Meredith that he would be the most famous sheriff that has ever been in this state."

Scarbrough's offer was illegal and would have been interpreted by most courts as a bribe. And his statement to the sheriff that he was acting alone in making the offer was an outright lie. In a memo dated June 14, Commission director Erle Johnston advised the governor that he had authorized Scarbrough to offer the money to Norvell.

"I know of no other investigator better qualified by judgment and temperament to handle such an assignment and assure there will be no repercussion against the Sovereignty Commission," Johnston said.

It was another example of how the Commission used carefully written reports to divert attention from its true mission.

Norvell was in serious trouble: caught red-handed at the scene of the crime with the gun in his hand and photographed by newsmen across the highway. That was Norvell's dilemma, as Scarbrough presented it. But if he told the court he was hired by a civil rights organization, he could pocket a sizable amount of money, plus receive a guarantee of leniency; if he told the court he acted alone, he would receive no money and go directly to jail.

For whatever reasons, Norvell stuck to his story that he acted alone. He may have been a forty-year-old unemployed white man who lived off the earnings of his wife—and he may have shot a man down in cold blood in full view of the entire world—but, by God, he was no liar and certainly had no intention of taking money from the government. He pleaded guilty to the shooting and received a five-year sentence.

Scarbrough joined the march as it made its way to Jackson. Joining the marchers on June 8 were Martin Luther King, who stayed a short while then returned to Memphis, Charles Evers, the Reverend Ed King of Tougaloo, and six others from Jackson. Unknown to the marchers, the Commission had planted an informant in their midst.

The informant's identity is unknown, but from the information contained in his report it is clear he was present when Martin Luther King had a private conversation with Meredith. The informant also reported that Evers was carrying a pistol. He was someone who was trusted by the inner circle.

Thirty years later, as the author read the informant's confidential report to Evers, the civil rights leader interrupted the author when Ed King's name was mentioned.

"I think he was an informer," said Evers. "I always thought it. Ed was at everything we had. He was too liberal at that time. It just wasn't normal. I never did trust him."

As news of the shooting dominated news reports, Memphis radio station WDIA, the first station in America to hire a black staff, broadcast a feature called "Speaking Out." The female announcer advised her listeners not to blame Mississippi for the shooting. The blame should be placed on "Memphis, if anything," said the announcer.

As the marchers passed through Batesville, Scarbrough noticed that everyone was in a holiday mood. "One thing I noticed was the whites were singing those freedom songs to the Negro rhythms just as well as the Negroes themselves were singing, and a great number of the marchers were dancing or slapping their hands," he said. "It must be a great temptation to the local Negroes to fall in line with them because the marchers appeared to be having such a jubilee time."

At that point, a number of newspaper reporters had joined the march. Scarbrough introduced himself to the reporters and asked what they thought about the shooting. "They stated the whole affair of Meredith's shooting and the march was a cheap publicity stunt," he said "The boy with the *Atlanta Journal* stated he would not have been here to start with had it not been for his paper calling him and telling him to get over here on the march at once. He stated it was one of the most uncalled-for and disgusting experiences he had ever had as a reporter. Of course, none of these people would write an item expressing their real feelings because if they did their jobs would be terminated."

When the marchers arrived in Canton, just outside Jackson, they were tear gassed by police when they attempted to camp on the grounds of the school. But the next day they made it all the way to the Capitol building, where they held a massive rally. It was at this historic rally that Stokely Carmichael first urged the use of "black power," a phrase that would have an explosive impact on the civil rights movement as the decade progressed.

During the week of June 21, one year after the disappearance of the three COFO workers in Neshoba County, civil rights activists gathered in Philadelphia, Mississippi, to participate in memorial services for the slain men.

The men accused of the crime still walked the streets.

Since the Meredith shooting had occurred only two weeks earlier, everyone was uneasy about the memorial service. Everyone was on edge. Before the services began, Sheriff Lawrence Rainey left town. He left Deputy Cecil Price, who, along with Rainey, had been indicted in the murders, in charge of the sheriff's department.

The Mississippi highway patrol sent observers to the city, as did the FBI and the Sovereignty Commission. Although civil rights activists had notified the city that a march was scheduled for that day, the city made no attempt to control traffic along the route.

As about 250 demonstrators, led by Martin Luther King, approached the courthouse several cars and trucks veered into the marchers, knocking a young boy to the ground.

A mob of about 400 white spectators heckled the demonstrators. Someone tossed cherry bombs among the marchers, panicking the demonstrators. Fistfights broke out. A photographer was slugged by someone in the mob, who then ran away before he could be caught. Two television crews also were attacked.

Deputy Price arrested one of the demonstrators, Clinton Collier, on four old traffic tickets, then prevented Martin Luther King, accompanied by FBI agent Joe Sullivan, from entering the courthouse. Highway patrol officers witnessed the confrontation, but did not intervene. Collier was not unknown to the deputy. He had been an unsuccessful candidate for Congress in a recent primary election.

At one point, the Ku Klux Klan held a rally at a ballpark in a black neighborhood. The rally was visible from the Council of Federated Organizations headquarters. According to Commission investigator Andy Hopkins, young black men in the COFO house began shooting at cars that came into the area because they feared the Klan was getting ready to invade the neighborhood.

"They first shot into the automobile of a white man who is alleged to have been drinking and either returned their fire or fired the first shot—no one seems to be clear on this matter," said Hopkins. "While the sheriff's force and the police department were chasing the white man that was involved in the shooting, the FBI joined in the chase and as they passed through the area, one of their cars was riddled with bullets."

Before leaving that day, Martin Luther King met with Sheriff Rainey, who had returned to town, to work out details for further marches. King returned to Philadelphia three days later, and the memorial services were concluded without incident. Later, King would confide to friends that his visit to Philadelphia was one of the most terrifying experiences of his life.

By the fall of 1966, public schools were being desegregated at a slow, but steady rate, and voter registration among blacks was soaring. By the end of the year, black voting strength in Mississippi had grown from 30,000 to more than 170,000. The person most responsible for those dramatic changes was Martin Luther King, or at least most white Mississippians ✳ perceived him to be responsible. As a result of his successes, both the FBI and the Commission stepped up their surveillance of his activities.

In mid-September, the Commission received a tip from one of its highly placed informants that King was going to Grenada to organize another demonstration. Johnston immediately notified the governor. "He will address a crowd Monday night and may also lead some of the negro children to the white school," said Johnston. "Two of King's chief aides, Ralph Abernathy and Hosea Williams, are conducting meetings on the weekend and they are praying for trouble and violence to make news headlines." ✳

The day before receiving the informant's tip, the Commission had received another report on civil rights activity in Grenada. According to that report, Andrew Young, one of King's top aides, already had arrived in Grenada to help organize the demonstration. The report, stamped "restricted," said that Young had told the highway patrol that if they did not protect the children, he would call in Southern Christian Leadership Conference forces from all over the country.

Because of its association with King, SCLC was one of the most hated civil rights organizations in the state. The Commission shadowed SCLC leaders, using informants and regular investigators to keep tabs on their every move. The reports show remarkable detail and provide information that could only be useful for sinister purposes.

For example, when SCLC scheduled a midsummer conference at the King Edward Hotel in Jackson, the Commission issued a report that provided the room numbers of those in attendance. "Dr. Martin Luther King has reserved rooms 1117, 1119, and 1121 . . . Room 1119 is a parlor," said one report. "Senator Edward Kennedy has reserved rooms 1126, 1128, and 1130. He is due to arrive Sunday. All of the SCLC top personnel will stay on the eleventh floor."

One of the topics of conversation at the King Edward Hotel was the upcoming demonstration in Grenada. Andrew Young and Ralph Abernathy presided over one of the meetings. Sitting at their side was the Commission's informant.

"The purpose of this meeting was to try and work out some strategy . . . on whether to send people there today or wait until after the convention," the informant reported. "They finally decided to wait until after the meeting tonight and then they would send all of their forces to Grenada this weekend and have day and night marches."

Also provided by the informant was information that, instead of attending a play at the Masonic Temple as planned, leaders stayed in their rooms "drinking beer and liquor." Accompanying the report were the license plate numbers of automobiles from Florida, Illinois, and Georgia.

The SCLC reports on King and Kennedy are examples of the detailed information the Commission gathered on a regular basis to distribute to persons unknown. It is the same type of information gathered on Michael Schwerner. Car tag numbers, room numbers, schedules of when subjects would arrive and depart. That type of information would have dubious value to any state agency operating under the law, but to one intent on causing harm to the individuals named in the reports, it was invaluable.

Above all else Erle Johnston was a journalist.

As a newspaper editor—and as director of the Commission—he considered the news media a crucial ingredient in the state's fight against civil rights and antiwar activists. He attended state and national press association meetings whenever possible, and he worked hard to maintain his friendships with other journalists.

Those friendships paid off on a regular basis.

When a television station in Seattle contacted the Associated Press office in Jackson to verify information submitted to the station by the Commission, Jim Saggus, the AP bureau chief, met with Johnston and examined Commission files on the subject in question. In a memo to the governor, Johnston said that Saggus had been able to verify "every bit of the information we had furnished" the television station.

Johnston was proud of the way he manipulated the media.

In late June, he went to Washington, D.C., to meet with Sam Schreiner, a senior editor at *Reader's Digest*. Schreiner told him he felt Mississippi had been unfairly treated by the national media. Johnston asked him if he would work with the Commission to help offset the "bad propaganda."

Schreiner said he would be delighted to help. He suggested an article penned by Governor Johnson. In a memo to the governor, Johnston told him about the offer from *Reader's Digest*. He said he would write the article, then submit it to the governor for his approval before sending it to the magazine.

In July, Johnston put together a package deal for radio station WBBM in Chicago, a CBS affiliate. The station had expressed a desire to air a program that presented Mississippi's point of view. Johnston thought it would be a good idea if the governor himself went to Chicago to be interviewed for the broadcast. He also invited reporters Kenneth Toler of *The Commercial Appeal* and William Chaze of the *Clarion-Ledger*.

The group flew to Chicago aboard the governor's DC-3.

In his report on the trip, Johnston does not mention the roles played by the governor or the reporters, but he describes his own two-hour interview for the station's *Nightline* program. The first hour was spent in question and answer, but the second hour was devoted to listener calls.

"About 21 calls got on the air and the switchboard reported there was a backlog of 733 calls that could not be completed because of the time limitation," he said in his report. "We believe the program was very successful in ... explaining some of the fallacies about the state that have been reported in news media."

In Mississippi, Johnston had carte blanche with the media.

Percy Greene, the black editor of the *Jackson Advocate*, regularly ran stories given to him by the Commission, and he accepted money from the Commission as an informant. Greene was a good catch for Johnston, and he often bragged about it in his memos. For his part, Greene toed the Commission line. In one editorial, he wrote: "The greatest need for the Negro in Jackson, in Mississippi and in the rest of the South is more and more 'Uncle Toms.' "

Johnston was successful in getting Jackson newspapers to drop the use of professional titles such as "Reverend" when referring to civil rights supporters. He was successful in killing stories he did not like and in planting Commission information in stories he did like.

In November, when a *Jackson Daily News* reporter came to him for help on a story about Ted Seaver, a white civil rights activist, Johnston provided him with background material on the twenty-seven-year-old former teacher. The published story, which said Seaver was "drawing on leftist labor union tactics to organize Hinds County Negroes into a 'Black Power' political bloc," went on to say that the Boston native had been fired from his teaching job in Vermont for "attitudes unbecoming a teacher." The story never explained what those "attitudes" were.

It was a scathing, wretched piece of yellow journalism, which included information that Seaver's current salary was being paid by the Michael Schwerner Memorial Fund. Seaver also was identified as a member of the Mississippi Freedom Democratic Party.

In another instance, Johnston was successful in getting the same reporter to write a story about how Charles Evers had deserted his child and forced the child's mother to apply for welfare. But when the reporter turned the story in, his editors balked at running it without proof the child was really Evers's.

In a memo dated November 28, Johnston said he had been told by *Jackson Daily News* editor Jimmy Ward that attorneys for the newspaper had advised against publishing the story without documentation. "We are working now to obtain the necessary proof and will resubmit it to Mr. Ward," he said in the memo.

The Commission was successful in obtaining a birth certificate on the child and other documents and turned them over to the reporter. Years later, for an article about the Commission, *Clarion-Ledger* reporter Jerry Mitchell tracked down the reporter to ask him about the story. "I don't think that was any big secret [about Evers's daughter]," he said.

When the author talked to Evers about the story in 1996—and showed him Johnston's memo—the civil rights leader said he didn't know what they were talking about. "I've got seven daughters from five different mothers and I've always admitted that—and I've always taken care of them," he said. "I don't think a man should be ashamed of his children. They [the Commission] should be the ones who are ashamed."

Johnston often wrote editorials in support of Mississippi's effort to fight desegregation and sent them to a friend at U.S. Press Association, a Washington-based editorial service that distributed editorials to over 3,000 newspapers. When the editorials were published, readers were not told who actually wrote them.

In a memo to the governor, Johnston said that he had received twenty-seven clippings from newspapers that used one of the editorials, "The Truth Finally Outs." One of the clippings was from the *Jackson Daily News,* which had reprinted the editorial, identifying it as one written by editors at a South Dakota newspaper.

Editors at the *Clarion-Ledger* and *Jackson Daily News* regularly went to the Commission with requests for information from the agency's secret files. Once Jimmy Ward called and asked Johnston if he had information on any "professional agitators" who had worked in other states before coming to Mississippi.

Johnston was happy to oblige.

Ward was given a dossier on a white, female activist from Berkeley, California, who had been arrested for civil rights activity in Alabama before participating in James Meredith's march earlier in the year. Johnston threw in a photograph for good measure, but asked that the Commission not be identified as the source of the information.

In one of his reports to the governor, Johnston referred to the incident, bragging that the story had been given wide coverage and resulted in the woman's leaving the state.

As the FBI expanded its Cointelpro program to include antiwar activists, the Commission and the highway patrol gave the Mississippi antiwar movement equal status with the civil rights movement. In the eyes of most Mississippians, it was just as radical to advocate peace as it was to advocate racial equality. Commission investigators were authorized to pursue either group.

In late December, investigator Tom Scarbrough was ordered to check with sheriffs and chiefs of police around the state to determine if activists were having any problems making their bonds. According to the law enforcement officers Scarbrough contacted, no one was having any difficulty obtaining the cash or property required for the bonds.

Interestingly, the tone of the interviews was beginning to change, however slightly, as law enforcement officers, for the first time, began to indicate a growing sense of impatience with the questions asked by investigators.

"All stated they did not object to any reputable bonding company making civil rights workers' bonds, that so far as they were concerned, that is a decision for the bonding company to make," Scarbrough said in his report. "Some of the officials however stated that quite a few of those arrested were conscientious objectors and were opposed to the U.S. policies in Vietnam."

Scarbrough contacted three of the state's largest bonding companies— Capitol Bonding Service, Nationwide Bonding Company, and Blaine Bonding Agency—all of which stated they would not make bond for civil rights workers because of the "high risk" involved. Scarbrough's investigation confirmed the Commission's fears that civil rights and antiwar activists had learned ways of bypassing the "good ole boy" system that the Commission had used successfully for more than a decade to harass them.

By the end of 1966, the United States had 360,000 soldiers engaged in combat in Vietnam. The war became an issue in Mississippi that year as Stokely Carmichael urged blacks to defy the all-white draft boards by refusing service in the military. Carmichael didn't know it at the time, but the situation was even worse than "all-white," for state officials had long been in the habit of appointing klansmen to the boards.

Attacking the antiwar movement was both easier and more dangerous than attacking the civil rights movement. The Commission was limited in what it could do to punish antiwar activists from outside the state, but within the state it could exercise the ultimate weapon: it could have them arrested and sent to Vietnam.

That was easy. All it took was a phone call. It was dangerous, however, since it was a violation of federal law and put the Commission at greater risk. For that reason, Commission campaigns against antiwar activists were taken to higher degrees of secrecy than those directed at civil rights activists.

The Commission often received help from the FBI, which earlier that year had elevated its surveillance of Martin Luther King. The civil rights leader had said very little about Vietnam, but public dissent was rising and Hoover was fearful that King, like Stokely Carmichael, would make it an issue.

The Mississippi highway patrol worked closely with the Commission in monitoring Vietnam War protests. They showed particular interest in a demonstration at the Jackson post office when it learned it was being sponsored by the Student Nonviolent Coordinating Committee and faculty members from Tougaloo College. Patrolmen took down the names of those participating in the demonstration and prepared background reports on each of them.

It was the sort of demonstration that concerned Hoover.

When the FBI learned that McGeorge Bundy, director of the Ford Foundation, was considering a financial grant to the Southern Christian Leadership Conference in the fall of 1966, Hoover asked a former agent, who had left the agency to become a vice president of Ford Motor Company, to have a talk with Bundy.

The FBI felt that if Bundy knew about the "subversive" people associated with King, he would reconsider making a grant to SCLC. When the former agent met with Bundy, he was surprised by Bundy's refusal to talk about King. According to FBI memos, Bundy told the man that he would only talk about King to people who had first-hand knowledge of the man.

The memo stated that it was doubtful that direct contact with Bundy by the FBI would have any different results. Hoover scribbled on the memo: "Yes. We would get no where with Bundy."

J. Edgar Hoover felt his power was slipping away. More and more Americans were treating the FBI with the same lack of respect Bundy had shown. The same thing was happening to the Commission. County sheriffs were no longer quite so happy to see Commission investigators come into their counties.

As the year ended, black voter registration was up across the South. The civil rights movement was gaining momentum. American casualties in Vietnam were averaging two hundred dead and over two thousand wounded per week. And protest demonstrations were spreading across the country.

CHAPTER 7

1967

After seven years on the job, Erle Johnston was beginning to feel the pressure. It wasn't easy putting in a full day running a top-secret spy agency and then commuting forty-five miles to Forest to put out a weekly newspaper, the *Scott County Times*.

Physically, he was wearing down. He wasn't alone, either. Andy Hopkins, his chief investigator, had frequent health problems after the Neshoba County murders and took extended leaves of absence. Then he was involved in a minor traffic accident while he was out on assignment. Soon Hopkins stopped coming to work.

By the fall of 1966, Commission members were asking questions. They instructed Johnston to send Hopkins a letter asking for the names of his doctors and written permission from him for Commission members to contact the doctors. The investigator was now being investigated.

"I assured the committee you would be happy to cooperate with them," Johnston said in the letter to Hopkins. "As I told members of the Commission, I certainly hope that you soon become fully recuperated and can get back on the job."

Hopkins chose to resign.

January began slowly enough. Johnston was tipped off by an informant that Martin Luther King was headed for Grenada again in February for another voter registration drive, so he knew that his workload would pick up soon; but, for the moment, he was free to focus on his "public relations" duties.

Mississippi could hardly keep tabs on subversives if it didn't know what "lies" the Communist Party was spreading about the state. The best way to know that was to subscribe to their publications. Of course, it wouldn't do for the Sovereignty Commission to have mail from the Communist Party delivered to the Capitol. What would people think?

At Johnston's request, *Jackson Daily News* reporter Mike Smith rented a box at the Jackson post office in his name for the purpose of receiving Communist literature ordered by the Commission. Johnston sent a memorandum to the postmaster that explained why Smith was receiving the literature.

That was the kind of public relations Johnston liked best.

In January, Tom Scarbrough, who had replaced Andy Hopkins as chief investigator, went to Washington County to determine if it was necessary "for white people to carry firearms in order to protect themselves from Negroes." After talking to his sources, he decided it was not going to be necessary for residents to carry firearms for protection, but he was concerned that "too many white people have given up" in their efforts to fight desegregation. That was the wrong way to look at it, he said, since it was obvious that blacks were not going to organize as a voting bloc. "It is true that the Negro vote is going to make a big difference in the next statewide election," he said. "However, since most of the civil rights groups are fighting between themselves, it is doubtful if the Negroes vote in a block except in a few counties."

In February, Scarbrough was sent back to Washington County to look into the activities of Stokely Carmichael, who had been spotted in the Delta "stirring up trouble." When he arrived in Greenville, Scarbrough was disappointed to discover that Police Chief William Burnley was unavailable for an interview; but Scarbrough was able to prepare a report on Carmichael after talking to several policemen, who told him that the civil rights activist had staged a demonstration at the jail in an effort to free a black man who had been jailed for civil disobedience.

"He made boastful statements that he would turn Greenville into a battleground, but apparently he could not stir up any enthusiasm in Greenville to support his boast as he left the next day to parts unknown and has not returned to anyone's knowledge," he reported. "The policemen stated that no one paid Carmichael any attention and it is their opinion even the Negroes in Greenville did not pay him very much attention."

Burnley's "unavailability" to meet with Scarbrough was indicative of a growing reluctance among local law enforcement officers to be associated with the Commission. It is tempting to think of all Mississippi sheriffs and police chiefs of that era as closet klansmen, but some, like Burnley, took their jobs to "keep the peace" seriously and did their best to uphold the law.

From Greenville, Scarbrough was sent to Carroll County, a picturesque rural area off the beaten path between Greenwood and Grenada. There are few blacks in the county and most of the whites are farmers who have worked the same sparse hillsides for generations.

In mid-February, Janet Maedke, a twenty-seven-year-old white woman from Wisconsin, accompanied by several black activists, went to Carrollton, the county seat, to integrate the town's main cafe. They were prevented from entering the cafe by the sheriff and then assaulted by the cafe owner as the sheriff watched. The window of Maedke's car was shattered during the altercation and the broken glass peppered her arm.

When Maedke and the black civil rights activists left town, they were followed by the cafe owner and another man, who pursued them on the highway at high speed and fired shots at them. After going at speeds that exceeded 100 miles per hour, they escaped and made it to a place of safety. When they stopped and examined the car, they found that one bullet had shattered a taillight and a second bullet had penetrated the trunk of the car.

After five days of hiding out, Maedke wrote a letter to a friend expressing her fear, disgust, and determination to continue with their efforts. She said she had not slept for days. She kept a rifle on the dashboard of her car and a shotgun on the backseat. She was convinced someone was going to kill her.

The case was turned over to the Sovereignty Commission after Maedke contacted Governor Warren Knowles of Wisconsin and asked for his help. Knowles called the U.S. Justice Department and spoke to John Doar, the assistant attorney general in the civil rights division. In a follow-up letter, Doar gave the governor a full report on the incident and told him Maedke should report the incident to the proper law enforcement officials. Copies of Maedke's letter to her friend and Doar's letter to the governor of Wisconsin somehow ended up in the Commission files.

Following Doar's advice, Maedke pressed charges against the cafe owner, but a jury composed of four blacks and two whites acquitted him of the assault charges. In his report to the Commission, Scarbrough said the sheriff described Maedke as a "typical looking, white beatnik" who associated with "no one but a low class of Negroes."

At the assault trial, according to Scarbrough's report, Maedke "was dressed in a very slouchy manner and was sitting among her usual crowd of Negroes." He said the sheriff saw one of the black men reach over and pat her on the knees and thighs during the trial. "Miss Maedke and her Negro companions had successfully integrated other places in Vaiden [a nearby town], before this incident," said Scarbrough. "It appears that they went to Carrollton for the purpose of making trouble."

That same month, the Neshoba County murders again made the news when a Jackson federal grand jury reinstated conspiracy indictments against seventeen of the original defendants. Added to the list were two new names—Sam Bowers, Imperial Wizard of the Ku Klux Klan, and Hop Barnett, a former Neshoba County sheriff.

The FBI also considered Bowers a suspect in a 1966 fire-bombing in McComb that resulted in the death of Vernon Dahmer, a black civil rights activist. Eventually, he stood trial for that murder—four different times. Each time, the trial ended in a hung jury.

Most Mississippians were shocked at the new indictments. Everyone had thought the Neshoba County murders were a closed issue. If the Commission took any comfort from the news, it was that federal prosecutors would have to take the case back to the courtroom of Senator's Eastland's college roommate, Judge Harold Cox.

Commission members were staunch believers in the system.

As the war continued in Carroll County over who could—and could not—eat in local cafes, a bomb exploded in the car of Natchez NAACP leader Worlest Jackson. He was killed by the blast. Charles Evers was stunned by the murder.

"When I saw him dead, I remembered when we had started the branch together in Natchez," he wrote in his memoirs. "The Sunday before he was killed he came to Fayette and asked me how we would change white men's hearts."

After the bombing, Evers organized a series of demonstrations in Natchez to protest the city council's refusal to appoint a black to the school board. During one of the demonstrations, a white laundry owner tried to run down the marchers with his car. A highway patrolman filed a report that said downtown Natchez "looked like a ghost town" because of the trouble. The Sovereignty Commission sent its best undercover operative, "Operator X," to the city to identify the "outsiders" who were causing the trouble.

Asked in 1996 by the author what he thought about the FBI's efforts during the Natchez demonstrations, Evers sighed and replied "not very much."

"The FBI told me they had word someone was going to assassinate me," said Evers. "They said they just wanted to let me know so I could be careful."

Evers asked what they were going to do to protect him.

"They said, 'We can't do anything about it unless they try.'

"I said, 'Get out of my face'—and I walked on past."

In March 1967, shortly after Captain Christopher Pyle was assigned to teach law at the Army Intelligence School, he had occasion to remove a book from his office shelf. Just as offices were provided with regulation desks and chairs, so, too, were they stocked with regulation books. Pyle opened the book.

Inside the cover was a rubber stamp imprint:

> This publication is included in the counter intelligence corps school library for research purposes only. Its presence on the library shelf does not indicate that the views expressed in the publication represent the policies or opinions of the counter intelligence corps or the military establishment.

That book was the Constitution of the United States.

Shocked, Pyle asked the school librarian why the Constitution had been stamped with a disclaimer. He was told that all the books in the library, even the ones containing federal laws, bore the same stamp. It was a throwback to the "red scares" of the 1950s, when United States senators took it upon themselves to purge certain books from library shelves. He was told not to worry about it.

Nonetheless, the incident had a lingering effect on Pyle.

By 1967, the U.S. Army had begun a secret undercover operation to gather information about the political activity of American citizens. More than 1,500 plainclothes agents were assigned to over 350 secret record centers. Their job was to gather information on individuals attending protest rallies, business executives who contributed money to political causes, and politicians who voted for unpopular legislation.

The Army agents dressed in street wear normal for the times. Some posed as news reporters and carried fake IDs. Others infiltrated civil rights and antiwar organizations. They attended meetings, photographed those in the audience, and took down names. By the end of the 1960s, they had compiled files on over 100,000 citizens.

The Army's counterintelligence units operated under several code names—Punch Block, Lantern Spike, Rose Bush, and Steep Hill, to name a few. They operated independent of the White House, and did not require civilian authority to initiate new programs, nor were they subjected to civilian oversight. The Army decided whom it spied on, and the Army decided what was constitutional and what was not.

That the secret Army units were aware of the activities being conducted by the Sovereignty Commission—and vice versa—is evidenced by an employment application the Commission received from a former army agent. For his files, Director Johnston noted that the applicant had served two years with Army Intelligence as a special investigator and was currently employed at a Jackson bank. He also noted, with apparent interest, that the applicant's wife was an editorial assistant at *Mississippi Farmer Magazine.* There is no notation as to whether he was hired.

~~~~~~

By 1967, the FBI had cut back its surveillance of Martin Luther King. That April, King made a decision that would have a profound impact not only on his career but on the lives of thousands of draft-age American males. Speaking before a huge crowd in the United Nations Plaza in New York, he stated his opposition to President Johnson's Vietnam policy. His words sent tremors all the way to Washington.

For the FBI, it was an excuse to increase surveillance again. A week after the speech, the FBI sent the White House and the Justice Department a revised edition of its file summary on King. The FBI noted that King's remarks were "a direct parallel of the communist position on Vietnam."

For the U.S. Army, it was an excuse to target King for surveillance by its secret agents. They had decided to monitor the New York speech the previous month in Chicago after white peace activist Dr. Benjamin Spock had called for a union of the civil rights and antiwar movements. Army agents recorded and photographed King's speech.

For the Sovereignty Commission, it was all it needed to lump the two movements together. Martin Luther King was the mortar that cemented the two groups. From that day onward, the Commission could, with smug justification, target the two groups with the same fervor and commitment.

From the beginning, the same white men and women who worked for civil rights in the South also opposed the war. Black civil rights workers were slower to join the antiwar bandwagon. For many, life in the military represented freedom, however limited, from the oppression prevalent in the civilian sector. Many whites considered the reluctance of some black leaders to support the antiwar movement a slap in the face.

Martin Luther King's denunciation of the war marked a turning point.

In January, President Johnson said in his State of the Union address that he felt the Selective Service System should be modernized. With troop strength in Vietnam approaching the half million mark, the draft had become the focus of protests around the country. By then, more than 20,000 men had refused to be inducted into the military. Thousands had fled to Canada.

In February, Senator Robert Kennedy offered a resolution in the Senate urging the president to overhaul the draft by executive order instead of waiting for legislation. As students prepared for a massive "Spring Mobilization" to oppose the draft, 200,000 marchers paraded through the streets of New York.

Noted British philosopher Bertrand Russell called for an international war crimes tribunal to hear evidence of American atrocities in Vietnam. The hearings were scheduled to take place in Paris in March. As a justification for the tribunal, Russell quoted Supreme Court Justice Jackson, who had served as chief prosecutor at the Nuremberg War Crimes Tribunal: "If certain acts and violations of treaties are crimes, they are crimes whether the United States does them or whether Germany does them. We are not prepared to lay down a rule of criminal conduct against others which we would not be willing to have invoked against us."

When King took his stand against the war, the national mood was tense.

Journalist David Halberstam was with King when he made the New York speech and then traveled with him to Cleveland, where four people had died in riots the previous summer. He said King's associates never questioned his commitment to the peace movement, but they did question the wisdom of taking a stand at a time when the civil rights movement needed his full-time attention.

King's boldness made his associates nervous. In the past, he had taken on Southern racists such as Bull Connor and George Wallace. Now he was taking on the president of the United States. They hoped he knew what he was doing.

At a press conference in Cleveland, King was asked about his New York statement. Did he think it would hurt his efforts on behalf of the civil rights movement? No, King answered. He didn't think it would hurt the cause or dampen President Johnson's commitment to it. A black reporter, who had just returned from a military hospital, said: "The war doesn't bother them. The soldiers are for it."

"Later, on the way to the airport . . . King's top assistant, Andy Young, commented on the fact that the Vietnam question had come from a Negro reporter," said Halberstam. " 'It always does,' Young said. 'Everytime we get the dumb question, the patriot question, it's a Negro reporter.' "

A minister said the black middle class was fearful of losing respectability on the issue. King agreed with him. "They're very nervous on Vietnam, afraid they're going to lose everything else," King explained. "Yes, they're hoping the war will win them their spurs. That's not the way you win spurs."

From Cleveland, the group flew to Berkeley, where King got into a heated argument with Whitney Young, the executive director of the National Urban League. Young had toured Vietnam the previous summer and saw the war as a vehicle for advancement for black men. King's position made him uneasy.

"Young told King that his position was unwise since it would alienate the President, and they wouldn't get anything from him," wrote Halberstam. "King angrily told him, 'Whitney, what you're saying may get you a foundation grant, but it won't get you into the kingdom of truth.'

"Young angrily told King that he was interested in the ghettos, and King was not. King told Young that was precisely why he opposed the war, because of what it was doing to the ghettos."

The FBI considered launching a Cointelpro operation against both King and Spock after rumors surfaced that the two might run as "peace" candidates in the 1968 presidential election, but the New York field office was successful in obtaining a postponement on the grounds that the war would be over by then or the Communist Party would be actively involved in the peace movement, thus making exposure of a King–Spock link to the Communists more attractive to the White House.

Hoover did approve a recommendation in March by agents who wanted to provide "friendly" newspaper reporters with embarrassing questions to ask King at press conferences. The agents wanted reporters to focus on King's foreign policy opinions, since they felt this would cause "extreme embarrassment" to the civil rights leader.

Later that year, FBI agents circulated an editorial published in a black magazine that was critical of King's Vietnam policy. The purpose of doing that, according to FBI memos, was to "publicize King as a traitor to his country and his race" and to "reduce his income" from a series of shows given by entertainer Harry Belafonte to raise money for the Southern Christian Leadership Conference.

In July, as racial riots broke out in Cleveland, Phoenix, Flint, and South Bend, Martin Luther King and other civil rights leaders made public appeals to end the rioting. Militant leaders such as Stokely Carmichael and H. Rap Brown called for a black revolution.

When Detroit exploded in rioting on July 23, the Army, operating independent of the FBI, sent in the 82nd Airborne, along with a team of secret agents. The commanding general ordered that the Army's secret agents be put on full alert in cities across the country. They were specifically ordered to put potential guerrilla targets—television stations, armories, power stations—under surveillance.

On July 28, Memphis was designated a target city by the Army.

By then, the Army's files on private citizens had grown so large they had to be converted to computers for storage. In addition to its own files, the Army had access to over 18 million Defense Department security clearance and criminal files, information on file at local and state police agencies, and the FBI's huge accumulation of domestic intelligence files (estimated at covering between 500,000 to one million persons).

"Several of the computerized systems were capable of producing round-up lists of civilian dissenters by name, address, ideology, and group membership," said Christopher Pyle, who left the Army to write about what he had seen. His first article on the subject was published in the *Washington Monthly.* Years later, he wrote a book about his experiences, *Military Surveillance of Civilian Politics.*

"Most of the files focused on incidents, but a large percentage dealt with the political beliefs, actions, and associations of individuals and groups," he wrote. "Some included detailed information on the financial, health, family, and sexual affairs of private citizens wholly unrelated to any legitimate purpose."

Not to be outdone by the Army or the Sovereignty Commission, the FBI stepped up its program of surreptitious entries, in which agents broke into homes and offices to plant hidden microphones. Hoover had banned the so-called black bag program in 1966, whereby agents entered homes and offices without warrants to photograph and steal documents, but he had allowed agents to continue those activities so long as they were for the purpose of electronic surveillance.

Years later, testifying before a Senate subcommittee, one of the agents who specialized in surreptitious entry said he rarely had to pick a lock. Most of the time, he said, he was able to obtain a key. Other times people simply left their doors unlocked. Another agent, who taught courses in "black bag" techniques, told the committee that he sometimes was asked to open safes. On one occasion, he said, he even installed hidden microphones in the homes of CIA agents.

In August, the FBI initiated a formal Cointelpro probe that it captioned "Black Nationalist–Hate Groups." The purpose of this new counter-intelligence operation, said one directive, was to "expose, disrupt, misdirect, discredit or otherwise neutralize" the activities of civil rights groups such as King's Southern Christian Leadership Conference, the Congress of Racial Equality, and the Student Nonviolent Coordinating Committee.

In another directive, FBI agents were told the Cointelpro operation was meant to prevent the "rise of a 'messiah' who could unify and electrify the militant black nationalist movement." Among those listed as potential "messiahs" was King, a real contender if he ever abandoned his "white, liberal doctrines."

For the past several years, the FBI had concentrated much of its civil rights—and anti-civil rights—efforts in Mississippi. The new Cointelpro operation meant that those already intense efforts would be pushed to the limit.

Sometime in late April or early May, Governor Johnson decided the Sovereignty Commission should hire more investigators so it could take on additional assignments. Johnston was offended, and sent the governor a memo suggesting that he meet with him and the Commission's three investigators so that he could personally instruct them about what he had in mind. There is no record of whether the meeting took place.

Two of the most troublesome areas of the state for the Commission were Washington County and its southern neighbor, Issaquena County. Washington County was troublesome because it was the home of liberal newspaper editor Hodding Carter III and had a reputation as a literary oasis. In addition to Carter, author of *The South Strikes Back,* those who called Washington County home were noted author and Civil War historian Shelby Foote; Walker Percy, author of *The Last Gentleman* and *The Moviegoer;* William Alexander Percy, author of *Lanterns on the Levee;* Ellen Douglas, author of *Family Affairs;* and Ben Wasson, a literary critic who was William Faulkner's first editor and agent. That historical accumulation of rebellious literati, when paired with liberal Jewish businessmen and progressive-minded farmers, made the county inhospitable for slow-talking Commission investigators intent on digging up dirt on civil rights activists.

Issaquena County was troublesome for different reasons. The most sparsely populated county in the state—it has never bothered to put up a traffic light and even today there is not one to be found in the entire county—was home to a hearty mixture of black landowners and white landowners who settled there after successful careers in professions that took them far beyond the boundaries of Mississippi. Neither group wanted trouble from political extremists or government investigators. Troublemakers weren't welcome in the county, and the few who were brave enough—or stupid enough—to travel the wilderness roads in search of ideological intrigue soon became discouraged by the miles and miles of virgin forests and blackbottom farmland that greeted them.

Issaquena County was home to one of Mississippi's most determined female black civil rights activists, Unita Blackwell. She had marched at Fannie Lou Hamer's side in demonstrations across the Delta, and she had led the Mississippi Freedom Democratic Party delegation to the national convention in 1964, where she befriended actress Shirley MacLaine. She later accompanied MacLaine on trips to China, thus achieving celebrity status in a state that rarely saw Hollywood stars in the flesh.

Commission investigators dreaded going to Washington and Issaquena counties. Their efforts there had never paid off, and going there seemed like a waste of time. That May, chief investigator Tom Scarbrough drew the short straw. Johnston asked him to go to Washington County to trace the origin of funding for the Citizenship Education Project. He had received information that the project was being funded by a group named "Voters League of Issaquena County."

When Scarbrough discovered that money for the project was being deposited at First National Bank in Greenville, he asked the county sheriff if he had any contacts at the bank who would provide confidential information to him. The sheriff said he didn't know anyone at the bank. "He asked me how I stood with Chief of Police Burnley," Scarbrough said in his report. "I advised the sheriff I had never been able to get any cooperation out of Burnley. He said that was about right, that neither he nor anyone else other than Mr. Hodding Carter. I asked him what he thought about Captain Long with the police department as Long had always worked with me pretty good. [The sheriff] said that it was his thinking that Long would come nearer getting the information I sought from the bank than anyone with the police department."

Scarbrough met with Captain Long and told him what he needed from the bank. Long told him that he had a friend who worked at the bank and he was certain he could get what Scarbrough needed. He told Scarbrough to meet him at his office later that afternoon. When he arrived at Long's office at the appointed time, he was told that it was not going to be possible to obtain the information. Long said his friend at the bank had received orders "from above" not to reveal any information about checks drawn on civil rights accounts. In his report, Scarbrough said he did not bother going to the bank himself, since he knew it would be futile. He did hold out a ray of hope. "Captain Long told me that he still thought he might be able to get the information but that his friend would have to have time to get it out of the bank without anyone's knowledge and if he received the information he would call me."

Scarbrough left Washington County, defeated once again. He didn't bother driving south to investigate the Voters League of Issaquena County. That *really* would have been a waste of time. Instead, he drove east to Grenada, where he hoped to learn if there was any talk of Martin Luther King returning to the city.

Scarbrough found Grenada more hospitable.

From the police chief, he learned that King had "lost his foothold in Grenada." If he returned, he would find he could not "stir up the trouble" that had taken place the year before. He said blacks were "tired of being bled for what money they could rake and scrape" together for King's organization.

"Grenada people are much better prepared for King's return than they were on his first appearance in Grenada soon after the Meredith march. . . .," Scarbrough reported. "It is hoped, of course, by all that King will not return to Grenada."

That month, Charles Evers attracted the Commission's attention with an announcement that he was giving state officials a June 1 deadline to appoint

African Americans to state draft boards. "I don't think Negroes should be called up by all-white draft boards," he told reporters. Evers, who had served in World War II and the Korean War, said that if changes were not made in the racial makeup of the draft boards he might ask blacks not to report for induction. Responding to Evers's comment was John Otis Sumrall of Quitman. When drafted, the young black man refused to take the induction oath. He filed a lawsuit challenging the authority of the all-white draft board.

Sumrall's case quickly made its way to the Fifth Circuit Court of Appeals, where a three-judge panel refused to delay his induction into the armed forces until the lawsuit could be heard. Sumrall was shipped off to war and the case evaporated into thin air.

At about that same time, another black man, Morris Davis of Jackson, announced that he also would refuse to serve in protest of the racial make-up of the local boards. Evers commended Davis on his stand. Said Evers: "No white man in Mississippi would allow his son to be sent to war by an all-Negro draft board."

By mid-June, Meredith was talking about organizing another march from Hernando, near where he had been shot in 1966. This time, he said, he would wear a bulletproof vest. He hinted he also would be carrying a gun.

The same Commission informant who reported on Meredith's activities also gave details of a closed meeting that Charles Evers had had with civil rights leaders at New Zion Baptist Church in Jackson. "The group decided to start a very quiet whisper campaign for William Winter in the governor's race and on or about July 8 will pass the word to all negroes to vote for Winter," said the informant. "Claude Ramsey with the CIO labor movement is behind Winter—so informed the group and actively sought their support for Winter, saying his group had endorsed Winter."

When the author showed Evers the informant's report in 1996, he said "that's exactly the way it was," meaning all the details were accurate. Referring to Winter's candidacy, he said: "He was the only one who wasn't calling us niggers at that time. He did everything but that, but at least he didn't call us niggers. Of those who were running, he was the only one we could support."

Running against Winter for governor were Congressman John Bell Williams, former governor Ross Barnett, and Bill Waller, who had unsuccessfully prosecuted Byron De La Beckwith in the Medgar Evers murder.

Throughout the campaign, Williams and Barnett went after each other like junkyard dogs, with the hottest issue being the desegregation of Ole Miss. Williams said that if he had been governor, there would have been no "under-the-table agreements" made with the Kennedys. Barnett denied ever making any "deals" with the Kennedys.

At a forum sponsored by the Citizens' Council, Williams was asked by the moderator how he would have handled the James Meredith affair. All the other candidates were there, including Barnett. Williams said he would have exhausted every legal means to prevent Meredith's entry to the university. If all else failed, he said he would have gone to the campus, faced the U.S. marshals, then stood aside when there was a show of force. "I would have said we are not surrendering, we merely submit in the face of overwhelming physical force," Williams said.

Barnett followed Williams to the speaker's stand. His eyes were blazing. His face was flushed. He said if he were not a deacon in his church he would call Williams a liar.

"Ross Barnett made no deal with anyone, and I dare John Bell Williams to prove it," Barnett said, his voice booming. "I'll never apologize for anything I've done."

When Winter was asked the same question, he responded with a one-sentence answer: "I would have handled it in a way that would not have resulted in bloodshed and violence—and I would have told the people the truth at all times."

When the ballots in the first primary were counted, Winter led with 222,000 votes to Williams's 197,000 votes, with Barnett coming in a distant third with 76,000 votes. Waller came in last with 60,000 votes. For Barnett, it was a bitter loss. He was the man who had "lost" Ole Miss. His political career was over and he knew it.

Since none of the candidates had a majority, Winter and Williams were required to face off in a second primary. During the campaign, both candidates said they were segregationists, but Williams said it with more enthusiasm; and when the votes were counted, he was victorious. In the general election, he defeated the Republican candidate, Reubel Phillips, by a three-to-one margin.

During the campaign, the Sovereignty Commission—at the request of the governor—had discontinued sending out its secret reports to lawmakers and other supporters. The governor wanted to keep the Commission out of politics for the duration of the campaign.

Not happy with that decision was Tom Hederman, editor of the *Clarion-Ledger*. He asked his city editor, Charles Smith, to find out why they were no longer receiving the secret reports. When Smith called the Commission office, Johnston explained that until after the election, the governor had asked that only he receive the reports.

"I explained we are determined that the Sovereignty Commission not be involved in politics and some of the reports naturally contained political overtones," Johnston noted in a report. "I also explained to Mr. Smith that if

Mr. Hederman wants to ask the Governor to have him put back on the mailing list, we will do whatever the Governor recommends."

The records don't indicate if Hederman asked the governor to put him back on the mailing list, but they do indicate that Johnston had a much cozier relationship with the *Clarion-Ledger* than previously had been revealed. In a routine letter addressed to the Houston Council on Human Relations, Johnston disclosed that one of the clippings he was enclosing from the *Clarion-Ledger* had, in fact, been written by him.

Exhausted after nearly eight years on the job, Commission director Erle Johnston released his resignation to the news media and informed the governor-elect that he would stay on the job only until a replacement could be found.

On the morning of June 24, James Meredith, accompanied by two black men, left Memphis in a light-blue 1965 Thunderbird on his way to the place where he was shot the previous year. When he arrived, he held a press conference that was attended by about thirty-five journalists.

Sixteen people participated in the march with Meredith, including Alfred Ross, a white intern on the staff of Senator Jacob Javits of New York. Outnumbered two-to-one by journalists, the marchers walked along the highway on their way to Senatobia.

Just north of Coldwater River, highway patrol officers discovered a child-sized mannequin on the shoulder of the road. It had a noose around its neck and was painted black. Taped to the mannequin were three shotgun shells and a sign: "Welcome to Mississippi."

Two miles south of Senatobia, the marchers called it a day at 4:30 P.M. Meredith got in the blue Thunderbird and returned to Memphis, where he spent the night. While they were gone, the highway patrol arrested three white men who were traveling in a pickup truck that contained materials for making a cross, a blackjack, a night stick, gasoline, and a hatchet. They were arrested and charged with having a concealed weapon and public drunkenness.

The march resumed early the next morning with Meredith and four marchers, who continued on to Grenada. Two women, one white, the other black, sought to join the march, but Meredith said no, on the grounds that he had asked no women or children to participate. Senator Robert Kennedy flew into Greenville and drove the sixty or so miles to Grenada to make a brief appearance at the march.

Also wanting to join the march, though for different reasons, was George Lincoln Rockwell, leader of the American Nazi Party. He flew into Memphis, where he met with supporters, but he decided against traveling into Mississippi after being told by the Mississippi highway patrol that he would probably be arrested if he went anywhere near the march. Many patrolmen may have been in sympathy with his racist, right-wing ideology, but he was an outsider, and outsiders just weren't welcome in Mississippi.

～～／～～

In January 1967, Abe Fortas went to the Hotel Deauville in Miami for a meeting with his friend, Louis Wolfson, a Jacksonville multimillionaire who had been indicted by a federal grand jury as a result of a Securities and Exchange Commission probe.

Fortas had bad news for Wolfson.

The two had met sometime back. Wolfson was a self-made millionaire who had turned a $10,000 loan into a fortune. By sheer grit and determination, the former all-South football star had transformed his family's scrap-iron business into a controlling interest in Merritt-Chapman and Scott, a heavy construction and marine salvage company that did an annual business of over $269 million a year.

Wolfson became the company president and diversified into a wide range of other industries, including shipbuilding. One of those businesses, the New York Shipbuilding Corporation, received contracts for the *Savannah,* the world's first nuclear-powered cargo ship, and the *Kitty Hawk,* the U.S. Navy's largest aircraft carrier.

Wolfson followed a game plan similar to the one formulated by Memphis businessmen, who had targeted defense industries as a source of multi-million-dollar contracts. Defense industries were attractive because they were susceptible to political influence, always issued contracts that were well padded, and provided enormous margins of profit.

Wolfson thought that Fortas, given his influence with the president and the other members of the Supreme Court, would be an asset to the team. Of course, he couldn't simply hire a Supreme Court justice to work for him. That would be unethical and illegal.

After conducting a little research, Wolfson learned that Fortas had accepted fifteen thousand dollars from his old law partners to teach a summer course at American University. It was an arrangement most legal scholars would have considered highly improper for a Supreme Court justice.

Wolfson saw an opening. He set up a charitable foundation that could pay Fortas for legal advice. It would be named the Wolfson Family Foundation. Fortas thought that was a splendid idea. In exchange for his services, Fortas would receive twenty thousand dollars a year for life, with the money going to his wife for the remainder of her life in the event of Fortas's death. Two weeks after he received the first check, Fortas wrote a letter to President Johnson in which he recommended Wolfson's firm, Merritt-Chapman and Scott, as a model that could be used for drafting policies of nondiscrimination.

Johnson could read between the lines.

Before anything good could happen to Merritt-Chapman and Scott, bad things started happening to Wolfson. That spring, the SEC sent to the Justice Department the first of two cases for criminal prosecution against Merritt-Chapman and Scott. The case would be prosecuted by Robert Morgenthau, the United States attorney for the Southern District of New York. Morgenthau was one of the most fearless—and least approachable—federal prosecutors in the system.

Wolfson asked Fortas what he should do.

In a handwritten note, Fortas told Wolfson, "For God's sake," not to resign as president of the company. Wolfson followed his advice and stayed at the helm. Later, Fortas told Wolfson that he had been responsible for Johnson's appointment of SEC chairman Manuel F. Cohen and would talk to someone about the case.

For reasons that are not entirely clear, Fortas had second thoughts about intervening directly in the case. He explained to Wolfson it would be like "lighting a fuse on our own dynamite." Supreme Court justices *just didn't do* things like that.

As Wolfson sweated the first indictment, a second was obtained in June. Four days after the second indictment, Fortas flew to Jacksonville for a meeting of the Wolfson Family Foundation. Wolfson told him he was getting concerned about the cases. Fortas told him not to worry, that it sounded like a "technical matter" to him.

While Fortas was in Florida, the White House called the Supreme Court looking for the justice. Fortas's law clerk, Dan Levitt, told the caller that Fortas was with Wolfson. The next day, Levitt was told by Fortas's secretary that the justice had received a check from Wolfson's foundation.

Aware of the SEC investigation, Levitt sent word to Fortas through his secretary that the relationship could get the justice in hot water. Fortas responded to Levitt through his secretary. His answer was simple: "Mind your own business."

But Fortas had been caught—and he knew it. When he returned to Washington, he dictated a letter to the foundation canceling the agreement and severing his association with the organization. But he didn't return the twenty thousand dollars.

Wolfson's problems grew during the summer, and that fall the Justice

Department publicly announced the indictments. Still, Fortas hesitated. He may have tried to intervene during that time—and he may not have intervened—the records are not clear. Not until December 15, did Fortas throw in the towel and send the foundation a check for twenty thousand dollars.

When the two men met at the Miami hotel, Wolfson had not yet been told Fortas had returned the check. Fortas became aware of that during their conversation, but didn't have the heart to tell him. Wolfson's wife was dying of cancer and Wolfson had been diagnosed with heart problems. The Justice Department wanted to put him in jail. Fortas didn't want to twist the knife.

When Fortas returned to Washington, Wolfson was still confident of their relationship. It wasn't until several weeks later that Wolfson's attorney informed his client that he no longer had a Supreme Court justice on the payroll. Fortas returned to his duties as a Supreme Court justice—and as a secret White House advisor—but he knew the Wolfson affair was a ticking time bomb that could explode in his face at any moment.

After Fortas delivered the fifth and deciding vote in the Miranda decision that extended Fifth Amendment privileges against self-incrimination to include police interrogation, the news media embraced him as the standard-bearer for New Deal liberalism. The media interpreted his Miranda vote as one that upheld the rights of the disadvantaged. It never occurred to them that the vote might have been cast to limit the power of the police and thus bolster the power of organized crime.

In a *New York Times* story headlined "The Fortas Liberalism: Justice Appears Devoted to Cause of Great Society," reporter Fred Graham said Fortas's record revealed "a deep commitment to the peculiar duality that marks Great Society liberalism: Compassion for the poor and empathy for big business."

In fact, Fortas's liberal facade was beginning to crack.

A careful analysis of his voting record shows that on occasions when money was not involved—voting rights, juvenile rights, etc.—he voted with the liberal majority. But on issues involving business—or on decisions to restrict the rights of the press—he voted against the liberal position. He was for less power for the police, more flexibility for big business, and more restrictions on the press.

In his *New York Times* story, Graham pointed out that Fortas had broken with Chief Justice Earl Warren and the other liberals on the issue of big business by calling for a "softer government line in antimerger and antimonopoly actions against big corporations." In his dissenting opinion, he said the high court should not encourage the Federal Trade Commission in a "machine-gun approach" to mergers, but should urge it to proceed with caution in its watchdog capacity over big business.

Graham did not know about Fortas's interest in the SEC investigation of Louis Wolfson when he wrote the story. Nor, apparently, was he familiar with Fortas's prior legal representation of Federated Department Stores in a lawsuit against the Federal Trade Commission. If he was aware of Fortas's hatred of a free press—and he may not have been—Graham kept that knowledge to himself.

Certainly, at some point, Graham and the other reporters who covered the high court, became aware of Fortas's desire to muzzle the press. Fortas used words such as "dirty" and "murderous" when discussing the press. Invariably, when casting votes in cases involving the media, Fortas sided with those who wanted to restrict the press in its coverage of crime and wrongdoing among public officials.

As the media were alternately dazzled and baffled by Fortas, he continued with what amounted to two full-time jobs. *Time* magazine wrote that: "Fortas is the true *éminence grise* of the Johnson administration. *No one* outside knows accurately how many times Abe Fortas has come through the back door of the White House, but any figure would probably be too low."

Fortas biographer Bruce Allen Murphy found that he and Johnson had 105 officially noted contacts between October 1966 and October 1967. But, he points out, even those figures are misleading: "The two men might go for a period of days without any contact and then Fortas might be in constant contact with Johnson, even to the point of virtually living in the White House day and night until a particular crisis was resolved."

In 1967, the crisis most often requiring Fortas's presence in the White House was the Vietnam War. Although Fortas had no foreign policy expertise, Johnson accepted his advice on the war, often to the exclusion of other, more qualified advisors.

Neither Fortas nor his political role model, E.H. Crump, had ever served in the military. Fortas was drafted, but he was in and out of service in the blink of an eye. Their views of the military were colored by the financial opportunities they saw in the equation. Crump and his friends had made a fortune off the military. So, apparently, had Louis Wolfson.

In November 1967, Fortas attended a top-level meeting in the White House to discuss the president's reelection strategy. When the four-hour meeting was concluded and everyone was leaving, the Supreme Court justice turned to one of the advisors and said, "I shouldn't be at these meetings."

"No, you shouldn't," replied the advisor.

Three days later, Fortas sent the president his analysis of the major question facing him: the cessation of bombing in North Vietnam. Fortas's analysis, marked "Top Secret" and not declassified by the federal government until 1985, advised against a bombing cessation.

"Again, I can only repeat that the proposal to halt the bombing makes no sense," Fortas wrote. "Its domestic good effects would be illusory. It's not what the 'doves' really want: [they] want us to quit seeking our objective in Vietnam. . . . On the other hand, if Hanoi wishes to talk or to de-escalate, it is preposterous, I submit, to suppose that they are waiting for a signal—and that the only signal acceptable is a halt in bombing."

As Fortas's trips to the White House increased in frequency—and as it became apparent to everyone that the Supreme Court justice was dictating foreign policy to the president—he became more relaxed with their relationship, even to the point of beginning his letters to the president with, "Dear Boss."

But just as his secret association with Louis Wolfson was ominously ticking away, out of sight but perhaps not out of mind, so was his secret relationship with the president beginning a countdown to disaster. Not only was Fortas violating his oath as a Supreme Court justice, he was offering the president *bad advice* that would ultimately guarantee the president's downfall.

That fall, the Sovereignty Commission stepped up its activities against antiwar activists. On October 5, Commission director Johnston told the governor he had received information that a group of Tougaloo students were going to hold a meeting to raise money to send a delegation to an upcoming peace march in Washington, D.C.

Of all the informants working for the Commission, the one so highly placed at Tougaloo was the most valuable in providing names and dates. He told Johnston the names of the organizers—all three of them white males, one of whom was from Washington County—and kept the Commission updated on their activities. Judging from the type of information provided, the informant probably served the college in an official capacity.

As the trial date for the Neshoba County civil rights case approached, Johnston seemed preoccupied and less willing to launch major new initiatives. That probably was because he had announced his intention to resign when the new governor took office. That fall, Johnston's heart just wasn't in his work. Actually, he and Governor Johnson were in the same boat: short termers.

Not one to sit idly by, Johnston concocted a plan to get himself and the governor some much needed (in his eyes) recreation at state expense. They planned a trip to Hollywood for mid-November. Traveling in the party would be Johnston and his wife, Governor Johnson and his wife, Dorothy, and a highway patrolman named Dick Carr (to protect them from Yankee marauders and Hollywood weirdos).

At that time, the reigning Mississippi celebrity was former Miss America Mary Ann Mobley, who had had the good sense to move to Hollywood to pursue a movie career. The star-struck Johnston wrote her a letter and asked if she and her "escort" would join the governor and himself for dinner while they were in Hollywood.

Mobley, who was making plans to marry her "escort," actor Gary Collins, in her hometown of Brandon, Mississippi, in late November, wrote Johnston back, inviting him to the wedding. She said she would be delighted to have dinner with "Mr. Paul" [the governor] and "Miss Dorothy" [his wife]. "I've told Gary so much about Mississippi and my Mississippi friends and I can't wait for him to meet four of the nicest," she said.

Johnston relayed that information to the governor.

"At this point I will need to know where you prefer to have dinner, and whether you want Mary Ann to suggest a place," said Johnston. "I am sure you do not care for any black tie or formal place, yet you might wish to go where some of the stars gather."

As Johnston worked out details of the Hollywood trip, federal prosecutors prepared for the most important civil rights trial in American history. On October 19, eighteen defendants went on trial in Judge Harold Cox's courtroom in Meridian on charges of conspiracy to deprive Goodman, Chaney, and Schwerner of their civil rights.

Those were the strongest charges the federal government could make against the men. Only the state could try them for murder, and the state had refused to do so.

As the trial got under way, federal prosecutors, led by Ole Miss riot veteran John Doar, noted a subtle change in Judge Cox's demeanor. The mural of slaves picking cotton was still on the wall directly behind his bench, but his attitude somehow seemed different. That may have had something to do with the impeachment proceedings that had been launched against him in 1964 by Senator Jacob Javits of New York and Representative Peter Rodino of New Jersey. The impeachment attempt failed, largely due to Senator Eastland's strong support of his former Ole Miss roommate, but it did let Cox know that the eyes of the world were upon him.

For Doar, it was not just an important case—the first time the civil rights division had ever tried a case in Mississippi—it was Doar's *last* case as a federal prosecutor. He had announced plans to retire from the Justice Department at the conclusion of the trial.

Facing off against Doar, were *all* the practicing attorneys in Neshoba County. All twelve of them. With eighteen defendants and twelve attorneys, the defense table had the look of a rather large family reunion picnic. Some of the men, such as Sheriff Lawrence Rainey, had their cheeks bulging with chewing tobacco.

The defendants and their attorneys seemed confident. They laughed and joked with each other. They reacted warmly with the spectators. They seemed impatient to get the whole thing over with, so they could go home and resume their lives.

Doar presented his evidence in a methodical manner to the all-white jury of seven women and five men. He traced the movements of the civil rights workers from the time they left Meridian to when they arrived in Philadelphia and were arrested and jailed.

One of the government witnesses was the Reverend Charles Johnson, who told about Michael Schwerner's activities in Meridian that summer. When he was cross-examined by one of the defense attorneys, he was asked if it were true that he and Schwerner had tried to get young blacks to agree to rape white women in the city.

Saying the question was "highly improper," Cox asked for an explanation. The defense attorney responded that he asked the question because he had been slipped a note from one of the defendants instructing him to ask it.

Cox looked agitated.

"Who is the author of that question?" he demanded.

The courtroom grew very quiet as the judge waited for an answer.

Finally, the defense attorney identified the defendant.

With the jury still in the courtroom, Cox eyed the defendants.

"I am not going to allow a farce to be made of this trial," he said sternly. "And everybody might as well get that through their heads, including every one of these defendants."

As the judge deflated the defense team, the courtroom got so quiet, according to observers, you could have heard a pin drop.

Doar's key witness was James Jordan, who had been named in the original indictments. After he agreed to become a government witness, he and his family were relocated in Georgia for their protection. When Jordan was delivered to the courthouse earlier that day by five FBI agents with guns drawn, he showed signs of tension. Before he could be called to the stand, he collapsed and had to be removed from the courthouse on a stretcher. With that, defense attorneys thought they had won the case.

To everyone's surprise, Jordan returned to the courthouse the next day surrounded by FBI agents. When he was called to the witness stand, he told the jury that he had been in the group that had abducted and killed the civil rights workers—and he told about burying their bodies.

In his closing argument, Doar confessed that this was only his second time to argue a criminal case. He assured the jury that the federal government had no intention of "invading Philadelphia or Neshoba County." He praised the courage of the three informants who had testified for the government. They were essential in cracking the case. "Midnight murder in the rural area of Neshoba County provides few witnesses," he said. He pointed his finger at Deputy Sheriff Cecil Price and said he had abused the power of his office and was responsible for the conspiracy.

After deliberating one day, the jurors returned to the courtroom and reported that they were deadlocked. Judge Cox instructed the jury to resume their deliberations. He made it clear he wanted a verdict.

The following day, the jury returned with verdicts.

The jury foreman handed a sealed envelope to the court clerk, who tore it open and began reading: "We, the jury find the defendant Cecil Ray Price not guilty. I'm sorry, Your Honor, may I start over?"

Cox nodded.

"We, the jury, find the defendant Cecil Ray Price *guilty* of the charges contained in the indictment. . . ."

Guilty verdicts against six additional defendants were announced. Named were Jimmy Arledge, Jimmy Snowden, Sam Bowers, Alton Wayne Roberts, Billy Wayne Posey, and Horace Doyle Barnette. Eight defendants were acquitted, including Sheriff Lawrence Rainey and Edgar Ray Killen, the Baptist preacher who was accused of helping to mastermind the plot. The jury was unable to reach a verdict on three of the defendants, including former sheriff Hop Barnett.

Cox allowed the unconvicted defendants to leave the courtroom while he explained the bond procedures to those who had been found guilty. He then released everyone on bond, except Price and Alton Wayne Roberts, whom he told to approach the bench.

Cox told them that it was his intention to deny them bond over the weekend because of inflammatory comments they had made in the courtroom and outside in the hallway. Said Cox: "I'm not going to let any wild men loose on a civilized society."

Reaction to the trial was mixed. The *Meridian Star* described the verdicts as a signal the Justice Department had broken "its losing streak." The *New York Times* described the verdict as an example of the "quiet revolution that is taking place in Southern attitudes."

At the sentencing hearing on December 29, Judge Cox gave Roberts and Bowers ten years each; Posey and Price six years; and Barnette, Snowden, and Arledge three years each. Cox later explained his sentences this way: "They killed one nigger, one Jew, and a white man. I gave them all what I thought they deserved."

The Justice Department was happy to get the convictions it got. But the trial left many questions unanswered. Where were the guns used in the murders? Why did informants not disclose the location of the guns? Or did they? Were they disposed of by the FBI? Why did the state not press murder charges after the men were convicted in federal court?

The defendants immediately filed an appeal and went home to their families. Although they had been released on bond while their appeals were being prepared, Lawrence Rainey was still sheriff and Cecil Price was still deputy sheriff.

Life returned to normal in Neshoba County.

⁓

You never knew what was going to fly at Ole Miss.

When Ole Miss and Memphis State alumni met in Oxford in September to watch their football teams renew an old rivalry, they were shocked at half-time—along with most of the students—when the Memphis State marching band formed the outline of two bunnies and played "Born Free" as Sue Bernard, a recent *Playboy* playmate of the month with no affiliation to either school, stepped out onto the field to dance with sixteen "Tigerettes" who had donned bunny ears and fuzzy bunny tails.

Alumni of both schools went nuts.

"The way she came bumping and grinding off the field was appalling," said one outraged alumnus. Others said the playmate should have her tight, round buttocks spanked—and hard. Ole Miss officials blamed the "incident" on Memphis State.

Memphis State band director Tommy Ferguson accepted responsibility for the blunder. "I made up the Playmate formation earlier and wondered what *Playboy* magazine would think of it," said Ferguson. "They liked the idea and said if we would introduce a Playmate at half-time, they would put a color picture of our band in the September football issue. Pages in *Playboy* go at $50,000, and when you get a deal like that you don't pass it up."

Mississippian editor Charles "Peanut" Overby wrote an editorial addressed to the band leader, saying, in effect: "Oh, well, you can't win them all." By 1967, Ole Miss had been radicalized by the Vietnam War, with many students openly critical of the president's war policy. As a result, the Commission increased its efforts on the campus, recruiting more students to serve as informants.

Overby's prowar editorials parroted the Commission's position. In October, in an editorial headlined "Protesting the protesters," Overby said the students who had marched on the Pentagon the previous weekend to protest the Vietnam War should be "tarred and feathered." Unlike most college newspaper editors across the nation, who were opposed to the war, Overby wrote editorials on a regular basis attacking the "peaceniks," saying "there is no significant number of persons in this country who oppose our troops in Vietnam."

Despite Overby's support of Johnson's war policy, the antiwar movement on the campus grew, as it did on campuses across the state. Where students once argued about race, they now argued about war and peace. The handful of black students on the campus shrank away from that debate, perhaps feeling they had enough problems of their own and didn't need to get involved in a second passion-driven issue.

Unlike black civil rights leaders, who had known about the Commission's operations from the beginning, student antiwar activists were not aware that Commission informants were watching them and reporting on their activities. There were no demonstrations or public displays of opposition to the war on the campus at that time, but students were beginning to attend out-of-state demonstrations and peace rallies on a regular basis.

There were no Ole Miss students in 1967 who had refused induction, but it was being discussed as a viable option. News that year from Canadian prime minister Lester Pearson, that his country would not prevent draft resisters from entering the country, was greeted with growing interest. Students often talked freely among themselves of fleeing to Canada. Others talked of joining the underground movement. Still others talked of joining the Army to disrupt its mission in Vietnam. All of which was dutifully reported to the Commission.

"Does the bombing of North Vietnam make sense? Is it likely to bring the war to an earlier end—or is it making peace negotiations more difficult? Is it worth what it costs, in terms of lives and planes lost, and political damage both in this country and abroad?"

Those questions, asked by contributing editor John Fischer in *Harper's* magazine, were typical of those asked by increasing numbers of Americans. Fortas's advice to Johnson that he should continue to follow a hard-line position on the issue was coming under attack—and the Johnson administration was reeling from the criticisms.

The same so-called liberal media that had embraced Johnson over his civil rights initiatives were now roasting him because of his Vietnam War policies. The *New York Times,* under the leadership of managing editor Turner Catledge, was, for the first time, really covering the war. Its daily news reports were horrifying readers not accustomed to such graphic descriptions of war and the deaths of fathers, sons, and brothers. *Harper's* magazine, under the direction of editor Willie Morris, was backing away from its earlier no-questions-asked praise of Johnson and assigning articles about the war to the nation's most thoughtful and probing writers.

One of the incongruous aspects of the Vietnam War was the fact that it was native Mississippians and Memphians who most often were at the core of the domestic battle taking place over the conduct of the war. The most ardent and vocal supporters of the war were Abe Fortas, Mississippi Senators James Eastland and John Stennis, and Representative John Bell Williams, who was trading in his congressional perks for the key to the governor's mansion.

Causing the most trouble for President Johnson were not the demonstrators, who were still disorganized and without leadership, but editors such as Morris and Catledge, both Mississippians, who continued to raise questions about the conduct of the war.

Especially troublesome was Catledge, who had begun his newspaper career in a confrontation with Memphis's Boss Crump, who had told him to his face that maybe he should leave Memphis if he couldn't handle the rough-and-tumble world of politics. Catledge did leave town. He went to New York, where he gave the *New York Times* the most aggressive leadership in its history.

When you consider the players involved in the Vietnam War debate, it is not surprising that the Sovereignty Commission would feel it had a role to play. The tri-state federation had an influence on the nation out of all proportion to its population and relative wealth. Few Americans understood that influence, just as few understood the power of the region's underworld lords, the Dixie Mafia and the Memphis cartel.

President Johnson's greatest fear was the entry of a third voice into that debate. That fear was realized in October, when Martin Luther King held a press conference after testifying before the National Advisory Committee on Civil Disorders. He said that if the government would not shut down the war, the government itself would have to be shut down by the people. He promised to return to Washington to lead massive demonstrations against the government's war policy.

Johnson was horrified. "We've almost lost the war in the last two months in the court of public opinion," he told his advisors. "These demonstrators and others are trying to show that we need somebody else to take over the country."

King reported to the Birmingham jail at the end of the month to serve a five-day sentence for defying a 1963 court order against racial demonstrations. When he emerged from the jail, he said it was his intention to camp in front of the White House to protest Johnson's policies. "It is time to get on the highway of freedom to Washington," King said. "We must let it be known that we will stay until our problem is solved. We must put our tents in front of the White House."

At every opportunity, King attacked the administration's war policy and Congress's reluctance to pass new legislation to upgrade the economic plight of African Americans. During that time, the government issued a report stating that American planes had caused $300 million in damage to targets in Hanoi. The report admitted, however, that seven hundred aircraft had been lost in missions over Hanoi, at a cost of $900 million. Those aircraft had to be replaced, creating an economic boom for the aerospace industry.

The war was funneling millions into companies that manufactured war supplies. King wanted to see those millions spent on domestic concerns. It was a position that made him unpopular not only with the government but with the Memphis cartel and the Dixie Mafia, both of which, according to sources, were making enormous profits off the war.

Peace activist Dr. Benjamin Spock released figures from the U.S. Agency for International Development showing that private investments in South Vietnam were bringing in profits of 20 to 30 percent a year. Those figures represented three or four times the profits that could be realized by the same investments in the United States.

In December, journalist David Halberstam returned to the pages of *Harper's* with an article about going back to Vietnam. His first visit had won him a Pulitzer Prize in 1964. He had returned from that earlier visit skeptical of the war, but hopeful of an American victory. This time around, that optimism was gone. "I do not think our Vietnamese can win their half of the war, nor do I think we can win it for them," he wrote. "I have a sense that we are once again coming to a dead end in Indochina."

As the body counts of American soldiers continued to rise—and as more information about the financial profits being reaped by American businesses surfaced—public opinion began to shift dramatically. Ordinary people were beginning to speak out. Like Halberstam, they began to feel the country was approaching a dead end.

At the end of November, Senator Eugene McCarthy announced that he was going to run against Lyndon Johnson in next year's Democratic primaries. His announcement energized the peace movement and put the White House on the defensive. Four days after McCarthy's announcement, Martin Luther King announced plans for a massive demonstration the following spring in Washington.

The White House didn't take McCarthy seriously.

King was a different story.

CHAPTER 8

1968

As the new year began, Sovereignty Commission director Erle Johnston was showing signs of emotional stress. In previous months, he not only had arranged a trip to Hollywood for himself and Governor Johnson, he had written Johnny Carson at the *Tonight Show,* requesting equal time to respond to a guest's unflattering comments about Mississippi. Carson apparently never acknowledged his letter.

Johnston floated rumors that he might resign.

Governor-elect John Bell Williams didn't rise to the bait.

Obviously frustrated about his future with the agency, Johnston leaked to the press the contents of a wrap-up report he had prepared for the new governor. For the most part, it was self-serving and filled with misrepresentations and outright falsehoods. Under the headline, "Sovereignty Commission 'Preventative Medicine,' " reporter Mike Smith, one of Johnston's contacts at the *Jackson Daily News,* described the report as the "never-before-revealed story" of how the Commission had "solved countless racial irritations." Johnston was depicted as a racial moderate who had worked hard to avert racial violence in the state. The news story was Dixie doublespeak. Johnston's report masked the Commission's illegal activities, and the Mississippi news media fell for it hook, line, and sinker, as always.

On January 16, 1968, atop a flag-draped platform in front of the Capitol, John Bell Williams was sworn in as Mississippi's fifty-fifth governor. Within the space of eight years, the leadership of the state had gone from bad to worse to catastrophic. John Bell Williams made Ross Barnett look like a flaming liberal.

Williams was a native of Raymond, a small community just outside Jackson. He was a graduate of the University of Mississippi and the Jackson School of Law. Prior to the attack on Pearl Harbor, he had enlisted in the Army Air Corps, where he was trained to pilot B-26 bombers. He retired from the army in 1944 after surviving a plane crash in South America that had cost him the use of an arm. At twenty-seven he became the youngest congressman in Mississippi history.

After twenty-one years in Congress, he really had no place to go except the Mississippi governor's office. His refusal to support Lyndon Johnson in the 1964 presidential election had cost him his seniority in Congress. As one of the founding members of the Federation for Constitutional Government, he continued to uphold that organization's goals of a segregated society existing beyond the reach of the federal government.

Unlike his predecessor, who had viewed his election as a promotion, Williams went into the governor's office with a chip on his shoulder. He had been driven out of Washington after twenty-one years by a coalition of liberal Yankees, none of whom had ever lost limbs in the service of their country. In his eyes, Mississippi was the political equivalent of a fortified bunker from which he could hurl verbal grenades at the enemy and huddle with like-minded Southern patriots.

Williams took his time making appointments. One of his first was David Bowen, a Millsaps College professor whom he made federal–state coordinator of federal funds. After Bowen's appointment, one of the file clerks at the Commission notified Johnston that they had found a secret file on him. Johnston pulled the file and took it to Herman Glazier, who had remained in the governor's office for a while to ease the transition.

Glazier told him to burn the file—and he did.

Later, David Bowen was elected to Congress, where he served five terms, representing the Delta district. By Mississippi standards, he was a liberal, a moderate on the issue of race, which is probably why the Commission spied on him. Of course, being a college professor in and of itself was usually enough to justify an investigation.

Coming under increased scrutiny early in 1968 was *Delta Democrat-Times* editor Hodding Carter III, after he became an advisor to Robert Clark, an African American who was elected representative from Holmes County. The Commission was concerned about Clark because he had announced plans to assist, in the words of the investigator, "aged negroes who do not now qualify" under welfare requirements.

The Commission's surveillance of Carter and Clark convinced investigators that the dreaded Mississippi Freedom Democratic Party was losing steam. They noted with interest that the FDP's publication had been suspended for lack of funds.

Also targeted by the Commission was a black Tougaloo College professor, Helen Bass Williams, who had been employed at the school since 1964. The language of the Commission's reports is indicative of the lack of respect showed African Americans. The reports described Mrs. Williams as a "50 year old negress." While there was nothing in the investigator's report to indicate that Mrs. Williams had ever done anything other than mind her own business, the investigator noted that her "politically [*sic*] sympathies are presently being checked."

There was one area of the state Johnston didn't have to worry about. *Mississippian* editor Charles Overby pushed the Ole Miss newspaper further to the right than it had ever gone before. Under his editorial guidance, the newspaper became a miniversion of the *Jackson Daily News* and *Clarion-Ledger*. On a daily basis, Overby attacked Vietnam protesters. In one editorial, Overby told of receiving an antiwar petition containing the names of more than four hundred student presidents and newspaper editors. He was asked to sign the petition since Mississippi was one of only four states not represented in the petition. Overby's response was not indicative of student opinion on the campus: "If . . . this editor has anything to do with it, Mississippi will continue to remain unrepresented on this epistle. In any other lifetime and in any other country the efforts of these protesters would be, at best, seditious."

Among the students on campus that semester were Haley Barbour, a candidate for student body president (by 1996 he had parlayed that passion for politics into the chairmanship of the national Republican Party), and Charles Sudduth, a philosophy major from Hollandale, a small town in the southern part of Washington County. Sudduth had attracted the attention of the police in his hometown by befriending the Freedom Riders who had arrived under the Council of Federated Organizations banner. He was seen speaking to them on the street corners and accepting their literature. By 1968, he had accelerated the interest of the Commission by filing for conscientious-objector status with the local draft board. "Don't ever ask for a CO application," he told a friend one day, after showing up on his doorstep, exasperated and shaken from what he said was an interview with the FBI. "The FBI comes and interviews you—and makes you feel like a damned criminal."

Sudduth said he felt the FBI was following him.

Actually, any one of several groups could have been following him. The FBI was concerned about antiwar activity and was keeping an eye on anyone who spoke out against the Johnson administration. The Sovereignty

Commission had informants all over the campus. That semester, even the *Mississippian,* under Overby's leadership, was using reporters as agents. In one instance, Overby allowed a reporter to buy a stash of marijuana for the purpose of attending a "pot" party. The reporter gave the contraband to Overby, who turned it over to campus authorities. The reporter, who remained anonymous, wrote about the party—and about a coed who took off all her clothes—and the story was run on page one of the *Mississippian.* The next day police arrested ten students.

After receiving threats at the newspaper, Overby swore to readers that he did not turn over the names of students involved in the pot party, only the marijuana. That may have been true, but, for the first time, students felt they were now being monitored by *everyone,* even their fellow students. After graduation Overby was hired by the *Jackson Daily News* to man its Washington news bureau.

That spring, Commission director Erle Johnston collapsed while at work. He was rushed to a hospital, where doctors treated him for a heart attack. Later, doctors discovered it was not a heart attack but a reaction to stress. Johnston had already hinted to the new governor that he wanted out. In light of that, why would he be under stress severe enough to cause him to collapse? Was something going on behind the scenes at the Commission? Were plans being developed for something big? Something heinous?

Johnston stayed out several weeks. He called his ailment "combat fatigue." When he returned, he sent direct word to the governor that he wanted out of the Commission. He was asked to stay on until a replacement could be found. Actually, Johnston did not seem to want to give up his government job so much as he wanted the job title changed. The pressure of supervising the agency's covert operations was getting to him, as evidenced by his collapse. He had always pretended the Sovereignty Commission was nothing more than a public relations agency. Now, he wanted the governor and the legislature to re-define the agency's mission.

Johnston enjoyed making trips to Hollywood and attending press association meetings. After eight years of dirty tricks and covert operations, viewing photos of dead civil rights workers and wondering who would be next to die, Erle Johnston was ready to have some fun. Governor Williams said he would think about it.

Johnston wasn't the only one having a nervous breakdown.

The entire country seemed to be falling apart in 1968. The March 8 edition of *Life* magazine contained stories that presented powerful images of two pressing issues—Vietnam and poverty in the cities. The Vietnam feature reported on the battle to retake Hue, which had been lost to the Viet Cong during the Tet offensive. The battle, which took twenty-five days, claimed the lives of 490 and left 2,252 soldiers wounded. A photograph showed wounded American soldiers, their bare legs bloodied and their terror-stricken faces wrapped with bandages, as they were piled aboard a truck for evacuation; the effect complemented, in a way only survivors of the decade could understand, photographs of hungry black children in America's inner cities. "The Negro and the cities constitute the nation's most alarming domestic problem," said the *Life* article. "Yet, except when violence flares up, people ignore its appalling realities."

Not ignoring those realities was Martin Luther King. He wrote an article that spring for publication in the April 16 edition of *Look* magazine. The headline said: "Non-violent protests return this spring, perhaps for the last time. Whites are welcomed. Even the militant Black Power groups have agreed to join in. But if the non-violent protests fail, holocaust could follow." In the article, King said: "If our non-violent campaign doesn't generate some progress, people are just going to engage in more violent activity, and the discussion of guerrilla warfare will be more extensive." He announced plans for a massive demonstration and said the "flash point of Negro rage is close at hand."

Students were marching in the streets. Men, by the thousands, were fleeing to Canada. American cities were ablaze. Blacks were rioting at every opportunity. Each evening on the television news, Americans were provided with body counts from Vietnam. For the first time in the history of warfare, ordinary citizens were allowed to view the horrors of war— through television—as it was actually happening. There was talk of revolution—and people on both sides were taking the talk seriously.

Into the breach stepped Robert Kennedy. On March 16, he announced his intention to run against Lyndon Johnson in the presidential primaries for the Democratic nomination. No one was surprised by that announcement, least of all Johnson, who already had been advised by J. Edgar Hoover that Kennedy had tried to call King to notify him of his decision.

On March 31, President Johnson went on national television to make an important announcement: he would end the bombing of North Vietnam in the hope it would lead to peace. Then, with tears in his eyes, he uttered words that stunned the nation: "I shall not seek and I will not accept the nomination of my party for President of the United States." He said he intended to devote every hour of every day in the remainder of his presidency to working toward peace. "I have concluded that I should not permit the presidency to become involved in partisan divisions that are developing this year." Some commentators praised the president for his decision. Others were skeptical, fearing there was a hidden agenda. Notified of the announcement at an airport, a shocked Robert Kennedy responded with an uncharacteristic "no comment."

Did Johnson really want peace? Or did he resign as part of a political strategy developed with his Memphis friend, Abe Fortas? And was there another shoe to drop? Was there anything that could happen—a national calamity, a disaster of some sort, a major riot—that would make the country turn to President Johnson and beg him to stay? What did Johnson have up his sleeve?

For the longest time, the nation held its breath.

From mid-December until late March, James Earl Ray had been on the road, driving his Ford Mustang from New Orleans, where he had stayed several days at the Provincial Motel—a favorite gathering place of Carlos Marcello and his associates—to Los Angeles, where he stayed nearly three months before returning to New Orleans on March 20. Ray looked different when he returned to New Orleans. While in Los Angeles, he had paid two hundred dollars for a nose job from a plastic surgeon who liked his fees in cash. In his autobiography, *Who Killed Martin Luther King?,* Ray said he went to New Orleans to meet a man named Raul, a mysterious underworld contact Ray claimed had hired him to smuggle contraband into the United States from Mexico.

By 1968, James Earl Ray, at forty, had done time for burglary, armed robbery, and forging United States money orders, an offense that cost him nearly three years at the federal penitentiary in Leavenworth, Kansas. When he wasn't in jail—or trying to escape from jail—he was on the run, constantly moving from city to city. Ray used an alias when he needed one. He had fake IDs, and if he required a firearm—he had a preference for .38–caliber pistols—he found a fence or an illegal gun dealer who would sell him what was called for with no questions asked.

When he arrived in New Orleans, Ray was told by an intermediary (whose identity he continues to protect) that Raul had gone to Birmingham. Ray was instructed to meet him there at the Starlight Club on March 23. Ray stayed the night in New Orleans, then the next day drove as far as Selma, where he spent the night. Leaving a paper trail that stretched from New Orleans to Selma, Ray apparently took the coastal route across Mississippi to Mobile, then north to Selma. Ray was careful not to spend the night in Mississippi or do anything that would leave a paper trail connecting him in any way with the Magnolia State.

At that time, Selma was notable for two things: it was the site of several early civil rights confrontations, and it was the place to go to buy illegal firearms. It was where, a few years earlier, an undercover agent for the Mississippi Sovereignty Commission had purchased two .38–caliber pistols and evaluated the potential of the building occupied by the firearms dealer for a possible future break-in. It has never been explained why Ray spent the night in Selma instead of driving the short distance on into Birmingham. Did he meet someone who helped him acquire a firearm? Did he meet someone who gave him instructions for his next job?

Ray stayed at the eight-dollar-a-night Flamingo Motel, then drove into Birmingham the next morning to meet Raul. They left together that same day and went to Atlanta, where they spent the night before returning to Birmingham. According to Ray, Raul gave him seven hundred dollars in cash and instructed him to purchase a rifle. Together, they looked through the yellow pages until they found a sporting goods store named Aeromarine Supply. Ray went to the store and purchased a .243 Winchester and a box of ammunition. When he returned to the motel, Raul told him it wasn't power-ful enough. He needed a .30–06–caliber, preferably a Remington. Ray re-turned to the store and exchanged the rifle for the one Raul had requested.

The next day, Raul told Ray he had to go to New Orleans for a few days. He instructed Ray to go to Memphis with the rifle and to check into the New Rebel Motel no later than April 3. Ray took his time driving to Mem-phis. On March 30, he spent the night at a motel near Decatur, Alabama. The next day he drove over to Florence to spend the night. On April 1, he drove into Mississippi and checked into a motel in Corinth. The following day, he drove another fifty miles or so and checked into the Desoto Motel, just south of the Mississippi–Tennessee state line.

Every step of the way, from New Orleans to Selma to Birmingham to the sporting goods store, then on into northern Mississippi, Ray left a trail that any first-year police cadet could follow. It wasn't his nature to leave a trail, so he pursued it with deliberation.

On April 3, as instructed, Ray checked into the New Rebel Motel.

That same morning, Martin Luther King and his SCLC staff arrived at the Memphis airport and drove to the Lorraine Motel, checking in just before noon. It was hardly a pleasure trip. King had come to Memphis on March 18 to show support for a strike called by the city's sanitation workers.

At a gathering of approximately 12,000 people at the Mason Temple, he urged all Memphis blacks, not just the sanitation workers, to strike. He called for a massive downtown demonstration on March 22, then left for meetings in Mississippi.

On the day of the scheduled demonstration, Memphis was paralyzed by a sixteen-inch snowfall. The demonstration was postponed to March 28. Unknown to King, the FBI had upgraded its surveillance of him. Now that King, code named "Zorro" by the FBI, had full Cointelpro status, agents had a virtual free hand. One of the dirty tricks that was approved—on March 25, while James Earl Ray was in or around Selma—was to send an anonymous letter to a civil rights leader in Selma in an effort to turn him against King.

Both the FBI and the Army viewed King's March 28 march with concern. The previous month in Los Angeles, H. Rap Brown, referring to the murder of Malcolm X, had proposed that the assassination of black leaders be avenged by "swift retribution" against police stations and power plants. Reacting to Brown's comments, J. Edgar Hoover told a House subcommittee that black nationalists were stockpiling weapons "for use against the white man."

Martin Luther King returned to Memphis on March 28 and led a group of about 5,000 marchers on a route that took them from a location near Beale and Pontotoc over to Main Street. They planned to follow Main Street north to City Hall.

As the marchers reached Main Street, young adults and teens at the rear ripped the signs from their poles and began breaking store windows. Then they started looting the stores. As the police moved in, King's aides commandeered an automobile and asked police to escort them to a place of safety. Police took them to the nearby Rivermont Hotel, an upscale Holiday Inn located on the bluff overlooking the Mississippi River. That night, police imposed a curfew and the city called out 3,500 members of the National Guard to assist the police. By then, the city was engulfed in a full-scale riot. Before it ended, four blacks would be shot, one fatally, approximately 150 fires would be set, and over 300 demonstrators would be arrested.

The next day King returned to Atlanta.

FBI agents sent Hoover a memo stating that the riot "clearly demonstrates that acts of so-called nonviolence advocated by King cannot be controlled." The memo said the same thing that happened in Memphis could happen in Washington when King arrived in April to hold the massive demonstration he had promised. FBI agents had noted with interest that King had spent the night at the Rivermont Hotel instead of the Lorraine, the black-owned motel where he usually stayed. On March 29, authorization was given for FBI agents to plant a fake news story with the media. The story said: "The fine Hotel Lorraine in Memphis is owned and patronized exclusively by Negroes but King didn't go there for his hasty exit. Instead King decided the plush Holiday Inn Motel, white owned, operated and almost exclusively patronized, was the place to 'cool it.' "

The bogus story was obviously meant to make certain that King returned to the Lorraine. Was it no more than a dirty trick, meant to discredit him among black leaders in the city? Was it meant to keep him away from the Holiday Inn, which had not been seeded with wiretaps? Or was there a more sinister purpose behind it?

The violence that took place in Memphis concerned King. If he did not return to the city to reassert his leadership as an advocate of nonviolence, he could lose ground to more radical leaders within the movement. The Memphis protest had seen a disorder. He did not want the same thing to happen at the demonstration planned for Washington. This is the reason he returned to Memphis on April 3.

When King and his aides checked into the Lorraine Motel, he was virtually surrounded by Memphis police officers, paid informants, FBI agents, and U.S. Army intelligence agents. The hotel itself was located just a couple of blocks from where Abe Fortas had spent his childhood and was within shouting distance of the birthplace of the Memphis cartel.

The Memphis police kept King under constant surveillance. Reports were made on his every move. An observation post was set up at a fire station that overlooked the Lorraine. Two black police officers were posted to keep King's motel room under constant surveillance.

The FBI was heavily involved in monitoring King's activities, although the bureau has always denied it installed electronic listening devices in the motel. The FBI did admit using paid informants to keep it advised of what was taking place at the meetings attended by King.

Also in place were agents from the 111th Military Intelligence Group of the U.S. Army. They were there to gather information on King and to evaluate the potential for violence in the city in the wake of the riot. They were shown to the roof of the fire station, from which they conducted photographic reconnaissance of the motel. Not far away, were U.S. Army marksmen, positioned on the roof of the Illinois Central Railroad building and the Taylor Paper Company water tower.

From the time King went to Memphis in late march, then traveled to Mississippi to make plans for the Washington march, little is known of the activities of the Sovereignty Commission.

Since the eyes of the world were on Memphis—and Commission investigators had visited the city often in the past to conduct investigations—it is reasonable to assume that Commission investigators were also present in the city on April 3.

That evening, Martin Luther King went to the Mason Temple to deliver a speech. The two Memphis policemen who manned the observation post at the fire station were told to go to the church to keep an eye on things. When they arrived, they were told by the minister that word was out that they were spying on King from the fire station. The minister advised the two men that they should leave the church for their own safety, which they did.

That night, King seemed distracted. He told a cheering crowd, "It really doesn't matter with me now, because I've been to the mountain top." The next day, April 4, King and his advisors remained in the motel all afternoon, conducting meetings under the watchful eyes of the Army, the FBI, and the Memphis police department. At approximately 4 P.M., Memphis Fire and Police Chief Frank Holloman—a former FBI agent—informed one of the men at the fire station that threats had been made on his life. He was ordered to leave his post and to move his family into a motel under an assumed name. He was taken home in a squad car, but he refused to take his family to a motel because it would inconvenience a sick relative who lived with them.

At 6 P.M. Martin Luther King stepped out onto the balcony of the Lorraine Motel. The sun was setting across the river, casting long, gray shadows that fell across the motel courtyard. The temperature was a chilly fifty-five degrees. King's driver, Solomon Jones, shouted that he should wear his overcoat.

"OK, I will," King answered.

Then the shot rang out.

King was struck by a .30–06 slug that tore into his neck and jaw. When his aides rushed from their rooms, they found him on his back, bleeding profusely. An unidentified white man walked up and covered King's face with a white towel. Then he disappeared. The civil rights leader was rushed to St. Joseph's Hospital in a fire department ambulance.

Thirty minutes later King was pronounced dead.

When news reached the FBI office in Atlanta, agents jumped up and down with joy. "They got Zorro!" one agent shouted. "They finally got the SOB!"

When news of Martin Luther King's murder went out over the radio, Memphis mayor Henry Loeb was in Mississippi, on his way to a speaking engagement at Ole Miss. He immediately turned his car around and headed back to Memphis.

Loeb knew he was in for a long night. Ever since the riot that had occurred on March 22, he had kept a loaded shotgun beneath his desk in the mayor's office. He just hoped there would be no more killing.

Hearing the same radio broadcast was James Earl Ray. Like Loeb, he was on the road in Mississippi, heading toward Alabama. The radio announcer said police were looking for a white man in a white Mustang. Unlike Loeb, Ray did not return to Memphis.

In the week following Martin Luther King's assassination, riots erupted in 172 cities, leaving 43 dead and more than 3,000 injured. There were more than 27,000 arrests. To assist the police, nearly 20,000 federal troops were called out, along with 30,000 national guardsmen. Hardest hit were Baltimore, Chicago, and Washington; riot-trained soldiers with bayonets attached to rifles patrolled black sections of the cities.

Memphis was no different. By the time Memphis mayor Henry Loeb returned to the city, violence was already taking place. It began with sniper fire in the black neighborhoods, then escalated to firebombing and looting. Loeb ordered a curfew, but the violence continued for three days, resulting in 229 fires and the death of one black demonstrator who was shot by police.

Within minutes of King's death, violence erupted in Jackson, Mississippi, where a white-owned supermarket was firebombed and two automobiles were burned. Most of the violence took place near Jackson State College, where later in the evening Charles Evers urged a jeering crowd to remain nonviolent in honor of Dr. King. About seventy-five policemen, wearing riot gear and armed with shotguns and carbines, barricaded the perimeter of the campus and fired tear gas grenades at groups of blacks gathered on the campus.

In Washington, the 116th Army Intelligence unit sent more than 120 agents out in unmarked cars, three men to a vehicle, to patrol the ghettos. After one of the cars was stoned—they were in inconspicuous four-year-old Plymouths—the white agents refused to go back out into the streets unarmed. With that, the leader of each group was assigned a .38–caliber snub-nosed revolver and a box of ammunition.

At the University of Mississippi, black students reacted with anger, some saying it was time to reassess the effectiveness of Dr. King's nonviolent philosophy. By 1968 several dozen black students had enrolled at the university and most were not shy about speaking their mind. "If Dr. King's tactics will not work, we must find new methods with which to express ourselves in order to gain our equality," a student from Jackson told the *Mississippian*. "The system is against the Negro," said another student. "We have been oppressed in every way possible and now it is time for us to do something about it."

A white student pulled up at a service station a couple of blocks from the campus. While the attendant was wiping the windshield, he talked about the rioting taking place in other cities, his voice seemingly rising with each wipe of the cloth.

"Somebody's gotta do something about them niggers," he said.

He leaned toward the door and flashed open his jacket. A revolver was tucked into the waistband of his trousers. "I'm ready for 'em," he said.

Within weeks of the murder, the Jackson Citizens' Council had its magazine *The Citizen* on the streets. "Did you ever see anything like it?" said an editorial. "Within a couple of hours after [King's death] . . . the nation's liberal establishment, official and unofficial, donned sackcloth and ashes and plunged into an orgy of public breast-beating. . . . We are sorry the man was shot. We are sorry he is dead. But somewhere the national sense of proportion seems to have become lost."

Although the King assassination was a state crime, the FBI took charge of the investigation immediately. Within twenty-four hours they had two solid leads: a white man in a white Mustang was seen fleeing the area immediately after the shooting, and a bundle containing a .30–06 Remington rifle—and a set of fingerprints—was found near the scene.

The bundle was a bedspread wrapped around the rifle, a zippered bag containing a pair of pliers, a cartridge box with nine .30–06 cartridges, two cans of beer, a portable radio, toiletries, a tack hammer, and an April 4 edition of *The Commercial Appeal*. Inside the rifle was a spent cartridge case.

The rifle was quickly traced to the Aeromarine Supply Company in Birmingham. The store manager told FBI agents he had sold the rifle to a man named Harvey Lowmeyer (one of James Earl Ray's aliases), and he provided a description of Ray. Within days, the FBI located Ray's Mustang, where he had left it in an Atlanta subdivision. The Mustang was registered to a man named Eric Starvo Galt (another of Ray's aliases).

In the days and weeks following the assassination, the FBI office in Memphis received many tips from citizens who thought they may have seen or heard something important. One of those was a black man named John McFerren, who strolled into the FBI office four days after the murder and told the agent on duty that he had heard a suspicious conversation on the afternoon of the murder. While shopping at the Liberto, Liberto, and Latch Produce Store, he had heard a "heavy set white male" telling someone on the phone to "kill the SOB on the balcony." Later in the conversation, he said, the man instructed the person he was talking to to go to New Orleans to get his money.

McFerren wasn't sure who the man on the telephone was, but he thought it might be a Memphis businessman, whom he identified by name. The FBI checked out McFerren's story and learned that the man had a brother who lived in New Orleans and was an associate of Carlos Marcello. After tracing

McFerren's tip to New Orleans, the FBI dropped its investigation into a link with the Marcello organization. By then, FBI director J. Edgar Hoover had announced that the King assassination was the result of a lone gunman and was not a conspiracy.

On April 11, the FBI sent out a bulletin advising that Eric Starvo Galt was wanted for questioning in connection with the murder of Martin Luther King. Soon they had a driver's license photograph of Galt, obtained from the Alabama Department of Public Safety. A printed bulletin was issued by the FBI that contained Ray's driver's license photograph and Eric Starvo Galt's name.

Only after wading through 53,000 sets of fingerprints did the FBI get a match with those lifted from the rifle found in Memphis. The fingerprints belonged not to Eric Starvo Galt but to a hard-case con artist named James Earl Ray. By the time a nationwide manhunt began for Ray, he was across the border in Canada and on his way to England.

On April 5, 1968, the day after Martin Luther King's assassination, White House aide Fred Panzer sent President Johnson a memorandum informing him that his job rating, as reported by the Harris Survey, had increased dramatically.

In March, 57 percent of those polled had disapproved of the way the president was doing his job. New polling results showed a complete reversal: Now 57 percent of those polled approved of his performance, while only 43 percent disapproved. Panzer said that Harris recommended that the president move an upcoming meeting in Hawaii to Washington in case there was trouble because of the assassination. "If you are not [in Washington, Harris] feels your public support will fall off," said Panzer.

Johnson took Harris's advice and canceled the meeting. That morning, he met with twenty-one civil rights leaders who had flown into Washington to advise him on the crisis. Then he went to the National Cathedral to attend a memorial service for Dr. King.

On April 8, the day before King's funeral, James Rowley, director of the Secret Service, advised the president not to attend the funeral. He said his opinion was shared by the FBI. Furthermore, he recommended for security reasons that Vice President Hubert Humphrey also not attend the funeral.

Johnson accepted Rowley's advice—at least partially. He decided not to go to the funeral, but did send Hubert Humphrey to represent him. On a memorandum, Johnson wrote, "Give V.P. whatever he needs," and instructed aides to provide Humphrey with a copy of the Secret Service report.

At the funeral were the two front-runners for the Democratic nomination—Hubert Humphrey, who was still unannounced, and Robert Kennedy, who had declared himself a candidate in mid-March. Recent Harris polls had placed Kennedy in the lead with 37 percent, Humphrey second with 24 percent, and Senator Eugene McCarthy in third place with 22 percent.

It was no secret that Johnson wanted Humphrey to have the nomination, if, in fact, he himself was not drafted by a groundswell of public opinion. The assassination had elevated Johnson considerably in the polls, for Americans always embrace the president in times of crisis. The murder had become a public relations bonanza.

Johnson was bitter about Kennedy's entry into the race. He told J. Edgar Hoover that Kennedy was trying to embarrass the administration while getting glory for himself. That March, Kennedy had reissued a book published in 1967 entitled *To Seek a Newer World,* which contained an updated section on Vietnam. In the book, which was widely quoted by the news media, Kennedy apologized for his earlier involvement in the Vietnam War. "It may be that the effort was doomed from the start, that it was never really possible to bring all the people of South Vietnam under the rule of the successive governments we supported," he said. "I am willing to bear my share of the responsibility, before history and before my fellow citizens. But past error is no excuse for its own perpetuation."

By the summer of 1968, most Americans were having second thoughts about Vietnam. Together, the two peace candidates—Robert Kennedy and Eugene McCarthy—had the support of nearly 60 percent of the Democrats polled.

But not everyone wanted the war to end. To some Americans, the war represented multimillion-dollar profits, especially for defense-related industries. Vietnam had been a godsend to the Memphis cartel, which, according to sources, had investment partnerships with various defense contractors.

As the California primary drew near, it became obvious that its winner probably would become the Democratic nominee. Kennedy was pulling ahead of McCarthy and the Draft LBJ movements were fizzling right and left. Kennedy was the man to beat.

On June 6, 1968, California Democrats gave Kennedy a 46 to 42 percent victory over his nearest rival, Eugene McCarthy. Before going downstairs to speak to his supporters in the ballroom of the Ambassador Hotel, Kennedy called his advisors in Washington, who told him that he also had won the South Dakota primary, taking 50 percent of the vote to LBJ's 30 percent.

That night, as he took a shortcut through the hotel pantry, Kennedy was gunned down by Sirhan Sirhan, who shot him several times with a .22–caliber revolver. Kennedy died the following afternoon after undergoing surgery to remove bullet fragments from his brain. When he heard the news, Charles Evers spoke for many African Americans when he said: "Robert Kennedy was the only white man in this country I really trusted."

During funeral services for Kennedy, Attorney General Ramsey Clark was pulled aside by an FBI agent, who whispered that James Earl Ray had been captured in London. The agent apologized to Clark for interrupting the service, but since Scotland Yard would not agree to hold the story he felt Clark should be told immediately.

As it turned out, Clark had been lied to by the FBI agent. The FBI was notified of the arrest the previous night, and Hoover had even leaked the story to one of his favorite reporters. Clark was furious when he found out about the deception. He called the bureau and told them he resented being lied to. He said the bureau would have to find another agent as a liaison with the attorney general's office.

On July 19 James Earl Ray was returned to Memphis nonstop from London aboard an Air Force C-135. When he arrived at the naval air station at Millington, just outside Memphis, he was hustled into an armored van and taken to the Shelby County Jail, where jailers had hung blankets over the windows to prevent "another Dallas."

After several months of legal maneuvering, Ray pleaded guilty and was sentenced to life imprisonment. At the hearing, he seemed confused and told the judge he didn't agree with Attorney General Clark's opinion that a conspiracy was not involved. Three days later, he changed his mind about his guilty plea and asked for a trial. But it was too late. He had been sent to the Tennessee state prison in Nashville.

Two weeks after the assassination of Robert Kennedy and the apprehension of James Earl Ray, President Johnson sent a ticking time bomb to the Senate. He nominated Abe Fortas to replace Earl Warren as chief justice of the Supreme Court.

At the same time, he nominated a crony, former Texas congressman Homer Thornberry, to fill the seat Fortas would vacate. Thornberry currently served with J.P. Coleman on the Fifth Circuit Court of Appeals, a jurisdiction many considered the private domain of Mississippi senator James Eastland. Johnson had notified Fortas the morning after talking to Warren (who wished to retire, but did not want to risk having a Republican president appointing his successor), but Johnson was scooped by the *Washington Post,* which reported Warren's retirement and Fortas's appointment in that morning's edition.

Senate reaction was mixed. That same morning before the nomination was even delivered, Tennessee senator Albert Gore, reacting to news reports, said on the floor of the Senate that he wished to congratulate the president on his choice. "I wish to commend to the Senate Justice Fortas, an eminent jurist, an able lawyer, and a patriot," said Gore. "He will write an indelible record as Chief Justice. It is with confidence that I make such a statement and it is with pride that I commend the selection." Not everyone shared Gore's enthusiasm. Washington insiders knew of Fortas's relationship with the president, and rumors had been circulating for more than a year about his ethics—or, more accurately, lack of ethics—as a Supreme Court justice.

The previous month, in an interview with United Press International, Fortas had compared the plight of blacks in America to that of Jews in Nazi Germany. For that reason, he said, Jews should help blacks in their struggle: "The cause of freedom is our cause and every man's fight to be free of discrimination is our cause." Not fooled by Fortas's racial posturing was Mississippi civil rights leader Charles Evers. "I don't know if he was connected to the [Sovereignty] Commission," Evers told the author in 1996. "We know he was a racist. He was a bigot."

Fortas could afford to appear to be liberal on the race issue when talking to the media. It didn't cost him anything. It was on issues that impacted his pocketbook—or those of his benefactors in Memphis—that he took a hard line. He was a hawk on Vietnam. The war was good for business. Every American vessel sunk in Vietnam meant additional construction contracts for friends such as Louis Wolfson.

Fortas took right-wing positions on the prosecution of Vietnam demonstrators and on limitations of free speech. Commenting on protesting students at Columbia University, he called their actions "totally inexcusable from the point of view of even primitive morality." Earlier in the year, he had published a book entitled *Concerning Dissent and Civil Disobedience,* in which he was critical of Vietnam War protesters who applied for conscientious-objector status because they felt the war was immoral. Said Fortas: "By participating in the particular war, the state takes the position that the war *is* justified and moral."

On the subject of the First Amendment, he was to the right of Attila the Hun. Commenting on Fortas's well-known hostility to the press, the *Evening Star* said he had used his "most strenuous language in condemning newspapers and magazines for printing stories that either threaten the reputation of public officials or private persons, or interfere with the privacy of individuals or families." The *Evening Star* also pointed out the shadowy nature of Fortas's power. "The popular impression here is that President

Johnson and Fortas have been in more-or-less continuous association and consultation for the better part of thirty years," said the newspaper. "Fortas insists that is exaggeration. But the confirmed facts of their relationship are enough to make exaggeration unnecessary; they are close confidants."

Within twenty-four hours of the nomination, President Johnson could see that there was going to be significant opposition to Fortas. The leader of that opposition was Senator Robert Griffith of Michigan, the Republican minority leader. Although the Democrats had a majority in the Senate, a number of their votes were from Southern senators opposed to Fortas's civil rights posturing.

The week before committee hearings were held on the nomination, Johnson received a tip from an informant on the committee, detailing the opposition's strategy. Griffith had decided to make an issue of the "cronyism" that existed between the president and his nominee for chief justice. Hearing that, Johnson ordered his secretaries to destroy papers and documents relating to Abe Fortas.

The chairman of the Senate Judiciary Committee was Senator James Eastland. He would be the first person Fortas faced. He would ask the first questions. He would set the agenda for the hearing. Eastland was accustomed to playing that role. He reveled in the power it afforded him. But Fortas's nomination put Eastland in a bind.

Even if Fortas's civil rights record was abominable (from Eastland's perspective), Fortas was "home folks" and was allied with some of the same Memphis power-brokers to whom he answered. If Eastland attacked Fortas because of his civil rights positions, he would damage the cartel. If he went easy on Fortas, he would come under criticism back home in Mississippi.

Neither Johnson nor Fortas were sure how Eastland would handle that dilemma. Then there was the matter of Thornberry's nomination. Johnson knew Eastland would be pleased to see a member of "his" appeals court move up to the Supreme Court. It would be a feather in Eastland's cap.

Not until the hearings actually began did Eastland's strategy become apparent. Going against Fortas's opponents, but showing no outward signs of embracing the administration's position, he made a series of procedural rulings that aided the justice's supporters. When it was time to begin the questioning, Eastland stole Griffith's thunder by leading off with questions related to Griffith's charges of separation-of-powers violations. He asked Fortas point-blank if he had overstepped the boundaries in the area of judicial appointments. Fortas said he had not.

That was a lie, but he was not challenged.

Eastland continued. "Now, the charge was made that you were adviser of the president in coping with steel price increases and helping to frame measures to head off transportation strikes—with the increasing intensity of the war in Vietnam Fortas is also consulted more and more on foreign policy."

Fortas answered: "All right, Senator. Let me say in the first place—and make this absolutely clear—that since I have been a justice, the president of the United States has never, directly or indirectly, approximately or remotely, talked to me about anything before the court or that might come before the court. I want to make that absolutely clear." Then later he added. "It is not true that I have ever helped to frame a measure since I have been a justice of the court."

The July hearings ended with a sputter.

Griffith was unable to produce a "smoking gun." There were a lot of things he didn't know about—such as the nature of Fortas's relationship with Louis Wolfson—but he knew in his heart that there was something not quite right with Abe Fortas. He stalled for time.

Throughout August and September, Griffith and his supporters filibustered in the Senate, delaying a vote on the nomination until they could obtain more information. Typical of the newspaper criticisms of Fortas was this analysis in the St. Louis *Globe-Democrat:* "President Johnson's nomination of Justice Abe Fortas . . . is patently not in the best interests of the nation. The Senate should refuse to confirm Mr. Fortas's nomination for a number of reasons. Justice Fortas's appearance before the Senate Judiciary Committee is notable for his lack of candor."

Fortas's supporters used the time to lobby for his confirmation.

Typical of the pro-Fortas efforts was a letter from a Memphis attorney to the Memphis *Press-Scimitar:* "True enough his decisions with respect to human rights are cast in a liberal mold. . . . With respect to business matters, the experience of Mr. Fortas as a business lawyer is evident. His decisions in anti-trust and similar type cases are certainly in the best interests of fair and free competition." In August, in an act of sheer desperation, friends of Abe Fortas went to Richard Nixon, who had just won the Republican nomination for president, and tried to cut a deal with him on the Fortas nomination. They argued that because Nixon's running mate, Spiro Agnew, was a hard-liner on civil rights, Nixon needed a mitigating voice on the Supreme Court. Nixon stood by his earlier statement that a new president should pick his own chief justice.

Despite the increasingly vicious sparring taking place in the Senate, President Johnson was hopeful the nomination would be approved. Then without warning, on October 1, the rug was pulled out from under the nomination. The Senate voted to put the nomination aside after failing to turn back the filibuster.

Fortas's reaction was swift. The day after the Senate vote he sent a letter to the White House asking the president to withdraw the nomination. "Continued efforts to secure confirmation of that nomination, even if ultimately successful, would result in a continuation of the attacks upon the court which have characterized the filibuster—attacks which had been sometimes extreme and entirely unrelated to responsible criticism," Fortas said in the letter. "Attacks of this sort would be especially inappropriate and harmful to the court and the nation if they should continue while the court is in session."

"With deep regret," President Johnson concurred with Fortas's decision. In a prepared statement, Johnson said: "I believed when I made this nomination, and I believe now, that he is the best qualified man for this high position."

The humiliating ordeal was over. Or at least they both thought it was. Abe Fortas was still a Supreme Court justice for life and Lyndon Johnson was still president—not for life but at least for a while longer. Of course, it was not over: it had just begun.

By late August, Governor John Bell Williams knew what he wanted to do with the Sovereignty Commission. He notified Erle Johnston that he had found a replacement for him. The new director would be Webb Burke, a career FBI man. It is hard to know what was going through Williams's mind at the time, but after a spring and summer of political assassinations, major riots, and political uncertainty, it is reasonable to assume that his selection of a new director was influenced by news events.

Webb Burke had a strong Mississippi connection. A native of Hattiesburg, he had attended Ole Miss, where he was a football hero. After graduation, he remained at the university for a short time as a football coach. He left to coach football at Southwestern University at Memphis—and was there while Abe Fortas was attending classes—but after a season or two he returned to Ole Miss, where he remained on the coaching staff for five years. That Fortas and Burke formed an association at Southwestern is fascinating to consider, for, if true, it would open the door to a wide range of possibilities.

When the Mississippi highway patrol was organized in 1937, Burke was chosen its first director. In 1940 he left the highway patrol to become a special agent with the FBI. Assigned to offices in Chicago and Philadelphia, he was then posted to the FBI's training division as a member of the firearms staff. Three years later, he was named agent in charge of J. Edgar Hoover's prized creation, the FBI Academy. The fact that Burke was made head of the academy shows the high regard Hoover had for his abilities.

Only those agents considered privy to the inner circle were placed in such high-profile positions.

Burke had a long career with the FBI—later serving in bureaus in Los Angeles, Newark, San Francisco, Denver, and Little Rock—before taking retirement in 1960. For the next eight years, he worked as a security consultant for various private companies before returning to Mississippi with his family to take over operation of the Sovereignty Commission.

Whether Governor Williams chose Burke on his own or was asked to hire him by the FBI is unknown, but if he was looking for a hard-liner, someone who could interface with the FBI and play big-league hardball, there could be no doubt he had found the right man.

Mississippi Representative A.C. "Butch" Lambert once called the CIA a "kindergarten" compared to the Sovereignty Commission. That analogy was never more apt than when Burke took over the Commission.

Erle Johnston didn't have much notice. Four days after Burke's appointment was announced, the new director reported for work. Johnston knew him by reputation, but had never met him. He spent the day with Burke, showing him the filing system, going over reports with him, then he packed up and went home to Scott County where he lived in relative obscurity until his death in 1995.

Governor Williams didn't say much about Johnston's departure, other than that he was leaving for health reasons. About Burke, he said: "[His] past experience in the law enforcement field should eminently qualify him for this sensitive but important position within our state government."

Thus far, it had been a busy year for the Commission. The King assassination had put a strain on the agency, as had a rash of bombings, most of which were directed against Jewish targets. Byron De La Beckwith was still under indictment for the murder of Medgar Evers, but the district attorney's office showed no indication of pursuing another trial. Informants told the FBI that Beckwith was traveling the state, recruiting for the KKK, but authorities could never get anything on him.

Concerned by the bombing of a Jewish synagogue in Jackson, the regional Anti-Defamation League, based in New Orleans, raised money to pay FBI informants in the Klan. Among the most valuable informants was Wayne Roberts, one of the men convicted of depriving Goodman, Chaney, and Schwerner of their civil rights in Neshoba County. Out on bond while he appealed his conviction, he was encouraged to provide information to the FBI about Klan activity.

On June 29, Roberts tipped off police that a prominent Jew in Meridian named Meyer Davidson had been targeted for a bombing. A klansman named Tommy Tarrants was apprehended by the FBI with a bomb outside

Davidson's home. Tarrants was wounded in a shoot-out, and his female companion, who was waiting for him in the car, was killed by police bullets. After that, the bombings stopped.

Not much is known about Webb Burke's early leadership since most of the files of that period were destroyed, but one of his first decisions was to terminate the existing staff of investigators. He divided the state into three investigative districts and hired three new investigators: Edgar Fortenberry, a twenty-year veteran with the FBI was hired to cover the south and southwest part of the state; Mack Mohead, who had worked for the District of Columbia police force for five years and for the Clarksdale police force for four years, was given the Delta counties; Fulton Tutor, a former two-term sheriff in Pontotoc County, was given the northern part of the state.

Any questions people may have had about Governor Williams's plans for the Commission were answered by the "dream team" of heavy hitters Burke assembled to carry out its mission. After Burke had put together the office team he wanted, he expanded the agency's use of private investigators, increasing those expenditures by more than 30 percent the first year.

~~~

Mississippi politics that fall were more strident than usual.

Earlier in the year, NAACP field director Charles Evers shocked the political establishment by running for the third congressional seat vacated by John Bell Williams. He was the only African American in the race. Running against him were Charles Griffin, Williams's longtime administrative assistant, and an assortment of others, including a television newsman and a former mayor.

When the votes were counted, Evers surprised everyone by leading the ticket. "They didn't know whether I was going to make a good congressman or not, but many of them wanted to give me a chance," Evers wrote in his autobiography. "A lot of whites started thinking and listening to our side, and they realized they had been wrong."

Well, not all of them. One evening Evers returned home from campaigning and found a car circling his house. Shots were exchanged, with one of Evers's fence posts the only casualty.

Since no one had received a majority of votes in the special election, Evers had to face the number two vote-getter, Charles Griffin, in a run-off. This time around, Griffin garnered all the white votes and was able to defeat Evers.

Even so, many white Mississippians felt it was a close call.

That summer, when Mississippi Democrats chose delegates for the national convention in Chicago, only three of forty-four delegates were African American. Evers was offended. A few weeks later, the liberal–black coalition that had changed its name from Freedom Democratic Party to the Loyal Democrats of Mississippi (the Loyalists) had a convention of its own. Newspaper editor Hodding Carter III was a member of this group, as was Claude Ramsey, head of the state AFL-CIO.

Evers joined forces with the Loyalists.

By the time the Loyalists went to Chicago to challenge the seats assigned to the regulars, Governor Williams had entered the fray, saying that if the national party wanted Mississippi's continued support it would have to vote for the regulars.

Faced with a choice between the Loyalists and the regulars, the credentials committee voted to seat the Loyalists. That meant Evers, Carter, Ramsey and the others in their group were recognized as the legitimate Democratic Party in Mississippi.

Governor Williams was outraged. He felt mistreated—and by the same liberals and blacks who had been tormenting him for as long as he could remember. He hinted that he would be supporting someone other than a Democrat.

As the Democratic convention erupted into violence—and the names of Vietnam War demonstrators became familiar to the news media—two names in particular attracted the attention of the Sovereignty Commission: Tom Hayden and David Dellinger. As part of the Freedom Rider "invasion" of 1964, both men already had dossiers compiled on their activities by Commission investigators.

How Governor Williams reacted to that information and what he did with the secret files on Hayden and Dellinger is not known. Judging from past responses in similar situations, it seems safe to assume that the Commission provided the Chicago police with whatever information was in the files.

The battle that took place in Chicago between the police and demonstrators left more than 700 civilians and 83 police officers injured. Police made 653 arrests. It was the bloodiest political convention in American history. Not surprisingly, the Mississippi Loyalists condemned Chicago mayor Richard Daley for the brutality unleashed upon the demonstrators by the police. The two most talked-about Democrats didn't even bother to attend the convention. President Johnson became the first incumbent president in twenty-four years not to attend his party's convention. Senator Edward Kennedy appeared in a film segment shown to delegates, but he, too, stayed away from Chicago.

Inside the convention hall the biggest battle was over the Vietnam War. When the dust settled, party nominee Hubert Humphrey had a platform that even Lyndon Johnson could have run on, but the delegates opposed to the war were successful in getting more than a thousand votes for their "stop the bombing" initiative, a figure that represented two-thirds of Humphrey's winning total.

The campaign that fall pitted Humphrey against both Richard Nixon and independent candidate George Wallace of Alabama. White Mississippi voters were clearly in no mood to support Humphrey, despite his prowar position on Vietnam. It was Wallace who laid claim to the loyalty of white Mississippi voters, although Nixon made serious inroads by allowing South Carolina senator Strom Thurmond (a cofounder of the Federation for Constitutional Government) to play a pivotal role at the Republican convention.

Thurmond's role in Nixon's strategy was so important that *Newsweek* described the senator as the "kingmaker" of the convention. Nixon's biggest threat at the convention was California governor Ronald Reagan. As the time approached for a vote, Nixon's head counters determined that the delegates from the South held the key to victory. Problem was they were leaning toward Reagan, whose home-spun conservatism seemed more to their liking than Nixon's "uptown" brand.

To get Thurmond on his side, Nixon agreed to consult with him before choosing a running mate. "I won't ram anyone down the throat of the South," Nixon told him. That sounded good to Thurmond, who ran with it, locking up the South for Nixon and painting Reagan into a corner. True to his word, Nixon chose Maryland governor Spiro Agnew as his running mate.

During the campaign, Governor Williams hinted it might be time for Mississippi to embrace the Republican Party (despite being a Democrat, he had supported Barry Goldwater in the last presidential election); but this year he campaigned openly for that Son of the South, George Wallace, whose speeches left no doubts about his intentions: "Well when I get to be President, I'm gonna call in a bunch of bureaucrats and take away their briefcases and throw 'em in the Potomac River. And if any demonstrator ever lays down in front of my car, it'll be the last car he'll ever lay down in front of."

As Wallace's popularity increased—the Louis Harris survey showed in mid-September that Nixon led with 39 percent, Humphrey was second with 31 percent, and Wallace trailed with 21 percent—the news media took his candidacy more seriously. Reporters traveled with him, just as they traveled with the major party nominees, reporting on his speeches and interviewing his supporters.

Asked by a *Newsweek* reporter why he was supporting Wallace, one man said, "It's not that we dislike niggers—we hate 'em." With his passionate speeches, Wallace became the most volatile candidate in the race. Said

Wallace, over and over again: "The people of the United States are going to take back government into their own hands."

That was language white Mississippi could understand.

~~~~

Unknown to the public, the U.S. Army was compiling its dossiers on dissidents into books that it was distributing to command centers around the nation. Volume 1 was a green-and-white glossy paperback published in 1968 at the Army Command's own printing plant in Baltimore. Five additional volumes were issued that year, but they were more crudely printed on legal-length paper and bound with a metal clamp.

The books were entitled *Individuals Active in Civil Disturbances,* but the title was misleading since the books contained information on a wide range of people. Targeted were members of the Southern Christian Leadership Conference, the NAACP, the American Friends Service Committee, Americans for Democratic Action, and the Presbyterian Interracial Council of Chicago.

Almost all of the people profiled in the secret books were civilians who had no association with the armed forces. Few had arrest records. Often the profiles of individuals were accompanied by photographs that had been surreptitiously taken through telephoto lenses.

The military called the collective lists of names the "Blacklist." Those were the people the military would round up and arrest when ordered to do so. The files were stored at Fort Holabird, Maryland, in a steel room in a warehouse that stood two stories high and half a city block long. More than seven million dossiers were kept in the warehouse, shelved, according to Christopher Pyle, in gray steel bookcases that stood over eleven feet high and stretched over fifty feet in length.

The contents of each file were determined by the Army officers gathering the material. The subjects of the investigations were never notified of the contents of the dossiers and were never allowed to correct incorrect information. The truth was whatever the Army wanted it to be.

Working independent of the Army investigators, the FBI continued building its own dossiers throughout 1968, but, unlike the Army, it played a more activist role with the information it acquired. In November, before Lyndon Johnson left office, Hoover ordered FBI agents to go after the Black Panther Party, which he characterized as "the greatest threat to the internal security of the country."

Two favorite tactics of the FBI were anonymous mailings and "pretext" telephone calls. For example, the FBI was successful in getting one of the Sovereignty Commission's chief targets, Stokely Carmichael, out of the country by having an agent call his mother and warn her that the Panthers were going to assassinate her son. Carmichael fell for it and flew to Africa, where he remained in hiding for years.

In another instance, FBI agents targeted a white woman who was working with a biracial organization named Action. They sent her husband an anonymous letter that read, "Look man I guess your old lady doesn't get enough at home or she wouldn't be shucking and jiving with our Black Men in ACTION, you dig?" Because of the letter, the man and woman separated, thus giving the FBI the "victory" it wanted.

～～／～つ

Two weeks before the election, President Johnson ordered a halt in the bombing of North Vietnam in hopes of jump-starting the Paris peace talks, which were broken off when Johnson had resumed the bombing earlier in the year.

The United States was flying an average of 300 missions a day into North Vietnam. The bombing, which had continued on and off for nearly four years, had cost the United States 915 aircraft and over 700 pilots killed in action.

Johnson wanted to leave office on a positive note and he also wanted to help Hubert Humphrey, who was still behind in the polls. He did neither. The North Vietnamese thought they could get a better deal from the new president—whoever he was—so they declined to return to the table. Johnson always believed that Nixon had actually promised them a better deal if they waited, but he never could prove it.

When the votes were counted after the November 5 election, Nixon won with 301 electoral votes to Humphrey's 191. The popular vote was much closer, with Nixon winning by only 500,000 votes. That margin was significant because the third candidate—George Wallace—had received almost 10 million votes. Wallace carried Mississippi, receiving 415,000 votes to Humphrey's 150,000 and Nixon's 88,000.

Nixon knew he would need the South to get reelected.

CHAPTER 9

1969 – 1979

In 1969 the Fifth Circuit Court of Appeals denied a new trial application from the men convicted of violating the civil rights of Schwerner, Goodman, and Chaney. It was going on five years since the murders, and the political climate had changed. None of Senator Eastland's appointments on the court was interested in going out on a limb for the men. There is no indication Eastland wanted them to: what was the point?

The men themselves were still free. Their lawyers were preparing an appeal to the U.S. Supreme Court. Anything could happen. Byron De La Beckwith was walking proof of that. Early in the year, a new Hinds County district attorney named Jack Travis dropped the murder indictment against Beckwith. His bond was refunded and he was allowed to carry on as if nothing had ever happened. Under the law, the case could be reopened, but no one thought that would ever transpire.

Beckwith was a free man.

Watching all this from a distance was James Earl Ray. Of all the accused civil rights killers of the decade, he alone was in prison. That in itself, he argued, should have tipped someone off that maybe he wasn't guilty. *Hell, nigger killers don't do time!* On his way to prison, he had told the sheriff that he had pleaded guilty "a little too fast." His lawyer, Percy Foreman, had talked him into it, he said, to avoid the electric chair. It sounded like a good idea at the time. No sooner did he reach the prison than he wrote the presiding judge, Preston Battle, to ask for a review of his guilty plea. Ray told the judge he had fired Foreman and was looking for a new lawyer.

Two days later, he hired J.B. Stoner, a race-baiting segregationist from Savannah, Georgia. Stoner wasted no time in proclaiming Ray's innocence. He said his client had been pressured into a guilty plea. Stoner was unable to convince Judge Battle that his client had grounds for a trial, but that did not mean that the judge himself did not have serious doubts about the case.

In March, Battle told *Newsweek* reporters he agreed with those who said the whole story had not been told. "I'd like the full proof," he said. One of the things that disturbed him and other critics was Ray's finances. Ray had money. Where had it come from? Who was Ray's financial backer? Those were critical questions, Battle explained to reporters, but not necessarily questions that would be answered in a trial, since Ray could not be forced to take the stand and the FBI claimed it had found no evidence of a conspiracy.

Battle's analysis made sense. Evidence of a conspiracy *was* strong, as was evidence that Ray had been set up to take the fall. There was even evidence that Ray may not have been the triggerman. But until such time as Ray was willing to identify his financial backer and explain how he had been set up, a trial would only raise more questions than it would answer.

Ray's strategy was to point a finger at the weaknesses of the evidence without pointing a finger at the individuals who set him up. He wanted to get out of prison without putting someone else behind bars. That may be because he was deathly afraid of the individuals who set him up, or at least the individuals he *thought* set him up.

What apparently never occurred to him was the possibility that he was the patsy for a double sting and had been manipulated into thinking his backers were someone other than who they really were. If he thought Carlos Marcello was his secret benefactor—as has been suggested by various authors—then he was mistaken, for the Dixie don would never have left such an obvious trail. The most likely scenario was that Ray was tricked into believing he was on Marcello's payroll.

During the 1968 presidential campaign, Richard Nixon said he would bring an "honorable end" to the war in Vietnam. Many people voted for him on that basis, thinking the operative word in that campaign promise was "end." After his inauguration, it became clear that the operative word was "honorable"—and it became equally clear that his definition of "honorable" was couched in terms of a military victory. Under Nixon's leadership, the war in Vietnam intensified, as did the government's secret war against American dissenters. In his inaugural speech Nixon said he had been embarrassed by protesters during the campaign, and he vowed that would never happen again. Nixon decided to add a new weapon to the government's intelligence-gathering arsenal: the Internal Revenue Service. At the request of the president, the IRS created a special team to monitor the activities of political activists for the purpose of auditing their tax returns and those of organizations to which they belonged. By the end of the year, the agency had files on nearly 50,000 individuals thought to be hostile to the president. Between July 1969 and September 1970, according to an IRS internal memo published in the *Washington Post,* the secret team reviewed the tax returns of approximately 1,025 organizations and 4,300 individuals.

Both the FBI and the Army Intelligence units stepped up their activities. J. Edgar Hoover was delighted to have Nixon as his new boss. Unlike Lyndon Johnson, who didn't trust him, and John F. Kennedy, who despised him, he sensed that Richard Nixon respected him and understood the value of his work. Hoover's assessment of Nixon the president was probably accurate, but his assessment of Nixon the man was woefully off the mark, as he learned early in 1969 when he sent word to the president that he had information for his eyes only.

That information was a report that the president's top three aides were homosexuals. Listed were H.R. Haldeman, John Ehrlichman, and Dwight Chapin. Hoover's information had come from a newspaper reporter who did double duty as an FBI informant. That revelation must have been painful for Hoover, since he himself was probably homosexual, as was his chief aide.

Nixon was stunned—and horrified—by the charges. The *last* thing the president wanted to know about his aides was details of their personal lives. Nixon liked to keep his distance from his aides and associates. Hoover's charges made him venture where he didn't want to go. He had no choice but to request a full FBI investigation.

Hoover asked assistant director Mark Felt to conduct the investigation. To Hoover's surprise, Felt reported that he was unable to find any evidence to support the charges. He recommended that the case be closed and it was. For their part, Haldeman, Ehrlichman, and Chapin must have wondered if Hoover's sources had been honestly mistaken or if this was only his plot to exert power within the president's inner sanctum.

⌒⌒

The war against integration in Mississippi was being waged mostly in the courts. Eastland shored up the Fifth Circuit Court of Appeals in 1969 with a new judge, Charles Clark of Jackson. It was Clark who had defended Governor Ross Barnett in the James Meredith case at Ole Miss. Now, with

Eastland's help, he could defend Mississippi on the Fifth Circuit Court of Appeals.

The Mississippi legislature looked to Governor Williams for leadership. The best thing the legislature could do for the state, said Williams, was to pass laws that would provide loans to parents who wanted to enroll their children in private schools.

Former representative George Rogers took advantage of the lull in civil rights activity to run for his old seat in the House. The seat became vacant through the death of the legislator who had held it for the intervening several years. This time the Women for Constitutional Government did not campaign against him, and he was reelected. When he returned to the Capitol, Rogers discovered that the Sovereignty Commission was not as communicative with the lawmakers as it previously had been. Said Rogers: "There were a lot of people in the Legislature who didn't want to know [what the Commission was doing]."

Later in 1969 the U.S. Supreme Court ruled that Mississippi schools would have to be desegregated "immediately." The *Jackson Daily News* story, written by Charles Overby, described the day of the Court's decision as "Black Wednesday," and went on to say that Senator Eastland "believes 'disaster' is impending for the state's public schools." Overby summarized comments from the state's congressional delegation as suggesting that the court decision would trigger "serious setbacks in public education."

Under Webb Burke's leadership, the Sovereignty Commission focused more on student dissidents and the antiwar movement than it did on civil rights activists. He increased the Commission's budget for private investigators by another 30 to 40 percent over the previous year—and he cultivated additional student informers at the University of Mississippi.

One of the Ole Miss informants, Charles Lamar Neill, supplied his information to Security Consultant, a Jackson detective agency hired by the Commission. One report supplied information on a "New Left" group Neill felt was planning to overthrow the school administration. In another report, Neill gave information about students who smoked marijuana. Years later, when *Clarion-Ledger* reporter Jerry Mitchell contacted Neill about his reports, the former student, who now lives in Seattle, said he didn't realize the detective agency was passing his reports along to the Sovereignty Commission. "What I did wasn't right," he told Mitchell. "I always thought the Sovereignty Commission was a very racist organization."

David Ingebretesen, the current executive director of the Mississippi office of the American Civil Liberties Union, was a student at Millsaps College in Jackson in the mid- to late 1960s. He recalls that although antiwar demonstrations attracted a variety of government spies, each agency usually could be identified by its cameras. "There was a pecking order," he says. "The FBI had Nikons. The highway patrol had Canons. The Sovereignty Commission had cheap cameras —they were Prakticas or something like that." Once when Ingebretesen was at an outdoor rally, he raised his voice to shout directions to a coffeehouse. Within seconds, agents from the Commission pulled up in cars with glow-in-the-dark numbers stuck to the doors.

There wasn't much antiwar activity in Mississippi in the 1960s, but what was there was monitored closely. In February, Bill Thomas, a reporter for *The Commercial Appeal,* which had a significant circulation in Mississippi, accompanied a Memphis man as he fled to Canada to avoid the draft. The newspaper supported the war, but Thomas, who had won the Ernie Pyle Award for his reporting in Vietnam, did his best to keep politics out of the story. His series of articles, entitled "Journey Into Exile" and published on the front page with a disclaimer that the newspaper did not approve of "this sort of thing," overdramatized the man's journey to Canada, but provided valuable information to others in the mid-South who were considering the same alternative.

Memphis had a favorite son already in Canada, singer/songwriter Jesse Winchester, who had left town three days after receiving his induction notice. Winchester's decision was especially painful for history-conscious Memphis because his family was among those who founded the city. One of the city's main thoroughfares is named Winchester Avenue. "I couldn't have gone to Vietnam," he explained to Roger Neville Williams in *The New Exiles.* "You feel it and you know when a fight is your fight, you know. . . . I mean, I just wasn't involved in that fight at all. It just wasn't my fight."

Shortly after James Earl Ray arrived at the state penitentiary in Nashville, state correction commissioner Harry Avery had a private meeting with the accused assassin at which Ray is said to have told Avery that the King murder was a conspiracy. Avery told Ray that he would go and get any money Ray had hidden away and he would deposit it in a trust fund for him. When Ray's attorneys learned of the meeting, they told the governor Avery had promised to "look after" Ray in prison if he would give him a handwritten account of the murder. When Tennessee governor Buford Ellington learned of the meeting, he asked for Avery's resignation. When he refused to resign, Ellington fired him. That same week Ray's application for a trial was turned down by Judge Preston Battle.

Avery cleaned out his office and went fishing.

Reporters tracked him down and asked for his version of his departure.

"I told him that if he wanted to tell me the full truth about this in his own handwriting and if anyone was interested in purchasing it, I would see that every nickel that anyone paid was placed in his trust fund," Avery told a reporter with Associated Press. "I did not want one percentage point of it at all—all I was doing was seeking the full truth."

<center>~~~</center>

By spring 1969, Abe Fortas thought he was on firm ground. He had survived Lyndon Johnson's abortive attempt to elevate him to chief justice of the Supreme Court. He was bloodied, but not beaten. Or so he thought.

At the end of October 1968, William Lambert, a reporter with *Life* magazine, received a tip that he should look into Fortas's relationship with Louis Wolfson. Four telephone calls later, the reporter was able to confirm that money had changed hands between the two men. Lambert dug deeper. Tough stories were nothing new to him—he was among the first reporters to write about mob activity in the Pacific Northwest—but what he discovered when he started asking questions about Fortas surprised even him. "Don't ask me any questions," one of his frightened government sources told him. "Don't even tell me anything—I don't want to know."

Early in November, U.S. Attorney Robert Morgenthau of New York called outgoing Attorney General Ramsey Clark and told him *Life* magazine was investigating the Fortas–Wolfson connection. The next day Clark went to Fortas's home to talk to him about the magazine's investigation. Clark later explained the visit by saying he wanted to hear Fortas's explanation, but the effect of the visit was to tip Fortas off about the investigation, giving him time to destroy any incriminating information.

Lambert asked Fortas for an interview, but the Supreme Court justice turned him down, saying in a letter to Lambert, "Since there has been no impropriety, or anything approaching it in my conduct, no purpose would be served by any such meeting."

If Fortas hoped Wolfson would go away, simply disappear out of his life, those hopes were dashed early in 1969 when Wolfson was convicted of stock manipulation charges. In April, Wolfson wrote Fortas and asked for a special favor. "I cannot go to prison right now," he said. "If you could do anything to get me a Presidential pardon—have President Johnson call Mr. Nixon. . . ."

Of course, Fortas did not dare intervene on Wolfson's behalf, not with *Life* magazine breathing down his neck. Shortly before Wolfson entered prison on April 25, he gave an interview to the *Wall Street Journal*. The article began: "If Louis Wolfson is to be believed, he could have obtained a presidential pardon last December, sparing him the anguish of a prison sentence." Wolfson explained to the reporter that he had turned down the pardon because "he didn't want any favors."

By that time, John Mitchell, the new attorney general, had been briefed on the Fortas case. The question for him was not whether Abe Fortas should have been nominated to become chief justice—that, after all, was a dead issue—it was whether Abe Fortas was fit to serve on the Court in any capacity. On May 7, Mitchell stuffed a packet of documents into an envelope and sealed it. Then he tucked the envelope under his arm and went to meet with Chief Justice Earl Warren. The envelope contained copies of letters between Fortas and Wolfson, and transcriptions of the minutes of two Wolfson Family Foundation meetings. After discussing the case with Warren, Mitchell left the envelope with the chief justice so that he could examine the documents at his leisure. Mitchell was of the opinion that the high court should police itself. If Warren could pressure Fortas into resigning, then the Nixon administration would not have to get involved.

In due course, Warren sent the documents back to Mitchell with a cover letter stating that he had made no copies. That was a lie, as researchers discovered more than a decade after the chief justice's death. Warren had made copies of all the documents. Whether Warren ever had a discussion with Fortas about the contents of the envelope is not known, but there is evidence that Fortas was aware of the fact that Mitchell had the information under lock and key in his private files. According to Wolfson, Fortas told him the whole affair had been sealed in the Justice Department and "would not get out."

Before the exposé in *Life* was published, Lambert contacted Paul Porter, Fortas's old law partner, to give Fortas an opportunity to respond to the allegations. Porter declined the invitation for Fortas, saying the Supreme Court justice would respond after the story was published. Fortas would take his chances.

The night before the story broke, Abe Fortas and his wife, Carolyn, went to a charity ball and waltzed the night away. The next day—as Washington buzzed about the damaging information in *Life*—Fortas took his seat on the high court and acted as if nothing had happened. He confided in three members of the Court, and all three, according to Fortas, told him to "stick it out."

Not encouraging him to stick it out were members of Congress. Representative Clark MacGregor of Minnesota asked the House Judiciary Committee to launch an investigation. Senator Robert Griffin of Michigan, who had led the fight in the Senate to block Fortas's nomination for chief justice, received death threats. "My office in Detroit tells me my life has been threatened," he told reporters. "The threat did relate to my position on the Fortas matter." He told reporters it was due to "incriminating evidence" he possessed about Fortas.

At a party for television news reporter Nancy Dickerson, Abe and Carolyn Fortas ran into the Howard Bakers of Tennessee. Those present described it as an "icy encounter." Although a fellow Tennessean, Senator Baker had opposed Fortas's promotion to chief justice and, unlike the other Tennessee senator, Albert Gore, he was not encouraging Fortas to stay on the court.

The controversy spilled over into Tennessee, where Hamilton S. Burnett, the chief justice of the state Supreme Court, called for Fortas's impeachment. When he read about the Fortas–Wolfson deal in the newspaper, it "made me sick," Burnett told reporters. "This violates every ethical principle of the judiciary—every principle of honesty," he said. "My whole training has been to believe that the Supreme Court and its members are always next to God in their actions. I can't understand how any one on the court should have a question in his mind concerning the acceptance of such a fee."

Rumors circulated of an impeachment movement.

As the controversy swirled about Washington, growing more damaging by the moment, Fortas went home to Memphis. There is no public record of whom he consulted while in Memphis, but it is obvious that in this, the most defining moment of his career, he would want to meet with his benefactors. On May 12, Fortas went to the campus of Memphis State University for a Law Day observance speech. Fortas used the forum to lash out at civil rights and antiwar demonstrators, and the students gave him a standing ovation.

Invited to sit on the speakers' platform with Fortas—but declining to do so—was Memphis mayor Henry Loeb. He had his reasons for snubbing Fortas. Although Loeb was a social conservative who agreed with Fortas's comments about civil rights and antiwar demonstrators—Loeb was mayor when Martin Luther King was assassinated—he was a political maverick who had always displayed a strong streak of independence. The day after the speech, Loeb received a letter from a constituent who took him to task for not attending the speech with Fortas. "It seems that there is going around a rumor that you were asked to be on the platform . . . and upon the invitation you stated that you would not because you did not want to sit on the platform with a crook," said the letter-writer. "I just wanted to bring this to your attention because I feel like it is a very vicious rumor which could hurt you."

Loeb responded by letter. "I reserve the right to go where I please or not," he said. "I did not choose to be on the platform with Justice Fortas, but said nothing against Mr. Fortas. . . . In all candor, I think the Judge was wrong, and that he should have resigned, but I said nothing about the Judge, except that I did not choose to be there."

By the time Fortas returned to Washington, it was clear to everyone involved—even to Fortas himself—that he would not be able to withstand the firestorm of protest now being leveled against him. Rumors were circulating that Fortas was somehow linked to a Las Vegas casino. Stories already had been published connecting him to a real estate tax shelter in Virginia. The Justice Department, for the first time, admitted it was looking into Fortas's financial dealings.

As it turned out, the casino link came through his involvement with Great America Corporation, a Nevada company that had ties to the Thunderbird Hotel in Las Vegas. In 1955 the hotel's gaming license was revoked on grounds that underworld figures had an interest in the hotel. Ironically, the Justice Department was already investigating Supreme Court justice William O. Douglas's connection with the Albert Parvin Foundation, which, according to federal prosecutors, was controlled by a group of Las Vegas gamblers.

The FBI was aware of the Douglas probe, of course—and of the Parvin Foundation's alleged link to organized crime—but what the FBI was not yet aware of, according to author Curt Gentry, was that Florida crime boss Meyer Lansky had a secret ownership of the Parvin Foundation casino. When Fortas resigned his directorship with Great America, his seat on the board was taken by a member of Fortas's old law firm. To Fortas's surprise, newspaper reporters were digging up details of financial transactions that had been well hidden for years.

The unanswered question was whether Fortas and Douglas were both linked to Meyer Lansky through a Great America–Parvin Foundation connection. There were rumors that Fortas and Douglas, longtime friends since they worked together at the SEC, had made investments together. When the author asked the FBI for Freedom of Information files on any Fortas–Douglas links to Las Vegas crime figures, he was told over the telephone that the Fortas–Douglas file no longer existed: It had been destroyed. That, of course, begs the question: If the FBI investigation did not turn up incriminating information on Fortas, why was the file destroyed?

The day after Fortas returned from Memphis he submitted his resignation to President Nixon. His letter said: "For the reasons expressed in a letter of this date which I have written to the Chief Justice, a copy of which, with his permission, I enclose, I wish hereby to tender my resignation as an associate justice of the Supreme Court which, with your approval, will be effective as of this date."

Nixon accepted his resignation with a curt, one-sentence reply.

Muhammed Kenyatta, a.k.a. Donald Jackson, moved to Mississippi from Pennsylvania in 1966 to work with the Child Development Group of Mississippi, one of several new community action groups brought into being as a result of the Civil Rights Act. After working with the organization for nearly two years, he left to enroll as a student at Tougaloo College.

In the 1960s, being a student at Tougaloo College was tantamount to waving a red flag in the face of the Sovereignty Commission and the FBI. Both agencies considered students at the college to be "subversives" because of their support of the civil rights and peace movements. By 1969, the FBI and the Sovereignty Commission both maintained "agitator" lists of individuals who were engaging in political activity not acceptable to President Nixon and Governor Williams. The Mississippi field office of the FBI incorporated its agitators list into the Cointelpro operation it was secretly conducting throughout the state.

Muhammed Kenyatta was one of their targets.

In April, the FBI forged a letter to Kenyatta on a letterhead used by the Tougaloo College Defense Committee. The letter notified Kenyatta that his conduct on campus was unacceptable, and he was warned that if he did not leave the campus local authorities would be contacted and measures less cordial than the written warning would be taken.

At about that same time, Robert Nichols, a white Jackson prosecutor, contacted the FBI regarding an investigation he was conducting on a community action group named the Jackson Human Rights Project. The Episcopal Church had asked Nichols for an investigation because it had agreed to make contributions to the group and, after paying one-third of the amount agreed upon, was having second thoughts. The church wanted Nichols to make sure the group was on the up and up. After exchanging information with the FBI, Nichols reported back to the church that he had discovered "extensive derogatory information" on two individuals associated with the group—Howard Spencer and Muhammed Kenyatta. As a result of his report, the church discontinued funding the group. Feeling himself to be discredited in the eyes of the student body because of the letter—and without a job because the church stopped funding the Jackson Human Rights Project—Kenyatta returned to Pennsylvania.

Not until 1975 did Kenyatta discover that he had been targeted by Cointelpro. He filed a lawsuit against three of the FBI agents assigned to the Jackson field office. In the course of the litigation, the FBI admitted that Kenyatta was on its agitators list and that he was a target of Cointelpro. FBI agents admitted forging the letter and they admitted supplying information to the city attorney. Kenyatta ultimately lost the lawsuit because he could not demonstrate to the court's satisfaction that the FBI's actions had damaged him. Kenyatta is now dead.

~~~~

In 1970 Mississippi was again in turmoil.

The year had begun with the refusal of the U.S. Supreme Court to hear the appeal for a new trial for those convicted of violating the civil rights of the three men murdered in Neshoba County. Five years after Schwerner, Chaney, and Goodman were killed, Sam Bowers and his six conspirators were taken off to prison. Mississippi could have prosecuted those men for murder, but declined to do so. Their only crime, in the state's eyes, was violating the civil rights of the murdered men. The murders themselves were inconsequential to the state.

Within three months of the final resolution of the Neshoba County case, all hell had broken loose on the campus of Jackson State College. Students at the historically black college were upset over the invasion of Cambodia by American troops, and they were upset over the escalating demands of the draft. Hadn't President Nixon been elected because he had a plan to end the war with honor? If that were true, asked the students, why was he expanding the war into Cambodia—and why were draft boards increasing the number of their call-up notices?

On May 14, after a series of protests against the war and several rock throwing incidents on the campus, Governor John Bell Williams ordered a call-up of the National Guard. But since the guardsmen would require most of the night to get to Jackson, Williams sent the highway patrol to the campus, where they joined a large force of city policemen.

Together, the highway patrolmen and the city policemen marched on the campus. Leading the way was a twenty-three-foot-long armored vehicle named Thompson's Tank (after a previous mayor). Inside the tank were ten men, armed with Thompson sub-machine guns and shotguns that were capable of launching tear-gas canisters. On the roof of the tank were two powerful spotlights. As the tank drove past the dormitories on the campus, it shined its spotlights along the walls and into the rooms. Walking beside the tank were officers armed with shotguns. Frightened women students peered out from the windows. Others shouted at the intruders: "Pigs! . . . Motherfuckers! . . . White sons-of-bitches!"

The tank and the army of shotgun-toting officers pulled up outside one of the dormitories and stopped. An officer in a white shirt tried to address the students with a bullhorn. The students were too upset to talk. A rumor had been circulating on campus that white policemen had murdered Charles Evers. His daughter, Sheila, was a student at Jackson State, and she had been unable to locate her father to find out if he was all right.

Suddenly, a bottle arced toward the tank and crashed onto the street, bursting into hundreds of tiny pieces. With that, the police officers opened fire. Students screamed and dived for cover. Shotgun pellets and machine-gun fire sprayed across the campus, mowing down students caught in the open, and ripping through the windows and walls of the dormitories.

When the firing stopped, police discovered that they had shot to death two students and wounded twelve others. Charles Evers was at the Chicago airport when several newsmen ran up to him, shouting that they had heard he was dead.

As they stood there—with Evers assuring them that he was alive—other newsmen ran over and started asking him questions about the killings at Jackson State. Evers was horrified. It was the first he had heard about the incident. He rushed to a phone and called home, reaching his daughter Sheila. She told him about what had happened and warned him not to return to Mississippi. "What happened at Jackson State College . . . was a case of students acting as students and Mississippi police acting as murderers," Evers wrote in his autobiography. "I've preached nonviolence because I don't think blacks can win the other way, but there comes a time when a man doesn't care anymore about winning."

The new attorney general, John Mitchell, asked J. Edgar Hoover to send extra FBI agents to Mississippi to investigate. They code-named the investigation "Jacktwo." Later, Mitchell went to the college campus to see for himself what had happened. As he looked at the broken windows in the dormitories and the bullet-riddled walls, he was overheard to say incredulously, "And only twelve were struck?"

When the FBI investigated the shooting, more than four hundred bullet holes were found in one dormitory alone, yet all the cartridges fired had disappeared from the scene. Immediately after the shooting, the Jackson mayor personally inspected the weapons of his police officers to determine if they were telling the truth that they had not fired any shots. He was not told that the spent ammunition already had been replaced. Not until a second grand jury investigated the shootings was there proof that the police and highway patrol had disposed of critical evidence.

After the killings, the spotlight of the nation was on Jackson State, just as ten days earlier it had been on Kent State University, where thirteen students had been struck down by gunfire from National Guard troops during a protest against the Vietnam War. In that incident four students were killed and nine were wounded.

In a telephone call with a White House aide, as reported by author Curt Gentry, Hoover gave his assessment of the killings: "The students invited and got what they deserved."

Not in agreement with that assessment were the parents of Allison Krause, one of the students killed at Kent State. In a letter written less than a month after the violent death of her daughter, Doris Krause, still grief-stricken over the loss, said, "I do not recognize the world any longer; it has changed beyond all nightmares."

When the President's Commission on Campus Unrest released its report in October, it accused the Jackson police and the highway patrol of "unreasonable" overreaction and suggested that the explanation given by police for the shooting was doubtful. Joseph Rhodes, the youngest member of the commission, said Mississippi was a police state, "ruled by terror."

Governor Williams denounced the commission, saying its members were biased, but, when the dust settled, it was Williams and the highway patrol who emerged victorious. The policemen responsible for the killings at Jackson State were never punished. The county grand jury said any action against the police would be "unjustified." The federal grand jury also refused to take action. No one in Mississippi was really surprised.

The federal grand jury investigation had been under the direction of that guardian of Southern culture, Judge Harold Cox, who instructed the jurors that people who engaged in civil disorder "must be expected to be injured or killed."

In April 1970, *Life* magazine published an exposé on Carlos Marcello. The magazine's investigative team, headed by David Chandler, reported on Marcello's operations in Louisiana in great detail, revealing his control of the Louisiana State Police and the district attorney's office.

Life pointed out that anyone who attempted to cross Marcello invariably got killed. For example, the magazine said that one of the state's most prominent syndicate gamblers, Harry Bennett, was shot to death by unknown killers in 1967 not long after some of Marcello's aides discovered he had met with federal prosecutors.

Sometime after that, said the magazine, one of Bennett's Gulf Coast partners, Donald James, was caught trying to swindle one of Marcello's associates out of $10,000. Marcello summoned the man to his office and ordered him to pay up immediately—or else. James paid up the next day, and Marcello put out word that he had paid up—*a day late*. Shortly after that, said the magazine, police found James's bullet-riddled body on the same spot where Bennett's body had been found two years earlier. Marcello never denied *Life*'s accusations.

In January 1972, Mississippi got a new governor—William L. "Bill" Waller, the man who twice unsuccessfully prosecuted Byron De La Beckwith for the murder of Medgar Evers. Most political observers considered his election victory a surprise.

The first Democratic primary, held in August 1971, had seven names on the ballot. In addition to Waller, it included Charles Sullivan, Jimmy Swan, Edwin Pittman, Roy Adams, Marshall Perry, and Andrew Sullivan. With the exception of Jimmy Swan, who worked racial innuendo into his campaign speeches whenever possible, most of the candidates avoided racial issues.

Charles Evers, who had planned to run as an independent in the general election, urged blacks to vote for Swan because he thought he would be an easier target in a two-way race. To the surprise of no one, Sullivan emerged from the first primary with an impressive lead. Coming in second was Waller. Going into the run-off primary, Waller was a decided underdog. Sullivan had name recognition across the state. Waller was well known in Jackson, the largest city in the state, but no one thought that—and the notoriety of the Beckwith trials—would be enough to enable him to beat an old political pro like Sullivan.

During the campaign, Waller surprised everyone by promising to appoint blacks to high-ranking positions in his administration. He was criticized for making overtures to black voters, who by 1971 made up nearly 30 percent of the electorate, but disenfranchised blacks had become a natural constituency for him after the Beckwith trials. He lost the trials, but blacks knew he tried, and that was important to them.

Waller handily defeated Sullivan in the run-off primary, then went on to defeat Charles Evers by a substantial margin in the general election. True to his word, he appointed blacks—for the first time in modern history—to high-ranking positions in departments dealing with prisons, education, and welfare.

Three blacks were hired for the highway patrol, which had no blacks on its staff of nearly four hundred officers. Cleve McDowell, who had made history by becoming the second black to enroll at Ole Miss, was appointed to the State Penitentiary Board. With Waller's help, he had made history again by becoming the first black to serve on the board.

As the prosecutor in the Beckwith case, Waller was aware of the Sovereignty Commission's interest in his activities, but today he says that to the best of his knowledge, "they didn't do anything."

"I never had an encounter where I was interviewed by the Sovereignty Commission or where they tried to influence me," Waller said. "Maybe my reputation was such they knew they couldn't."

After he took office as governor, Waller didn't make any changes in the Sovereignty Commission. Webb Burke was left in charge and his entire staff was left intact. Of course, the Commission got new members on its board by virtue of the election. Joining the board for the first time was the new lieutenant governor William Winter. The Commission was allowed to go about its business as usual. Waller was biding his time.

Mississippi senator James Eastland had his biggest year yet in 1972. It was the year he became president pro tempore of the Senate, which meant that he had filled the slot held years earlier by Senator McKellar of Memphis. This meant that if anything happened to President Nixon that prevented him from serving out his term of office—and Vice President Spiro Agnew became president—then Eastland would assume the duties of the vice president in the Senate.

That same year the mother of a Mississippi war resister met with Eastland in his plantation office in Doddsville. The meeting had been arranged after the woman had asked to meet with him about her son. The woman took her eighty-one-year-old father with her as a witness.

The woman told Eastland she had heard that the U.S. attorney was being selective in whom he did or did not prosecute. She talked to him about the growing movement in Congress for a declaration of amnesty for war resisters who had left the country. The woman, with the help of her father, stated her case, the whole time wondering if the senator—the third most powerful man in the United States government—had been drinking or if his bright-red face was always flushed that way. "Would it help if I got people to send you letters?" she asked.

Eastland seemed evasive. It was as if they were talking about two different things. The meeting made him restless. She wondered what was on his mind. Finally, he told her.

"It's going to take more than letters," he said.

"Oh," the woman responded.

After that, there was nothing else to say. The woman and the old man left the senator's plantation office confused about their conversation. On the trip back home, they drove in silence for the longest time. Then the woman looked at her father, her face reflecting the dawning recognition of what had transpired in the office.

"He was asking for a bribe," she said, astonished at the boldness of her words. "Did you see the way he looked when he said it?"

The old man smiled. He understood Mississippi politics as well as anyone. "You're right," he said. "I guess, if a few thousand dollars is what it will take, I'd be willing . . ."

Outraged, the woman interrupted him. "Why, we wouldn't do that!" she said, understanding, perhaps for the first time, why her son had left for Canada.

Governor Waller endured the Sovereignty Commission for almost a year and a half, then in the spring of 1973, without any advance warning, he pulled the plug on the secret agency. The legislature had passed a two-year appropriations bill for the Commission, as it had done without question since 1956, but when the bill arrived on Waller's desk he vetoed it. That meant the Commission would cease to exist on July 1, the date its current funding expired.

Director Webb Burke was surprised by the veto. He told reporters he was given no advance warning from the governor that funding would be terminated. "We will continue like we are until we hear something further from the governor," said Burke.

In a brief veto message, Waller said the work done by the Commission would be transferred to the highway patrol. "The Sovereignty Commission," he said, "performs no real indispensable services to the people of this state." The legislature was stunned by the veto, but did not try to override it. Contacted by reporters, Burke said: "I definitely don't think we've been utilized as a negative force . . . we've been accused of a lot of things we're not guilty of."

When the Commission's offices were closed, its extensive filing system was transferred to a storage area accessible to the highway patrol, which had the authority to use the files as it saw fit. The Commission itself may have been put out of business, but the business of the Commission was merely transferred to other hands.

In the summer of 1996, the author met with Waller in his Jackson law office to talk about the Commission. He was affable, friendly as one Ole Miss graduate is to another, but he was clearly uncomfortable talking about the secret agency. He seemed especially concerned about how the author's book would affect the state's image.

"When you get through with it, will you give me a chance to rebut any charges against it?" he asked. The author explained to Waller that he had nothing but praise for him and did not anticipate that there would be any-thing in the book he would feel personally compelled to rebut. As far as rebutting charges against the Commission, the author told him he did not feel it would be his place to defend an agency he single-handedly had destroyed.

"My opinion [of the Commission] was based from the outside and seeing them operate," said Waller. "I vetoed their appropriations because it was a joke. Certain politicians would use Burke to go out and get information secretly they could use in their campaign or for fund-raising. But as a state agency it had very limited activity and very indefinite goals and assignments."

Waller said he was not surprised the legislature did not try to override his veto. "There were maybe a half dozen ultraconservative legislators who wanted to keep it around as a personal tool," he said. "People have a way of getting even with a governor and sometimes after a veto they don't say anything, they just lay in ambush. But I never got any response [to the veto]. I got overridden on several of my vetoes, but not on that one."

Today, Waller downplays the significance of the Commission. "They were strictly an ideological censor group . . . a conservative watchdog cen-sorship group on the Keystone Kops level," he said. "They didn't really have any operations. They were more of a censors group. They were trying to find out who was on the liberal side of an issue and then making a record in their files." The only personal contact he had with the Commission, he said, was as a prosecutor. "One time Burke wanted to help me with a prosecution," he said. "I can't remember what it was related to. I got word that Burke had some information—it could have been for a grand jury investigation, a crime—I remember very well he brought his file into my office and opened it up and it was three or four newspaper clippings. He didn't have any evidence. He was a clipping service. He had interviewed no one. He didn't have any evidence."

At first, the author was troubled by Waller's subtle defense of the Com-mission. Why would the person who destroyed the Commission want to rebut anything negative said about it? The more the author talked with the former governor, the more he realized his reluctance to criticize the Com-mission—his willingness to downplay the seriousness of its missions—was based on that peculiar pride Mississippians have for their state and not an attempt to cover for the Commission. It was as if Waller were saying to the author, "I killed the Commission, what more do you want from me? It's gone—can't we just forget it ever existed?" You almost have to be a native-born Mississippian to understand how that form of denial works. It is unique to the "Magnolia State."

Before leaving Waller's office, the author decided to share some of his research findings with him, more out of respect than anything else. If the man who destroyed the Commission—and therefore deserves the gratitude of all Mississippians—was going to tell reporters that the agency was nothing more than a Keystone Kops operation, perhaps he needed more information, so as not to be embarrassed later. "Did you ever know the Commission opened a private bank account, one that would allow them to handle money without its going through the state auditor's office?" the author asked.

The former governor's face sank into a frown. "Why, no," he said, his voice lowering almost to a whisper. "Did they really?"

Less than three months after the demise of the Sovereignty Commission, Byron De La Beckwith reared his omnipresent head again, perhaps in reaction to the decision of his former nemesis to put an end to the secret agency.

In September 1973 the FBI office received a tip from one of its informants that Beckwith was planning to bomb the Anti-Defamation League headquarters in downtown New Orleans. For some mysterious reason, the FBI notified the local police and turned the case over to them. Eight days later, after a brief stop in Jackson where it was alleged he picked up the bomb, Beckwith was spotted by police on Highway 49 in his 1968 white-and-blue Oldsmobile 98.

Beckwith's route into New Orleans took him over the five-mile span across Lake Pontchartrain. When he reached the other side, the New Orleans police were waiting for him. It was a little after midnight when they pulled him over.

Beckwith got out of his car and was greeted by police officers who told him to put his hands on the hood of his car. One of the police officers patted him down and discovered a .45–caliber automatic tucked into his pants.

"You're under arrest for carrying a concealed weapon."

"I always carry a .45," Beckwith answered.

The police officer then shined his flashlight into Beckwith's car. On the front seat was a wooden box over which had been pulled a black bag. The officer asked Beckwith if he had ever been arrested. "Yes sir, I was arrested before," Beckwith said. "They say I killed a nigger in Mississippi."

When the bomb squad arrived and opened the box in Beckwith's car, they found six sticks of regular-strength dynamite and a five-pound cartridge of high-grade dynamite. Into the dynamite had been inserted a blasting cap. Connected to the blasting cap were a ticking alarm clock and an Eveready battery.

Beckwith was taken to the parish jail to await arraignment. As he was moved about the facility, reporters spotted him and shouted out questions to him.

"Are you a member of the KKK?" one reporter asked.

"I've been accused of it," he answered.

When Beckwith's case went to trial in January 1974, it was in federal court, and for the first time he faced a jury that contained blacks and women. Beckwith took the stand in his defense and admitted that the .45–caliber automatic belonged to him. He had a permit for it, he said. When prosecutors asked him about the bomb, he said he had never seen it before and had no idea how it got into his car.

The jury reached a unanimous verdict: not guilty on all counts.

Beckwith was delighted. He told reporters he was thinking about running for political office in Mississippi—maybe he'd try for a seat in Congress.

Not delighted by the verdict was New Orleans's new district attorney, Harry Connick (father of the popular singer of the same name). Beckwith left New Orleans, but he did not leave the thoughts of Harry Connick.

Connick brought his law partner, Bill Wessel, into the case and asked him to find a way to prosecute Beckwith on state charges. Under Louisiana law, persons accused of certain misdemeanors could be tried by a five-member jury. Beckwith was still accused of illegally transporting dynamite into Louisiana, a misdemeanor.

Finally, in May 1975, Beckwith went on trial in state court on the dynamite charges. This time, to his horror, the jury consisted of five black women. Beckwith was playful throughout the trial, sparring with the prosecutors, but the jury was not impressed. After deliberating only thirty-five minutes, the jury returned a guilty verdict.

Beckwith was given the maximum sentence—five years in prison.

After a two-year delay for appeals, he entered the Louisiana State penitentiary in Angola in 1977. He was kept in a solitary cell just off death row so that guards could protect him from the general population, a large percentage of which was black. In 1980, with two years of his sentence taken off for good behavior, Beckwith was released and allowed to return to Mississippi.

The Vietnam War ended in March 1973 with the withdrawal of the last American troops, but it ended badly, giving the United States its first overseas military defeat. By the summer of 1974 President Nixon was under siege as a result of revelations stemming from the Watergate break-in and cover-up. There was talk in Congress of impeachment action against the president and possible criminal prosecution for obstruction of justice.

A *Newsweek* poll published the first week in August showed 276 members of the House in favor of impeachment, with 59 undecided, and 99 leaning against. None of Mississippi's five congressmen was in favor of impeachment. Both Mississippi senators—James Eastland and John Stennis—stood behind the president. By then Gerald Ford had replaced Spiro Agnew as vice president—Agnew had resigned in October 1973 after pleading nolo contendere to felony charges—and the question was not so much whether Ford would become president as *when.*

Nixon resigned on August 9, 1974, less than two weeks after the U.S. Supreme Court ruled he must turn over secretly recorded White House tapes to prosecutors investigating crimes associated with Watergate. Shortly after becoming president, Gerald Ford issued a pardon to Nixon for any crimes he may have committed in office and he declared an amnesty for all Vietnam War–era draft-resisters who wished to return to the country and perform two years of alternative service. While Ford's pardon to Nixon made some people angry and some people happy, his amnesty plan made almost everyone angry and not too many happy.

Mississippi war-resisters had a somewhat different perspective. Most had been prepared to perform alternative service from the beginning, but that option had been denied them by the Sovereignty Commission and by draft boards who had targeted them because of their support of the civil rights and antiwar movements. Several returned to Mississippi, though most of the war-resisters affected by Ford's plan turned it down. Lying in wait for the war-resisters returning to Mississippi was the highway patrol, which had access to the Sovereignty Commission's secret files and had, in effect, picked up the fallen banner.

〜〜〜

By 1976, most of the men convicted in the Neshoba County case were out of prison. Many returned to the Meridian–Philadelphia area. Cecil Price started driving a truck for an oil company. Lawrence Rainey, who was acquitted, was unable to hold a job in law enforcement after the trial. When last heard from, he was working as a mall security guard. Sam Bowers returned to his hometown of Laurel and resumed his job with an amusement company. In a 1996 interview with the *Oxford American,* Bowers, now seventy-two, didn't discuss the Neshoba County case, but he did offer his perspective on Christianity.

"Well, there's nothing, really nothing, unique about my ideas," Bowers told writer Charles Marsh. "I'm a Pauline, Galilean, Calvinist, reformed Lutheran Christian. I believe that the empirical resurrection of Jesus Christ is the one single and central fact of manifested history."

Periodically, Mississippi officials were asked by reporters if the men were ever going to be tried by the state on charges of murder. Over the years, official reaction ranged from "We're looking into that" to a final admission that it was too late because "those files were lost a long time ago."

Early in 1977, the *Delta Democrat-Times* reported that two bills that would transfer ownership of the Sovereignty Commission files to the highway patrol had been prefiled for the upcoming legislative session. Although the highway patrol had had access to the files since the Commission office was shut down in 1973, the two lawmakers who filed the bills—Gulf Coast representatives Dennis Dollar and Glenn Endris—said they felt ownership of the files should be formalized.

When the legislature convened in January, the Dollar and Endris bills spurred a passionate debate over what to do about the Commission—technically it could be revived any time the governor signed a new appropriation by the legislature. Mississippi had a new governor in 1977—Cliff Finch, a bulldozer-driving attorney from Batesville who was elected in 1975 by a self-described "Redneck–Blackneck coalition." In some ways, Finch was a loose cannon his first year in office, an unpredictable administrator who never seemed in touch with the reality of government.

Clearly, it was time to do something with the Commission files. Everyone seemed to agree that the Commission should be abolished. The disagreement arose over what to do with the files. The bills sponsored by Dollar and Endris were killed. No one wanted the files officially to be turned over to the highway patrol, although everyone knew that the agency already had made copies of any files it wanted to keep. Many legislators wanted to destroy the files. Others said they should be preserved.

Among those wanting to see the files preserved were the state's black legislators. Said black lawmaker Horace Buckley: "I thought all the book burning and manuscript burning ended in the 12th century. By your vote to burn those files you are, in my opinion, condemning those people you have worked with." Another black lawmaker, Doug Anderson, said: "If there is evil in those files, we should keep them to learn a lesson."

Former lieutenant governor William Winter also went on record as being opposed to the destruction of the files. When the author interviewed Winter in 1996, he said he had not changed his mind about preserving the files. "My concern is the same as that expressed by [others] that, however the records are handled, they should be handled with a sensitivity to the innocent individuals who may be included in the files," he said.

By the time the dust settled from the 1977 session, the legislature had voted to abolish the Commission and to preserve the files. But there was a catch: the files were ordered sealed for fifty years. Governor Finch signed the bill in March, and the files—six filing cabinets containing thousands of names—were sealed and delivered to the Department of Archives and History.

Sitting in the legislature when the vote was taken was Representative George Rogers. He had seen the Sovereignty Commission come full cycle. "I voted to seal those records," said Rogers. "I knew there was a lot of junk in there, investigative reports that could damage people's reputations. The press wanted to make them public. I voted to seal them, not because I didn't want people to know, but because I was concerned about what was in the files."

Shortly after that vote was taken—and the files were sealed—Rogers resigned from the legislature to work for the Central Intelligence Agency, and the American Civil Liberties Union filed suit in federal court to have the files opened. The lawsuit ended up in the courtroom of Judge Harold Cox, who promptly dismissed the case. The ACLU appealed and won. The lawsuit was reinstated by the appeals court.

"We agreed to take the case . . . to give victims a chance to sue for damages and to see what actions were taken by the government to promote segregation," said David Ingebretesen, director of the Mississippi office of the ACLU. "Our position was that the files should be opened. The state was opposed to opening any files at all. There is damaging information about state officials. Damaging information about prominent individuals. Damaging information on people who had relatively clean records [on the surface]."

That fall, the ACLU filed a motion to take the deposition of Elbert Hilliard, director of the Mississippi Department of History and Archives, the keeper of the files. Hilliard was provided with a list of sixty-six names and asked to identify which of those individuals named had been the target of files kept by the Commission. Included on the list were Hodding Carter III, Claude Ramsey, head of the state AFL-CIO, Bennie Thompson, and other leaders in the civil rights movement. When Hilliard responded to the court order, it was revealed that Carter, Ramsey, and Thompson all had files, as did thirty-three other people named on the list.

Despite the publicity, Carlos Marcello thrived, as did his organization. By the end of the decade, he was again under FBI scrutiny, only this time federal agents were successful in planting electronic surveillance devices in his private office. By then, New Orleans had a black mayor, Ernest Morial. In 1979, a secretly recorded conversation between Marcello and an undercover agent for the FBI revealed Marcello's continuing hatred of African Americans.

"The mayor's a nigger here," said Marcello. "He's black. . . . He wants to do it on his own . . . . He's a nigger, and a nigger's gonna be a nigger even if you give him some authority."

"How come you elected a nigger mayor?" the agent asked.

"Cause these assholes went to sleep."

Marcello didn't know it then, but he was headed for a fall.

CHAPTER 10

1980 – 1989

In October 1980, the Mississippi attorney general's office asked the federal appeals court to dismiss the Sovereignty Commission lawsuit brought against the state by the American Civil Liberties Union. Assistant Attorney General J. Stephen Wright argued that the state officials named as defendants in the lawsuit were no longer in office.

Jack D. Novik, an ACLU lawyer from New York, argued that the work done by the Commission had been parceled out to other agencies after the Commission was abolished and might still be going on.

The ACLU won that round, and the case was allowed to go forward.

Working in favor of the ACLU was the 1979 election of William Winter to the governor's office. As lieutenant governor, Winter had argued for preserving the files. Although the state attorney general was elected by popular vote—and not appointed by the governor—it was helpful to the ACLU's cause to have a governor who was not opposed to its efforts. Winter was no wild-eyed liberal; he was a serious-minded historian, a former editor of the Ole Miss *Mississippian,* and he did have a strong personal sense of justice.

Mississippi politics had changed radically by the 1980s.

The 1980 roster of the legislature reflected that change. Fifteen of the House's 122 members were black, and 1 of the state's 52 senators was black. That doesn't sound significant by today's standards, but for a state emerging from the racial horrors inflicted in the 1960s and 1970s by governors such as Ross Barnett, John Bell Williams, and Paul B. Johnson, it seemed nothing short of a miracle.

There was only one woman in the legislature in 1980: Representative Betty Jane Long of Meridian, one of the only four remaining legislators who had served on the Sovereignty Commission. Racial politics had changed the playing field for the legislature, from one that raised questions about whether blacks should be allowed equal rights to one that raised questions about how the economic pie should be sliced.

The fact that the Sovereignty Commission was no longer in operation did not mean that its work was not being carried out. The same dark forces that had supported the Commission from its inception were still in place. Nothing had changed. If money, not race, was the issue in the beginning, it was still the issue. The ACLU lawyer was right: Just because you could no longer see the Commission did not mean it did not exist.

With the official demise of the Sovereignty Commission, the Federation for Constitutional Government had gone underground—and stayed there. Carlos Marcello was still the anchor in Louisiana and south Mississippi. The Memphis cartel was still calling the shots in Tennessee and northern Mississippi. The region's underworld families sought political solace wherever they could find it.

Keeping pace with the political changes in the mid-South were the region's newspapers, which underwent a radical shake-up in the early 1980s. On the surface those changes were heralded as little more than routine changes in ownership. But that was only part of the story. In Jackson, the friendly editorial competition in the daily press between Jimmy Ward and Tom Hederman's nephew, Rea Hederman, continued throughout 1980 and 1981. Ward was feeling increasingly threatened by Rea's liberal encroachments and his growing power base within the Hederman family. The news division of the *Jackson Daily News* was thriving under managing editor Robert Gordon's leadership, and whether by design or default, the editorial pages were Ward's last stand against the new order.

It was Hodding Carter III who had begun the newspaper shake-ups, when in January 1980 he and his family sold the *Delta Democrat-Times* to the conservative, California-based Freedom Newspaper chain. It marked the end of an era. Mississippi's only newspaper with a moderate to liberal philosophy was gone in the blink of an eye.

The *Delta Democrat-Times* sale was just the first jolt of several.

In 1982, the Hedermans announced the sale of the *Clarion-Ledger* and the *Jackson Daily News*—as well as six Mississippi weeklies—to the Gannett Company. In December, Rea Hederman and other family members purchased the *New York Review of Books* for a reported five million dollars. Rea moved to New York, where he began a new life.

In January 1984 Jimmy Ward, who had been ailing with throat cancer for several years, retired on his sixty-fifth birthday, completing twenty-six years as editor of the *Jackson Daily News*. A farewell to Ward, published in the Sunday joint-edition of the *Clarion-Ledger–Jackson Daily News* was headlined: "Fiery editor's retirement ends an era." Five weeks later Ward was dead. The following year, almost to the day, Tom Hederman died at the age of seventy-three. It truly was the end of an era.

Gannett put Charles Overby, the former Ole Miss student editor, in charge of both newspapers. At the time, no one was quite sure what that meant, only that the state's newspaper balance of power had been altered. But Overby was more of a transition editor than anything else and didn't remain at the helm for long. Soon he was transferred to other newspapers, and by 1996 he had been appointed chairman and CEO of The Freedom Forum, a foundation established by the Gannett newspaper chain to promote free-speech issues.

By mid-decade Gannett's Mississippi strategy became apparent when it suspended publication of the *Jackson Daily News,* making the *Clarion-Ledger* its flagship daily in the state.

Changes in Mississippi journalism were mirrored in Memphis. From the day organized crime appeared in Memphis, it had been attacked by both *The Commercial Appeal* and the *Memphis Press-Scimitar.* Of the two newspapers, it was usually the *Memphis Press-Scimitar* that was the more aggressive. In October 1983, to the surprise of everyone, Scripps-Howard, which owned both newspapers, abruptly ceased publication of the *Memphis Press-Scimitar.* Overnight, Memphis had become a one-newspaper town.

Within the space of two years, the remnants of the Sovereignty Commission had witnessed its two biggest supporters—the *Clarion-Ledger* and the *Jackson Daily News*—change hands, then watched as the latter died a slow death. And the Memphis cartel had seen its biggest foe, the *Memphis Press-Scimitar,* shrivel up and disappear. That left only *The Commercial Appeal* in place as an adversary, and, by 1985, with the forced retirement of tough-as-nails editor Michael Grehl, there were signs that the newspaper's opposition to organized crime was cracking.

On April 7, 1982, *The Commercial Appeal* ran an obituary editorial on Abe Fortas, who had died the day before of a heart attack at the age of seventy-two. The editorial, written by Scripps-Howard staffers in Washington and not the local staff, made no mention of the fact that Fortas was a son of Memphis.

The editorial politely blamed his resignation from the Supreme Court on a "lack of discretion," and went on to praise his court decisions upholding the rights of criminals. It was a low-key, and uninformed to the point of awkwardness, send-off to a man who had had a profound impact on the course of American history. The last years of Fortas's life were a nightmare for him. His old law firm, Arnold and Porter—the one Fortas had helped build from scratch—refused to take him back as a partner. Feeling he was soiled goods, his old friends had abandoned him. His Memphis associates had no use for him whatsoever after his fall from power.

Fortas's last major foray into the public arena came in December 1969 when he spoke at the National Press Club—despite his deep hatred of the media, the media seemed always eager to embrace him—and launched a blistering attack on President Nixon's war on crime. In particular, Fortas voiced concern that Nixon planned to "unshackle the police" with preventive detention of suspects and use of the so-called no-knock provision that would allow warrant-armed police to enter premises unannounced to search for drugs.

To the reporters present, it seemed Fortas was upholding the liberal tradition. To those who knew him better, who knew of his past and his Memphis associations, his attacks against increased police powers took on an entirely different meaning.

In 1970 Fortas formed a Washington law firm with a Chicago lawyer named Howard R. Koven, and they set up offices in Georgetown, near Fortas's home. Fortas told the *Washington Post* it was his intention to "enjoy life, do some good and have some fun."

In 1977, just when it seemed that Fortas was regaining his public equilibrium, *Washington Post* reporter Bob Woodward obtained a transcript of a conversation Fortas had with Louis Wolfson just after Wolfson's release from prison. Fortas had asked for the meeting with Wolfson when he learned that Wolfson had scheduled a press conference to discuss his case. Fortas urged Wolfson not to release copies of the letters they had exchanged and asked if he could rewrite Wolfson's press release.

According to the transcript, Fortas said the release of the letters would be "very bad" for him: "If you release those, I tell you that you will inadvertently and unwittingly be doing me harm. . . . Things are quiet now and I have reached a point where I think I can resume my life." Fortas's attempt to control Wolfson's press conference only got him into deeper trouble when Woodward, in a front-page story, reported on the meeting between the two men and quoted from the transcript of their conversation.

Ironically, Fortas won his last legal battle, although he didn't live long enough to know it. In March 1982, Fortas returned to the august halls of the

Supreme Court to argue on behalf of a client. Puerto Rico's two major political parties were embroiled in a dispute over how vacancies in the island's legislature should be filled following the death of a sitting member. Fortas presented his argument to the high court, then two weeks later—before the court's decision was announced—he died of a burst aortic valve.

Not so lucky with his legal battles was Carlos Marcello.

By 1979, the year FBI wiretaps recorded his conversations about New Orleans's first black mayor, Marcello's long-running battle against the federal government's deportation order was still in the courts. It had become the longest and costliest deportation case in American history.

Although it was not in the cards for Marcello to be deported, the case did indirectly lead to his downfall. It began in 1979 with a newspaper column written by Jack Anderson. To Marcello's surprise, the column, which was carried by the New Orleans *Times-Picayune* in July 1979, identified him as "the most powerful mobster in the nation." It also said that he was the House Assassinations Committee's "chief suspect in the John F. Kennedy assassination plot."

Jack Anderson was the least of Marcello's problems.

By 1980, the leader of the Dixie Mafia had been ensnared in a federal probe named "Brilab," an acronym for bribery and labor. Marcello's problems had begun with an attempt to influence an Immigration official and ended with charges he attempted to bribe a federal judge who was about to preside over a racketeering and extortion case involving some of his associates.

This time Marcello's luck abandoned him and he was convicted. On April 19, 1983, he entered a federal penitentiary in Texarkana, Texas, to begin serving a ten-year sentence. After serving almost six years there, only a few hours' drive from Memphis, he was transferred in 1989 to a federal prison in Rochester, Minnesota. That October, with time off for good behavior, the seventy-nine-year-old Marcello was released and allowed to return to Louisiana. He died in 1994.

Marcello's conviction sent shock waves radiating up from New Orleans, through Mississippi, and into Memphis, and from there to every Cosa Nostra outpost in the country. As Anderson had pointed out, Marcello was the single most powerful don in America. His departure brought about major changes in the criminal underworld.

When Marcello went to prison, his financial empire—and by then he had acquired an impressive collection of legitimate businesses—was transferred to his brothers, who, by all reports, took over operation of those businesses without getting involved in his underworld activities. The Dixie Mafia was left to fend for itself.

Mississippi politics took a bizarre turn in the mid-1980s when Bill Allain, the Democratic candidate for governor, was accused of being homosexual. Two weeks before the 1983 general election, supporters of Republican candidate Leon Bramlett leveled charges that Allain had had relations with a transvestite prostitute.

At that time, Allain was 20 to 30 percentage points ahead of Bramlett in the opinion polls. After the charges were made, Allain's popularity plummeted to the point where the two candidates were running neck-to-neck. Allain denied the allegations.

Bramlett challenged him to take a lie detector test—and he did, releasing results that showed he was telling the truth when he said he was not homosexual. Two days before the election, *The Commercial Appeal* urged voters to make up their minds using information they had received before the homosexual charges were made. "Not only has the gubernatorial race between Allain and his Republican opponent, Leon Bramlett, proved to be the dirtiest in the state's history, it has proved to be a textbook example of how vulnerable free elections can be to the manipulations of unprincipled men and women," said the editorial.

Allain won the election, rumors and all, proving once again the fiercely independent nature of Mississippi voters. The election also proved the strength of *The Commercial Appeal* with voters in north Mississippi. Not since the *Memphis Commercial* was consolidated with *The Appeal* in 1894 had the newspaper made endorsements in Mississippi elections.

Interestingly, Judge J.P. Coleman had been courted by Democrats in 1983 to leave his position on the Fifth Circuit Court of Appeals to run against Bill Allain for governor. He declined, citing his age, seventy, and the declining health of his wife, Margaret.

Throughout the 1970s, Coleman headed a three-judge panel that handled Mississippi's decade-long battle with civil rights lawyers and the Justice Department over reapportionment of the legislature. For the most part, Coleman fought against efforts to force the state into single-member districts to increase the chances of blacks to win office. It was a battle Coleman and his colleagues lost in 1979, which is the reason the 1980 legislature had sixteen black members, an increase of thirteen over the previous session.

Tired and in failing health, Coleman retired from the bench in 1984. In a tribute, Chief Judge Charles Clark said he and his colleagues on the bench would "miss him sorely." Coleman died on September 29, 1991, of complications from a stroke he suffered the previous year.

Also dropping to the wayside was Senator James Eastland, who had surprised everyone in 1978 by not running for reelection. His seat was won by Republican Thad Cochran, the current incumbent. The second Senate seat was occupied by veteran Senator John Stennis, thus giving Mississippi a Republican and a Democrat in the U.S. Senate. Republican upstart Trent Lott had his eye on Stennis's seat, and won it upon the senator's retirement, over John Hampton Stennis, the senator's son. Today Lott is the Republican majority leader in the Senate.

Although segregation was not a battle call for new leaders like Lott and Cochran, it was still very much alive as an issue in the 1980s, as demonstrated by a 1982 interview with Citizens' Council director William Simmons. The interview, conducted by United Press International, quoted Simmons as saying the race war in Mississippi was still raging. "If segregationists today are more discreet, it's a matter of survival," he said. "A fear of the power of the government has silenced them. But there's a deep and widespread resistance still."

Simmons said he still worked full-time for the cause. "I don't think it's a lost cause any more than the ministers of the gospel would think that because everyone's not a Christian theirs is a lost cause," he said. "If I believe in something, I believe in it, period."

In 1989 James Earl Ray got the worst news of his two-decade-long legal quest when the Supreme Court denied his application for a trial on the grounds that his Sixth Amendment rights had not been violated. "Why, if official America is so firmly convinced that I pulled the trigger of the rifle that killed Martin Luther King, is there so much reluctance to allow me to have a trial and fully air the evidence?" Ray wrote in his 1992 book. "Instead of letting this cloud hang over the assassination, and over me, why not allow twelve citizens on a jury to decide, once and for all, whether I am guilty of killing Martin Luther King?"

To his attorney, William Pepper, the answer was simple: "Cover-up."

~~~~~

On July 27, 1989, Judge William Barbour ruled that the Sovereignty Commission files must be opened to the public. The ruling, which found for the plaintiffs—the ACLU, the Reverend Ed King, Ken Lawrence, Rims Barber, and others—sent shock waves across the state.

"This court finds that the state of Mississippi acted directly through its state Sovereignty Commission and through conspiracy with private individuals to deprive the plaintiffs of rights protected by the Constitution to free speech and association, to personal privacy, and to lawful search and seizure, and statutes of the United States," he said in the ruling. "Deprivations were accomplished through unlawful investigations and through intentional actions designed to harass and stigmatize individuals and organizations engaged in speech and conduct protected by the United States Constitution. The targets of Commission activity were designated by members and agents of the Commission. There is no record that a search warrant or any other judicial sanction of Commission acts was either sought or received. The avowed intent of the Commission and its co-conspirators was to chill or preclude the plaintiffs from speech, assembly, association, and the petition of government."

Additionally, Barbour ruled that the law passed by the legislature in 1977 sealing the records was unconstitutional, and he permanently barred the state from enforcing a law making disclosure of the records a crime. Barbour's decision did not mean the long ordeal was over: The state could appeal the decision and keep the matter in the courts almost indefinitely.

In 1989, the governor was Ray Mabus, who was well into the second year of his term. As state auditor, he had attracted considerable attention in his efforts to ferret out corruption in government. He had entered Ole Miss well after the trauma of the riots and, like many other Dixie Baby Boomers, had found that entire era of segregation an embarrassment and a moral travesty.

After Barbour's decision was made public, Mabus announced that he was opposed to appealing the decision. The governor's office would not stand in the way of those who wanted to open the files. Ray Mabus was no Ross Barnett. That left one remaining hurdle: Attorney General Mike Moore.

David Ingebretesen, director of the Mississippi ACLU, requested a personal meeting with Moore. "[The issue] obviously didn't engage him at all," says Ingebretesen. "He said, 'That's all that Sixties stuff isn't it?' I said, 'Yeah, that's what it is'—and that's what changed the state's position. The state's leaders had no vested interest in protecting what was in the files. That was important to us [that the state didn't appeal] because it allowed us to move ahead."

With the state of Mississippi terminating its fight against making the contents of the files public, all that remained was agreeing on a procedure for opening the files. To the surprise of Ingebretesen, and nearly everyone else associated with the case, two of the plaintiffs, the Reverend Ed King and John Salter, filed an appeal with the Fifth Circuit Court of Appeals asking that Barbour's order be overturned.

King and Salter said they were concerned about the privacy of the individuals listed in the files. Opening the files without some kind of safeguards similar to those attached to information released under the Freedom of

Information Act, they argued, would only compound the damages suffered by the individuals targeted by the Commission.

David Goldstein, the New York attorney who filed the appeal, based his argument on the belief that the files contained substantial amounts of information of a "highly sensitive intimate personal" nature and "the most vicious sort of rumors and gossip." Basically, Goldstein argued that the files should not be open to the public, only to those whose names were in the files.

Ingebretesen was stunned by the appeal. "I think [King] is very sincere in what he is doing [but] . . . I think he's very wrong here," he said. The appeal meant that two of the primary critics of the Commission had become, almost overnight, its only remaining defenders. To those involved in the case, it was the latest of many mysterious twists and turns.

Shirley Payne, the ACLU lawyer handling the case, was not optimistic of an early resolution. "It still may be many years before members of the general public or victims of the espionage agency can have a look at what the files contain," she told reporters.

⌁

James Earl Ray was not the only accused assassin having problems as the decade ended. Byron De La Beckwith was again in the spotlight as Hinds County District Attorney Ed Peters reopened the Medgar Evers murder case in 1989.

Peters's decision to reopen the case came as a result of news reports that the Sovereignty Commission had screened potential jurors for Beckwith's second trial. Peters asked U.S. District Judge William H. Barbour for permission to review the sealed files to determine if jury tampering had taken place. Barbour denied his request.

"The decision of the district attorney as to whether to try Beckwith again should be based on whether he thinks the evidence available to him at this time is sufficient to obtain a conviction," wrote Barbour in his opinion. Besides, he said, evidence of jury tampering would not be admissible in any new murder trial.

Assistant District Attorney Bobby DeLaughter told reporters he was disappointed in the judge's decision, but said, "There are other ways we can gather information [on possible jury tampering] and we'll be continuing to do that."

CHAPTER 11

1990 – 1998

Byron De La Beckwith led a quiet life after his release from the Louisiana prison in 1980. Unable to find a job and penniless, he returned to Mississippi, where he set up housekeeping in a house trailer near Cruger, a rural community not far from Greenwood.

Beckwith tried to fade into the kudzu-smothered woodland that surrounded his house trailer, but occasionally a newspaper reporter would get directions to his home and, much to Beckwith's displeasure, show up on his doorstep unannounced. He always turned them away.

One of the last to knock on his door was a young *Jackson Daily News* reporter named Jim Ewing. As a representative of one of the most conservative dailies in the South, Ewing was hopeful that if anyone could get an interview with the reclusive Beckwith, he would be the one. He was wrong. Beckwith politely turned him away, saying he was afraid he would be misquoted by the "Jewish owned press."

Ewing wrote a story anyway, to mark the twentieth anniversary of Medgar Evers's death. The headline was "Byron De La Beckwith Lives Quietly in the Delta."

Shortly after that encounter with Ewing, Beckwith moved to Tennessee and married Thelma Neff, a retired nurse he had met after his release from prison. She owned a small house on Signal Mountain just outside Chattanooga. When Beckwith moved in, he hung a large Confederate flag out over the porch. It is not surprising that Thelma, who led a rather routine life as a nurse and mother, shared Beckwith's right-wing views on race and politics.

Generally speaking, rural Tennessee either leans to the radical right or to the radical left, with not much ground left in the middle. Thelma leaned to the radical right.

What is quite amazing, at least from a historical perspective, is the fact that Thelma, as a young woman, had dated Senator Estes Kefauver. Of all the political figures who had paraded in and out of prominence over the past half century in the South, only Kefauver had gone on the offensive against the tri-state federation, organized crime, segregationists, and others of that ilk—and Thelma had been his sweetheart!

As the decade wore on, the Beckwiths shared their love of political activism by working together on an assortment of issues, such as campaigning to get fluoride out of the local water supply. Occasionally, they returned to Mississippi, where he introduced her to his friends—and at least one of his former enemies, Bill Waller, whom he happened upon at a campaign rally in Blackhawk. Beckwith flagged down the startled candidate for governor and introduced him to Thelma. They even shook hands.

The Beckwiths returned to Signal Mountain and finished out the decade, convinced they were making progress in their quest to elevate Beckwith to the historical place of honor they felt he deserved. Unknown to the Beckwiths, Hinds County District Attorney Ed Peters and his assistant Bobby DeLaughter were looking for ways around their failed attempt to gain access to the Sovereignty Commission files.

As the new decade began, the missing pieces to the Medgar Evers puzzle fell into the laps of Peters and DeLaughter, piece by piece. First, Delmar Dennis, a former FBI informant, confirmed he had heard Beckwith say that killing Evers "gave me no more inner discomfort than our wives endure when they give birth to our children." Second, Evers's wife, Myrlie, presented the prosecutors with the 963–page transcript of Beckwith's first trial. The transcripts had mysteriously disappeared from the court records, and the lack of a transcript had often been cited by prosecutors as a reason for not reopening the case.

With transcript in hand, and new evidence to cite as a reason for a third trial, Peters went to the Hinds County grand jury and asked for an indictment charging Beckwith with the murder of Medgar Evers. The new evidence was based on the testimony of two black men who said they saw Beckwith at the church Evers visited a few hours before his murder. The indictment was handed down on December 14, 1990.

A stunned Beckwith, now seventy, said he would fight extradition to Mississippi. Thelma told reporters he was too ill to withstand another trial. As if to reinforce that point, Beckwith entered a Nashville hospital within a week after the indictment and underwent surgery to clear a blocked carotid artery.

"He's been a good man all his life—I'm so mad," Thelma told reporters for the *Clarion-Ledger.* "He's been through hell. He's done more good than any fifty people I know. He's a good Christian and everybody loves him."

Not so sure of that was Mississippi governor Ray Mabus, who signed an extradition request within hours of receiving it and sent it by overnight delivery to Tennessee governor Ned McWherter. Although McWherter approved the request in quick order, Beckwith challenged the extradition, first in state court, then in federal court, and it was not until October 1991 that Beckwith was returned to Mississippi, where he was held in the Hinds County Detention Center without bail.

Not until January 1994 did Beckwith go on trial.

First Beckwith, with Thelma at his side, went to Batesville, where a jury was picked. Then they returned to Jackson for the actual trial. It was an unusual scenario, but the presiding judge, L. Breland Hilburn, felt the odds of finding an impartial jury were better in Batesville, a small town on Interstate 55 about an hour's drive from Memphis. They selected the jurors, eight blacks and four whites, and then bused them to Jackson, a drive of nearly three hours.

Beckwith didn't testify at the trial. He was seventy-three and in failing health. His attorneys said his memory was not strong enough to allow him to testify. The trial, which lasted less than a month, was filled with emotion but offered few surprises.

One of the biggest surprises was the addition of the Reverend Ed King's name to the defense witness list. King was never called to testify, but the fact that the man who was fighting to keep Commission files secret was linked to Beckwith through a witness list was enough to send a wave of gossip through the courthouse. According to King, the reason he was on the witness list was that he was at the church on the day Beckwith was alleged to have been there—and he had not seen him there. When King heard an account of the grand jury testimony, he was horrified to realize, as he told the author in 1996, that the white man in the church identified as Beckwith was really himself.

When the twelve jurors lined up in front of the judge and announced their verdict—guilty—Beckwith showed no emotion, but Evers's widow, Myrlie, and two of their children cheered and embraced in the courtroom. Reporters described a "roar" that thundered from spectators in a hallway outside the courtroom. In a room set aside for media interviews, Myrlie said, "All I want to say is yea, Medgar, yea!" To *Clarion-Ledger* reporter Jerry Mitchell, she said of Beckwith, "I don't have to say accused assassin anymore."

As Beckwith was led out of the courtroom, Thelma sat quietly and watched, wiping away tears. "He's not guilty and they know it," she sobbed. "He's sick and everything."

Beckwith's attorneys appealed the conviction, but the courts refused to allow him out on bail. Thelma blamed the Anti-Defamation League for her husband's woes, saying the group had framed him in the Louisiana bomb conviction, but Special Assistant Attorney General Pat Flynn blames Beckwith's woes on the fact that the *Clarion-Ledger* had reported on the Sovereignty Commission's involvement in his earlier trial. Said Flynn in a motion filed with the state supreme court, "Beckwith would probably have gotten away with his crime entirely if the contents of the Sovereignty Commission files had not become knowledge years later."

Ed King told the author that although he thinks Beckwith is a "despicable sicko" and is guilty of murdering his friend Medgar Evers, he does not feel Beckwith got a fair trial, because of grand jury testimony he considers incorrect.

By early 1997, Beckwith was still in the county detention center and his appeal was still before the state supreme court. He has had several strokes since the trial, leaving his speech slurred and his vision impaired. His son, Byron De La Beckwith VII, told reporters that he thinks others will be implicated in the Medgar Evers murder once the Sovereignty Commission files are unsealed.

"There are people that have framed him and have used him, and there's proof that they have lied, and the courts won't do anything about it," said the younger Beckwith. "I really believe if they would open the thing, they would find out there was a conspiracy."

Beckwith's appeal with the state Supreme Court was denied late in 1997.

In January 1990 the *Clarion-Ledger* ran a series of articles on the Sovereignty Commission. The articles, written by reporters Jerry Mitchell, Michael Rejebian, and Beverly Pettigrew Kraft, effectively allowed the newspaper—for the first time—to capture the mantle of moral leadership in mid-state affairs from the foundering leadership of *The Commercial Appeal* in Memphis. The articles were bolstered by editorials from editorial page director David Hampton, who had worked as a political writer and columnist for the *Jackson Daily News* under Jimmy Ward's editorship.

Hampton was never attuned to Ward's right-wing politics and his columns, even while Ward was still editor, addressed issues from a more moderate perspective. Acknowledging the wrongdoing of the newspaper's involvement with the Commission during the previous decades, Hampton's anti-Commission editorials and a series of solid news articles gave Mississippi readers their first comprehensive glimpse into the machinations of the spy agency.

Interestingly, the public debate about the Commission seemed to intensify the efforts of Ed King and John Salter to keep the files closed. In September 1990 the Fifth Circuit Court of Appeals reversed Judge Barbour's ruling ordering full disclosure and gave him a choice of removing names and identifying information pertaining to people who are not named—or removing names only.

It became apparent throughout 1990 to the end of 1993 that it was former civil rights activists themselves, and not the state, who were most interested in blocking public access to the files. As a result, Ed King and John Salter came under intense criticism from former friends who felt they had sold out.

"Ed has been a friend for thirty years—and I can't turn my back on him—but he has gone off the deep end on this one and I don't understand it," said longtime activist Rims Barber, himself a plaintiff in the case. "I've tried to sit down with the man to see if we could come down to some reasonable accommodation."

King has told reporters the criticism from former friends "hurts."

"I have been damned as a white racist, as a paid agent of the state, as one who has accepted financial bribes," King told reporters. "The smears and attacks have been an important part of the way this case was waged."

Barber said court documents indicate there are over one hundred references to himself in the Commission files. "You've got to open the files and have names—otherwise it's a piece of fiction," he said. "The question is, do you want [the files] to be fiction or nonfiction?"

In September 1993, as hearings over how the files would be opened continued, Judge Barbour kept his focus on the end result. "It's not an issue of whether the files will be open," he said during one hearing. "The questions are: when and to what extent."

That same year, the first year of President Bill Clinton's administration, the Justice Department and the FBI showed renewed interest in the files. For reasons that have yet to be explained, someone at the upper levels of the Justice Department devised a plan to enable the FBI to gain access to the sealed files. That was accomplished by asking a federal judge in Washington, who was hearing a judicial redistricting case, to issue a court order allowing the FBI access to the Mississippi files on the grounds that they might contain information applicable to the case.

H.T. Holmes, director of the archives and library division of the Mississippi Department of Archives and History, is today the actual custodian of the sealed files. He was not in charge of the files in 1993, but he was employed in the archives in 1993 and was there when the Justice Department and the FBI arrived to inspect them. A portion of the building was set aside for them to work in and they were given full access to the files.

"We had someone with them at all times," Holmes said. "They were never left unsupervised." They were allowed to make photocopies of the documents, he said, and "left with a box of copies." When the author interviewed Holmes in 1996 and asked if he thought it was possible they could have taken original documents from the archives, Holmes wasn't certain. "I've never thought about it," he said. "That's the first time that question has been raised."

ACLU director David Ingebretesen is concerned about the integrity of the files, but he is confident that if the Justice Department and the FBI removed anything he would be able to detect the missing files. "By then Ken Lawrence [one of the original plaintiffs] had read everything in there," he said, referring to the fact that in the early stages of the court case representatives of both the plaintiffs and the state were allowed total access to the files. "If anything is missing we will be able to find it. He cataloged [everything in the files]."

As the debate over what would be opened continued, Mississippi attorney general Mike Moore entered the case on the side of King and Salter, asking the judge to declare the files sealed until opened by the individuals named in the files. The ACLU opposed that approach since it would allow guilty parties a veto over information in the files about themselves.

"The ACLU nationally takes the position documents about an individual should remain private unless that individual gives consent," said a spokesperson. "It's the position of this affiliate that the situation involving the Sovereignty Commission was so severe and of such long-lasting impact on events here, that the only way we can move forward is to know finally what's in the files, what the state did and to whom."

In May 1994, four years after ordering the files opened, Judge William Barbour issued a ruling on how the files would be opened. It was a victory for the ACLU and those who had argued for full disclosure.

Barbour ruled that individuals named in the files would fall under one of two categories, victims or state actors. There would be no separate category for public officials. Victims should have a say in how—or whether—their files are opened, he ruled. He defined "victims" as anyone who was subject to "investigation, surveillance, intrusions or the dissemination of false and misleading information."

State actors—those who worked for the state as public officials, employees, or informants—would have no such rights because "those persons were responsible for violating the constitutional rights of the victims."

Under the plan devised by Barbour, the state was ordered to place advertisements in *USA Today*, the *Wall Street Journal* and the *New York Times* notifying victims of their rights to see information about themselves and to block public dissemination of any information about themselves deemed in violation of their privacy rights. The state was also directed to place advertisements in the twelve daily newspapers published in Mississippi. The advertisements were ordered to run once each week for two consecutive weeks. Barbour acknowledged the state's objections on the basis of the costs of the advertisements, but he said cost was not a factor. "While these prices are expensive, they are not too onerous a burden for the State to bear for notifying possible victims of illegal Commission activity," he ruled.

Under the time frame established by the judge, state officials were given twelve months in which to assign a "victim" or "state actor" status to each individual listed in the files and to submit an advertisement for the approval of all parties involved. All advertising would have to be completed within forty-five days of the end of the twelve-month period.

Once the advertisements were published, individuals named as victims would have ninety days in which to request copies of information about themselves. The state would have ninety days in which to respond to those requests. If after responding and providing the information requested, the state receives no response, the individual would waive all rights to privacy. If the individual asks that his or her files remain closed, the state would be required to comply with that request and those files would remain sealed permanently.

By the judge's calculation, all files not closed at the request of victims would be open to the public within eight months from the date the advertisements first ran. In his May 1994 ruling, as he had done throughout the case, Judge Barbour minced no words in his descriptions of the Commission's activity: "The understood purpose of the Commission . . . was to maintain racial segregation in the South despite orders to the contrary by the United States Supreme Court. As the secret intelligence arm of the State, the Commission engaged in a wide variety of unlawful activity, thereby depriving the Plaintiffs of their constitutional rights to free speech and association, to personal privacy and to lawful search and seizure."

Reaction to Judge Barbour's ruling was predictable.

"I think the opening of those files will achieve no purpose but open old wounds that are forty-years-old or over and have been forgotten," complained Representative Charlie Capps of Cleveland. "We have enough present problems in Mississippi without opening old wounds that will probably create new problems." Not surprised about opposition from the legislature was Rims Barber. "Some of the old timers don't want to give up, but a court order is a court order," he said. "The records will be opened one way or the other. We'll either do it right or sloppy. I hope the legislature chooses to do it right."

Caught in the middle was the Mississippi Department of Archives and History. Director Elbert Hilliard made a direct appeal to the legislature for money to carry out the court order. "I feel uneasy about this whole situation," Hilliard told reporters. For the first time in twenty years as state archives director, he said, he was spending money he did not have.

Supporting Hilliard in his efforts was former governor William Winter, now president of the board of trustees for the Department of Archives and History. No one understood better than Winter the history of the files and the importance of preserving them for history. Ironically, he was there when they were created, serving as an ex officio member of the Commission during some of its darkest years.

Compounding that irony was the fact that William Winter led the Democratic Party delegation to the 1996 convention that renominated Bill Clinton for president. If there was a common denominator in Mississippi's efforts to right the wrongs of the past, it was William Winter, a survivor of more than just old political wars.

As criticisms of the decision flowed in, and the legislature quibbled over funding for the archives to carry out the court order, Ed King and John Salter did the unthinkable: they appealed Barbour's decision, gouging old wounds and buying more time for those who did not want the files opened.

In May 1994, the Reverend Hosea Williams, one of Martin Luther King's closest associates, stood before a Tennessee parole board in Nashville and argued for James Earl Ray's release from prison.

When speaking to the board, Williams didn't attribute blame in the King murder, but he has told reporters in the past that he thinks it was the FBI, not Ray, who was responsible for the killing. Williams was standing on the balcony with King when he was shot. You would think his opinion would count for something.

The parole board listened.

Ray, who had served twenty-five years of his ninety-nine-year sentence, looked pale and tired, his aging body worn down by a quarter century of efforts to get a trial. He told the board he was innocent. He pointed out that for more than two decades he has been asking for a trial—not a new trial since he never had one in the first place—but simply a trial, period. He pleaded for an opportunity to prove his innocence in court.

In the end, the parole board ignored Williams's argument and Ray's appeal, and told Tennessee's most famous prisoner to try again in five years, shortly after his seventy-first birthday. Looking dejected and weary of the fight, the graying Ray was taken back to prison. There was something fragile about him, something in his walk that made you wonder if he would be around for the next parole hearing in 1999.

The board's rejection was the second for Ray in as many months.

The month before the parole board hearing, Shelby County Criminal Court Judge Joseph Brown responded to a request for a new evidentiary hearing by Ray's lawyers with a ruling that stated Tennessee law does not provide a means for a defendant to benefit from new evidence after he is convicted of a crime. The only avenue left, said the judge, was a plea to the governor for clemency.

Judge Brown did, however, leave a door open for Ray.

Although Brown agreed with prosecutors that Ray had exhausted his state court remedies, he did agree, to the surprise of prosecutors—most notably District Attorney John Pierotti—to allow Ray's attorneys to bolster his appellate court case by subpoenaing and questioning witnesses under oath in his courtroom. Said Pierotti: "I could be doing a lot of other things that would be productive. It's garbage. The whole thing's garbage."

Ray's attorneys, William Pepper of London, England, and Wayne Chastain of Memphis, both seem uniquely suited for the case. Chastain is a former reporter for the *Memphis Press-Scimitar,* and reported on the assassination before leaving journalism to become a lawyer. Pepper, the lead attorney, is a former civil rights and antiwar activist who was an associate of King from 1967 to 1968. He was the executive director of the political coalition that hoped to put King forward as a third-party presidential candidate in 1968. After the assassination, he walked away from political activism and moved to England. He did not get involved with James Earl Ray's case until 1977, when he interviewed him in prison at the request of the Reverend Ralph Abernathy.

Pepper left that interview convinced of Ray's innocence, and has spent the past twenty years attempting to get his client a trial. In 1995 Pepper published a book, *Orders To Kill,* in which he argued that King's assassination was the result of a conspiracy of government leaders and organized crime families.

It has been a rough decade for Pepper.

When the 1992 Thames/HBO teletrial on the James Earl Ray case was aired in 1993, Pepper was optimistic it would open the doors to a real trial for Ray. The trial had pitted himself against Hickman Ewing, who had been hired to do the television prosecution. To Pepper's delight, the made-for-television jury, after hearing all the evidence, handed down a "not guilty" verdict.

Shortly after the trial, the London *Observer* ran a story stating that a Memphis man named Lloyd Jowers had admitted to knowledge of the assassination and had cleared Ray of any involvement. As a result of the story in the *Observer,* television newsman Sam Donaldson interviewed Jowers on ABC's *Prime Time Live.* Jowers told Donaldson he had hired a shooter for the assassination, after being paid $100,000 to set it up. He said he had been visited by a man named Raul who gave him a rifle and asked him to hold onto it until final arrangements could be made.

To Pepper's dismay, the media largely ignored the *Observer* story and the *Prime Time* telecast. At the urging of Pepper, District Attorney Pierotti said he would interview Jowers, but apparently never did. In his book, Pepper was highly critical of both Ewing and Pierotti, neither of whom, he felt, was interested in seeing justice done.

A twenty-eight-year veteran of the prosecutor's office, Pierotti has shown little interest over the years in the Ray case. He is best known in Memphis for a series of high-profile murder prosecutions. Ewing is best known for prosecuting public officials accused of criminal abuses of power. For that reason, in the summer of 1996, he was asked to assist in the prosecution of the so-called Whitewater cases in Little Rock, Arkansas.

The author spoke to Pepper and to his partner, Wayne Chastain, several times in an attempt to arrange an interview with James Earl Ray. After one conversation, Pepper said he had talked to Ray about the interview and that he had agreed to do it. Later, in November 1996, Pepper said Ray was ill in the hospital, and would be unable to do the interview. By Christmas, Ray had been admitted to a Nashville hospital for treatment of a liver disorder. Early in 1997, family members told reporters Ray was seriously ill and might require a liver transplant. By the end of the year, he had been released from the hospital and returned to the prison, but his lawyers said he was critically ill and could not long survive without a transplant.

In January 1995, retired North Dakota university professor John Salter notified the Fifth U.S. Circuit Court of Appeals that he wanted to withdraw from the fight to keep the Commission's files closed to all but the victims. That left Ed King as the only stumbling block.

By 1995 King, at fifty-nine, was on the payroll of the state of Mississippi, working as a sociology professor at the University of Mississippi Medical Center in Jackson. If he saw a conflict of interest—a state employee fighting to keep state records secret—he never acknowledged it to his friends, many of whom, like Rims Barber, were mystified by his behavior. To them, he suggested he was on a Great Crusade, like the one he had participated in during the 1960s when he was a familiar face at civil rights rallies and meetings across the state. Not many old friends found that argument credible.

That spring, Fred Hiatt, an editorial writer with the *Washington Post,* wrote a signed column in which he compared what happened in Mississippi to what happened in Eastern Europe during and after World War II. He agreed with King that victims' names should be released only with their permission. As an example, he cited an East German case in which a prominent dissident discovered after the fall of the Berlin Wall—and the release of secret files maintained by the East German police—that her husband and fellow dissident had been informing on her for years.

"Mississippi is far from being Eastern Europe, of course, but certain principles are universal," wrote Hiatt. "Opening the [Mississippi] files will hurt some people there, too. Some depicted in the files as stool pigeons may in fact be innocent. Some civil rights activists who were hurt once could find themselves defamed again."

On June 11, 1996, the appeals court issued its ruling.

The three-judge panel rejected King's argument and upheld Judge William Barbour's decision to open the Commission files. The court said it saw no constitutional problems with the method Barbour devised for opening the files, but it did invite the judge to give victims more time to file rebuttals to information contained in the files before the information is made public.

"We are not willing to find that the plan provision regarding rebuttal time is an abuse of discretion," said the court. "However, it is a close question."

ACLU executive director David Ingebretesen was elated by the decision, as was Rita Schwerner Bender, whose husband Michael Schwerner was among those murdered in Neshoba County. "The records should be opened," she told Jerry Mitchell, a reporter for the *Clarion-Ledger.* "Given recent events in this country . . . somehow racism again is OK, which makes understanding the history of what happened more important than ever."

King told the author in a 1996 interview that it disturbed him that people would attack him for his stand on keeping the files closed unless opened by individual victims. "It is a little crazy that everything I stand for, as a white Mississippian who was accepted and trusted for years by Medgar Evers . . . can be destroyed because someone sees some greater good is sick and a violation of what we stood for in the movement," he said.

The author asked him about allegations that he was an informant for the

Commission. King declined to either confirm or deny the allegations, citing his conviction that to do so would violate his rights. "I think everything I did, whether public or private as a priest, has been fairly consistent," he said. "I am certainly a human being and a sinner. That's the only defense I can offer. If some people see that as evidence as to why I am doing this, they will have to interpret it that way. . . . I would like [my] reputation not to be destroyed . . . but my primary responsibility is to the victims, especially the ones I don't even know. Whatever happens to me, happens."

To the surprise of no one, King appealed to the Supreme Court. If the high court chose to hear the case, it would put everything on hold for at least another year, maybe longer. Was there no end to this nightmare?

Mississippi watched and waited as summer faded into fall.

Finally, as tempers frayed among those waiting for justice, the Supreme Court announced its decision: on November 18, 1996, the high court said it would not hear the case, thus affirming the lower court's decision that the files should be opened.

The twenty-year battle to reveal the secrets of the Sovereignty Commission was finally over. And hopefully so was the nightmare.

In the spring of 1996, the author located Cleve McDowell, the second black student to enroll at Ole Miss. He was living in Drew, Mississippi, where he had a successful law practice. Since the author was a student at the university at the time McDowell enrolled at the school, they spoke briefly about the not so good "good ole days." The author had gotten in trouble with other students for remaining in the cafeteria when McDowell entered (everyone else picked up their trays and moved to another part of the room). "Oh, you were the one," McDowell said with a laugh. "I think I do remember you." The author told McDowell that he wanted to interview him for this book, and he said fine, though he sounded apprehensive about talking about the Sovereignty Commission. A date was set for the interview.

The author drove nearly 400 miles to Indianola, Mississippi, the place McDowell chose for the interview, but when he arrived, McDowell was nowhere to be found. After waiting around for an hour or so, the author drove to McDowell's office in Drew. His assistant told the author he hadn't seen McDowell and didn't know where he was. The author waited around for a while longer, then started back to Nashville. Unfortunately, that interview would never take place.

In March 1997, McDowell was shot to death at his home in Drew during a robbery attempt. Taken was a 1995 Cadillac and a small amount of cash.

The man arrested for the crime later pleaded guilty and was sentenced to a prison term at the Mississippi State Penitentiary at Parchman, not far from Drew. An editorial in the *Delta Democrat-Times* said: "Whether you agreed with his politics or not, this was a man who deliberately chose to make a difference. . . . His memory will continue to burn brightly in the hearts and souls of those who have benefited from his activism."

~~~~~~

Early in 1997, the state of Mississippi published advertisements throughout the state and in several national publications, including *USA Today* and the *New York Times,* advising anyone who thought they might have been victims of the Commission to contact the Mississippi Department of Archives and History to receive information about their secret files. Those who responded to the ad received a questionnaire requesting information about the respondent's birthdate, where he or she lived during the years 1956–1977, and an explanation as to why they thought they might have been investigated by the Commission. Also demanded was an affidavit, which would have to be witnessed by a notary public, that required the respondent to provide details of their civil rights activity in Mississippi.

Once state officials had determined if the respondent was among the 87,000 individuals named in the secret files, the respondent would be given the option of keeping his files secret or allowing them to be released to the public. By the end of the summer, nearly one thousand people had responded to the ad. Of those, 360 were identified as being named in the files. Only a small fraction of the individuals named in the files chose to keep their records secret.

As the date approached for the opening of the files, new problems arose. Ed King asked the court to keep the records of four deceased civil rights activists closed. They had asked to see their files, but had died before that could happen. Family members responded that King did not have their permission to speak for their deceased relatives and they, in fact, wanted the files opened. Nonetheless, King's action had raised new legal issues about the files and the year ended with the records still sealed to the public.

Early in 1998, questions were being asked about the content of the files. Skeptics feared state and federal officials had too many opportunities to remove incriminating information. In its heyday, Commission members had bragged of files on over 120,000 individuals and several thousand organizations. Now state officials said the files contained information on over 87,000 individuals. If true, that leaves files on nearly 30,000 individuals unaccounted for.

What happened to the missing files?

When the files were removed from the Commission office in 1973 and stored in a warehouse where the Mississippi highway patrol and other law enforcement agencies had access to them, there was no record of who maintained them and no trace of who removed particular files. "On the night they came to move the files [in 1977], the files were loaded into two trucks," said Ingebretesen, who learned of the incident from various sources. "One truck went to the archives. No one knows where the other one went."

In 1995, eighteen years after all the files were supposedly securely locked inside the archives, a well-known Jackson street scavenger named Billy Earl discovered a cache of secret documents. "He was picking up trash and found a trunk that was packed full of Sovereignty Commission stuff," said Ingebretesen. "Most of it was innocuous—photocopies of mug shots of civil rights activists—but how many times things like that were repeated, I don't know."

Finally, in January 1998, Judge Barbour set another date for the opening of the files—March 19, barring further appeals. Commission victims and their families were optimistic the twenty-year court battle would end at last, but justice had not proved to be a faithful ally to Mississippi's long-suffering and dispossessed, and it was difficult for anyone involved in the case to believe it would really happen.

As the March 19 deadline approached, officials at the Mississippi Department of Archives and History prepared for the expected unveiling of the files. Computer terminals were in place, one for the media and two for the general public, and an index of the Commission files was prepared for public viewing. In all, more than 132,000 pages of reports, notes, letters, and newspaper clippings were scanned into the computer system. There was talk of someday making the entire collection available on computer disk.

When the appointed day came, to the surprise of almost everyone, the doors to the archives swung open. After twenty years, the public was allowed to peer into the repository of one of America's darkest secrets. Of course, at least half the files had been purged over the years from the system and it would take years for researchers to unravel the tangled web that remained, but it was a start—and that was something. Addressing the fact that Commission records show that orders went out to destroy the content of some of the more explosive files, the *New York Times* said in a editorial that "what remains is a record off state-sanctioned terror that demands to be remembered."

The Sovereignty Commission no longer exists, but it would be a mistake to assume that the powers that once propelled the Commission no longer exist. On the contrary, many of the individuals and organizations who helped create and sustain the Commission are alive and well, still in the business of corrupting government officials and building secret financial empires.

In that sense, the Commission is alive and well, but no longer called the Sovereignty Commission. Or the Federation for Constitutional Government. Or the Dixie Mafia. Or the Citizens' Council. It is no longer anchored to a government agency. Nor does it have a mailing address or a public board of directors.

But it is there, as it has been for decades.

This book has described forty years of killings, bombings, assaults, break-ins, smear campaigns, violations of selective service laws, invasions of privacy, ruined lives, and betrayals of public trust by elected officials and newspaper editors. Some of those crimes were committed by the Sovereignty Commission. Others by the leaders of the Federation for Constitutional Government and the Dixie Mafia, and still others by the families in the Memphis cartel. Over the years, the leadership of those organizations has changed, and in some instances, vanished entirely, but in the past forty years the baton has often passed from father to son, from storefront to corporation, over a geographic area that has remained unchanged.

Many of the bad things that happened in America in the 1950s, 1960s, and 1970s were hatched, nurtured, and released upon an unsuspecting public by persons in the Mississippi–Tennessee–Louisiana nexus described in this book. It was, as Judge Barbour said in his original ruling, a massive conspiracy of government, the media, and private power-brokers. We are just beginning to understand the enormity of that conspiracy.

One of the biggest disappointments to emerge from the secret files has been documentation of FBI involvement in Commission activities. The FBI provided former agents as investigators, read and approved copies of speeches to be delivered by Mississippi officials, worked with the Commission in a variety of ways, and, in its final years, had a former high-ranking agent, Webb Burke, actually in charge of the Commission. The most damaging evidence against the FBI can be found in what the bureau did not do. It has had intimate knowledge of the Mississippi Sovereignty Commission since 1956, the year a former FBI agent helped organize the filing system, but in forty years of congressional investigations, there is no evidence the bureau ever offered that information to Congress or to the American people. It took a courageous federal judge in Jackson, Mississippi, to make that information available.

Retired FBI agent Joe Sullivan knew Webb Burke from the days when Burke was in charge of the FBI's weapons division. "As far as I know, he wasn't fraternizing with the Jackson agents, and that always surprised me. He was always a real gung-ho FBI type and I would have expected him to [have more contact with active agents]," he says.

Sullivan said he knew the Commission was watching his agents, but not to the extent revealed in the secret files. Nor was he aware of the private banking account used by the Commission. "We probably made a mistake of not making a more intensive probe of the Commission; I think that was perhaps the key to a lot of the problems," he says. "I was aware they had money. I always suspected the White Knights were funded in some fashion by the Commission. In the years that followed, I wished we had done some probing in that area. We had nothing that would allow us to subpoena the documents."

One of the FBI's biggest critics is the Justice Department's own task force set up to review the Martin Luther King assassination. This task force found that the FBI was reluctant "to provide the Civil Rights Division and the Attorney General, with timely reports on the course of the murder investigation." The task force also criticized the FBI for not finding out why James Earl Ray went to Alabama and for not finding out where he obtained the money he used to pay his expenses: "In light of the fact that a good deal of mystery still surrounds James Ray and the assassination, particularly the means by which he financed his life style and travels, we concluded that on the basis of the information which was uncovered, the Bureau should have pursued this line of the investigation more thoroughly."

Whether the FBI actively supported the Commission during its reign of terror—or was unaware of the activities of its former agents—is really beside the point. Either way, the result was the same, and the lives of many innocent Americans were destroyed.

Dealing with the Mississippi Sovereignty Commission files has been a painful experience for everyone involved, but former Mississippi governor William Winter feels it will offer all Americans, not just Mississippians, an opportunity for some much needed soul-searching.

"In addition to the obvious lesson—that we must never again succumb as a society to the hysterics that overwhelmed us in the 1950s and 1960s—I guess the main lesson is that the way to respond to actions of government, legislative or judicial, is not to do it as we did [then]," he said. "The second lesson is that government needs to be as open as it can be, that any sort of clandestine effort, influencing public policy and private attitudes, is counter-productive. Government needs to be open."

William Winter, the keeper of the files, the gatekeeper to the past and the future, paused, thinking about what he had said. It is an emotional subject for all involved. He has seen the best and the worst. Finally, his rich, old-style Southern voice, still oratorical after an absence of more than a decade from public office, broke from that brief reverie with a final thought that offered hope and despair in the same breath:

"I hope that we don't ever repeat those old experiences."

Notes

Chapter 1

Newspaper articles about the Federation for Constitutional Government can be found in the December 29 and 30, 1955, editions of the *Commercial Appeal* and in the December 30 and 31, 1955, editions of the *New York Times.*

Leander Perez's quote on African Americans can be found in *Leander Perez: Boss of the Delta* by Glen Jeansonne. Additional information about Perez and John U. Barr can be found in *Earl K. Long: The Saga of Uncle Earl and Louisiana Politics* by Michael L. Kurtz and Morgan D. Peoples.

In the 1920s and 1930s, the activities of E.H. Crump and Senator Kenneth McKellar were described as "bossism." The word "cartel" was not in vogue then to describe organized crime. In an effort to simplify—and categorize—descriptions of activities taking place in Memphis and elsewhere, the author has adopted the use of the word "cartel" as a replacement for "bossism," "Mafia," and "mob."

Information about Memphis's battles with cocaine addiction, prostitution, and gangsterism for the first three decades of the century can be found in back issues of *The Commercial Appeal,* the *Memphis Press-Scimitar,* and in police reports on file at the main branch of the Memphis and Shelby County Public Library. When Scripps-Howard shut down the *Memphis Press-Scimitar* in 1983, its clip files and photographs were donated to the University of Memphis libraries, which now own the copyright to all of the newspaper's articles and photographs.

Memphis was a favorite target of magazine crime writers throughout the 1920s and 1930s. Although the businessmen sponsoring the sale of drugs on Beale Street were never identified by the magazines or the local newspapers, their activities were well documented. All of the Memphis families today suspected of illegal activities have business histories that place them on or near Beale Street during the wide open days of "cocaine by the box."

George Rogers currently lives near Washington, D.C. He is retired from the CIA, but works as a computer security consultant for private businesses.

Hilton Waits was the nephew of the author's maternal grandfather, Audie Turner. Waits was an early influence on the author and played a significant role in the author's education on the subject of Mississippi politics.

The circulation area of the *Deer Creek Pilot* extended to the author's hometown of Hollandale, Mississippi. The author grew up reading the newspaper and had an awareness of the DeCell family from an early age. Despite Hal DeCell's association with the Sovereignty Commission, the author always knew Hal and his wife, Carolyn, to be honest, hard-working people who showed a professional interest in developing writers, including the author. In the late 1970s, articles written by the author for other newspapers were often reprinted by the DeCells in the *Deer Creek Pilot.*

All of the Crump–McKellar letters referred to in this book are on file in the archives of the Memphis and Shelby County Public Library. The library permits researchers to view the documents by appointment only. The McKellar collection contains approximately 1.8 million items. McKellar's list of Memphis projects was dated July 1, 1955, and is a listing of seventeen projects. There are numerous Crump–McKellar letters in the collection dealing with their attempts to have the IRS punish a rival. Roosevelt's letter to McKellar is dated January 18, 1944, and begins, "Dear Kenneth." The letters between McKellar and Roosevelt, and between McKellar and Crump, provide insight into the relationship of the three men. Crump's letters and papers are still in the possession of the Crump family and have never been made available to researchers and scholars.

Just prior to the date the author began his research, the Memphis library reported that numerous Franklin D. Roosevelt letters to Senator McKellar were stolen from the collection. Also reported stolen were letters from J. Edgar Hoover to unidentified recipients. As the author was winding up research on this book, he learned that some of the stolen letters had been recovered. The author was not allowed to view them since they were still in the possession of law enforcement authorities and had not been returned to the library.

Information about FBI reports that Carlos Marcello "had the keys" to Governor Long's office can be found in *Earl K. Long: The Saga of Uncle Earl and Louisiana Politics.*

Former attorney general Francis Biddle provides an account of the Hoover–McKellar confrontation in his memoirs, *In Brief Authority.* Additional information about that exchange can be found in *J. Edgar Hoover: The Man and the Secrets.*

Information about Judge John D. Martin was taken from the John D. Martin Collection in the Memphis and Shelby County Room of the Memphis and Shelby County Public Library. Abe Fortas's letter to a friend can be found in the Mississippi Valley Collection at the University of Memphis.

An account of Senator James Eastland's confrontation with C.B. Baldwin can be found in a June 10, 1949, Associated Press dispatch from Washington.

The law creating the State Sovereignty Commission can be found in Volume 2, Title 3, of the 1972 Mississippi Code (annotated). All Sovereignty Commission documents referred to in this chapter and in subsequent chapters can be found in the Governor Paul B. Johnson Collection at the University of Southern Mississippi, Hattiesburg, and in the state auditor's files at the Mississippi Department of Archives and History, Jackson. For several years, various "secret copies" of Sovereignty Commission documents have circulated and have been offered for sale by brokers. The author is wary of those documents since some of the ones he has examined appear to be forgeries. As a result, the author used no Sovereignty Commission materials in this book that cannot be viewed at the University of Southern Mississippi or the state archives.

All Sovereignty Commission documents referred to in this book have the names of the victims intact. The author has deleted those names from this text in those instances in which he felt privacy issues were a consideration. In no instances were the names of state actors or informants deleted.

Chapter 2

The Commission's early financial records can be found in the state auditor's file at the Mississippi Department of Archives and History. Hal DeCell's reports are in those files.

The author's descriptions of Tom Hederman and Jimmy Ward are derived from personal observation: he worked for both men. The author is the only living person to ever write editorials for both the *Jackson Daily News* and its chief competitor, the *Delta Democrat-Times* in Greenville.

Information about J. Edgar Hoover's filing system was derived from a number of sources, including Curt Gentry's *J. Edgar Hoover: The Man and the Secrets*; the final report (Book III) of the Select Committee to Study Governmental Operations (U.S. Senate); Kenneth O'Reilly's *Hoover and the Un-Americans*; and Athan Theoharis's *From the Secret Files of J. Edgar Hoover*.

The best source for information about FBI break-ins and wiretaps is the 1976 final report of the Select Committee to Study Governmental Operations, created under authority of the U.S. Senate (see Book III). The committee details the FBI's activities during the 1960s and concludes that the FBI conducted more than five hundred "warrantless surreptitious microphone installations" between 1960 and 1976. Reported the Senate committee: "Surreptitious entries were performed by teams of FBI agents with special training in subjects such as 'lock studies.' Their missions were authorized in writing by FBI Director J. Edgar Hoover or his deputy, Clyde Tolson. A 'Do Not File' procedure was utilized, under which most records of surreptitious entries were destroyed soon after an entry was accomplished." Brennan's memo to Sullivan was obtained under the Freedom of Information Act by author Athan Theoharis for his book, *From the Secret Files of J. Edgar Hoover.*

When Senator Kenneth McKellar died in October 1957, the *Memphis Press-Scimitar* published a lengthy obituary that disclosed, for the first time, to Memphis readers that McKellar had become a wealthy man through his investments in the South Memphis Land Company. The obituary, written by Clark Portenous, offers a good summary of the senator's career. Before his death, McKellar made a list of the projects he had given to Memphis. The list can be found in his papers in the archives of the Memphis and Shelby County Public Library.

News stories about the debate over whether to abolish the Sovereignty Commission can be found in the *Jackson Daily News* (March 8, 1958).

A good source for information about Senator Kefauver's committee can be found in *Facts on File* (May 3, 1951; March 1, 1951; September 4, 1952; December 27, 1951; and March 29, 1951).

Chapter 3

The Associated Press reported in a May 19, 1959, dispatch that FBI agents were burning four boxes of papers at an incinerator.

"Waits is Unanimous Choice for Mississippi's Speaker," the *Commercial Appeal* (December 3, 1959). "Veteran Legislator, Called by Some the 'Best,' Recalls Past Sessions, Compares Financing Then with the Present," *Clarion-Ledger* (February 26, 1956). "Coleman Given Strong Support on Session Play," the *Commercial Appeal* (August 28, 1959).

The author was present during the 1959 special session of the Mississippi legislature. He served as a page under appointment of Representative Hilton Waits and worked with the legislators who created the Sovereignty Commission. Steven Turner, who helped write the Mississippi Constitution of 1890, is the author's great-grandfather.

John Martin's correspondence with E.H. Crump, Senator Kenneth McKellar, and Senator James Eastland can be found in the McKellar and John Martin collections at the Memphis and Shelby County Public Library.

In *Mafia Kingfish,* John Davis gives an account of Aaron Kohn's attempt to prosecute Carlos Marcello and is the source of the "stupid little man" quote attributed to New Orleans FBI agents. Additional information can be found in the Time-Life book, *Mafia.*

E.H. Crump's letter to Senator McKellar chastising him for anti-Semitic remarks is dated May 22, 1944, and can be found in the McKellar collection.

The author was present on the day Ross Barnett was sworn in as governor.

The most detailed account of the FBI's electronic surveillance of Martin Luther King can be found in the final report issued by the Senate Select Committee to Study Governmental Operations (Book III).

Chapter 4

An account of Abe Fortas's visit to Memphis can be found in the *Memphis Press-Scimitar* (April 4, 1961).

"Sparks of Dissension Dart Sovereignty Commission," *Jackson Daily News* (March 19, 1961).

"Coleman Appoints Winter to Tax Collector Post," *Memphis Press-Scimitar* (April 4, 1956).

"Reporters are Banned at Meeting Sponsored by Mississippians," *Memphis Press-Scimitar* (November 8, 1961).

An account of Senator Estes Kefauver's hearings on the drug industry can be found in Joseph Bruce Corman's biography of Estes Kefauver, *Kefauver: A Political Biography.*

The author's account of James Meredith's enrollment at Ole Miss is derived from Meredith's book, *Three Years in Mississippi;* newspaper stories from the *Jackson Daily News,* the *Clarion-Ledger,* the *Memphis Press-Scimitar, The Commercial Appeal,* and *The Mississippian*; Erle Johnston's published account; David Halberstam's *Esquire* story; the Kennedy–Barnett tapes; and the author's own recollections of the event.

In 1993 the Organized Crime/Drug Branch of the Criminal Investigative Division of the Justice Department published a booklet entitled *An Introduction to Organized Crime in the United States.* The booklet offers an excellent look at the organization of Cosa Nostra families across the country. Memphis was not included since it has never been under Cosa Nostra control.

Chapter 5

The author was a student at the University of Mississippi when James Meredith was joined on campus by Cleve McDowell. He was on campus when word went out that President John Kennedy had been assassinated.

Details of Dennis Hale's confrontation with the Sovereignty Commission were derived from Commission reports in the Paul B. Johnson collection at the University of Southern Mississippi.

Abe Fortas's correspondence about Puerto Rican issues can be found in the LBJ Library. An account of his involvement with the cigarette lobby can be found in Bruce Allen Murphy's *Fortas: The Rise and Ruin of a Supreme Court Justice.*

Information about the Coordinating Committee for Fundamental American Freedoms, including its budget, can be found in *Facts On File* (April 1, 1964), and in Robert Loevy's *To End All Segregation: The Politics of the Passage of the Civil Rights Act of 1964.*

Glen Jeansonne discusses Leander Perez's association with the Delta Development Corporation of Delaware in his book *Leander Perez: Boss of the Delta*, (p. 80).

Details of the trip to Memphis by Erle Johnston and John Sullivan to talk to the Reverend Ed King's mother are contained in a Commission report on file at the University of Southern Mississippi.

Information about Allen Dulles's visit to the Sovereignty Commission offices can be found in Commission reports on file at the University of Southern Mississippi and in United Press International's *Retrospect 1965.*

The author's account of the Medgar Evers slaying and the trial of Byron De La Beckwith was based on newspaper stories in the *Jackson Daily News* and the *Clarion-Ledger*; *The Mississippian*; Sovereignty Commission reports; *Ghosts of Mississippi*; Associated Press; United Press International; *Evers*; *Local People: The Struggle for Civil Rights in Mississippi*; an interview with the Reverend Ed King; and various other sources.

J. Edgar Hoover's visit to Jackson, Mississippi, was covered by the local media. His letters to and from Colonel T.B. Birdsong are on file at the University of Southern Mississippi.

Minutes of the Mississippi State Sovereignty Commission for July 19, 1963, contain information about the Satterfield connection to the agency; Satterfield is also discussed in the agenda prepared by Erle Johnston for that meeting.

In a pre-interview telephone conversation that took place in the summer of 1996, Cleve McDowell told the author about the Commission visits to his family and teachers.

Concerning U.S. Representative Gerald Ford's appointment to the Warren Commission, FBI agent William Sullivan wrote in his memoirs: "The director wrote in one of his internal memos that the bureau could expect Ford to 'look after FBI interests' and he did, keeping us fully advised of what was going on behind closed doors."

Chapter 6

A list of Abe Fortas's business interests can be found in *The Commercial Appeal* (July 21, 1965). His letters to John Macy and Walter Jenkins can be found in the LBJ Library.

The memo from Charles Snodgrass to Colonel T.B. Birdsong regarding the Sharkey County klansman can be found in the Paul B. Johnson collection at the University of Southern Mississippi.

The author was present at Robert Kennedy's speech at Ole Miss.

Wendell Paris was interviewed in 1996.

Information about the anonymous letter the FBI sent to Martin Luther King can be found in the final report of the Senate Select Committee to Study Governmental Operations (Book III).

A report on Senator Eastland's efforts to cause trouble for the racially mixed couple traveling through South Carolina and details of the FBI tip on Jackie Robinson's travel plans are on file at the University of Southern Mississippi.

The author's account of the shooting of James Meredith is based on Sovereignty Commission documents and newspaper articles.

The author's account of the memorial services held in Philadelphia for the slain civil rights workers is based on Sovereignty Commission documents and newspaper articles.

Judge Cox's remark that he gave the Neshoba County defendants the sentences he thought they deserved is from Seth Cagin and Philip Dray's *We Are Not Afraid.*

Frank Chavez's letter to Robert Kennedy was reported in James D. Squires' *The Secrets of the Hopewell Box.*

Chapter 7

The code names used by the Army's counterintelligence units are from *Military Surveillance of Civilian Politics.* Many of the details of the Army's use of surveillance were garnered from the final report of the Senate Select Committee to Study Governmental Operations. Of particular interest is the chapter entitled "Improper Surveillance of Private Citizens by the Military" (p. 787).

Some of the details of James Meredith's second march were taken from Mississippi highway patrol documents on file at the University of Southern Mississippi (memo to Colonel Birdsong from C.A. Marx dated June 21, 1967; memo to Colonel Birdsong from Charles Snodgrass dated June 28, 1967). Other details were gleaned from newspaper articles.

Abe Fortas's relationship with Louis Wolfson was reported by Bruce Allen Murphy in *Fortas: The Rise and Ruin of a Supreme Court Justice*; United Press International; Scripps-Howard; Associated Press; and the *Memphis Press-Scimitar.*

The Memphis cartel has benefited from military expenditures for projects in Memphis and by joint ventures with companies in other states, according to the author's research.

Details of the Neshoba County trial can be found in *We Are Not Afraid*; *The Klan*; *Ghosts of Mississippi*; and various newspaper articles.

Martin Luther King's threat to camp on the lawn of the White House was reported by United Press International on November 4, 1967.

Sovereignty Commission reports on Janet Maedke and letters from Maedke are in the Governor Paul B. Johnson collection at the University of Southern Mississippi.

Christopher Pyle's account of his experiences can be found in *Military Surveillance of Civilian Politics.*

Information about the FBI's plan to launch a Cointelpro operation about Martin Luther King and Benjamin Spock can be found in the report issued by the Senate Select Committee to Study Governmental Operations.

Author William F. Pepper was able to establish July 28 as the date the Army designated Memphis a target city for secret operations.

Details of FBI "black bag" operations can be found in the report issued by the Senate Select Committee to Study Governmental Operations.

Abe Fortas's letter to President Johnson recommending Wolfson's firm, Merritt-Chapman and Scott, is discussed in *Fortas: The Rise and Ruin of a Supreme Court Justice.*

Abe Fortas's recommendations regarding a cessation in bombing in North Vietnam can be found in the LBJ Library in the National Security File, Box 127 (the memo is dated November 5, 1967).

Chapter 8

"Haley Barbour in top race," the *Mississippian* (March 6, 1968).

The "marijuana" stories were published in the *Mississippian* during the week of February 18, 1968, and contained the following note from editor Charles Overby: "This story was assigned to a *Daily Mississippian* staff member last week to determine the availability of marijuana on this campus. The actual marijuana he bought (minus the names and places connected with the purchase) has subsequently been turned over to the University administration."

The author's account of James Earl Ray's actions before and after the assassination were compiled from Ray's memoirs; his attorney's book *Orders To Kill* (William F. Pepper); the report of the Justice Department's task force to review the FBI, Martin Luther King Jr., Security and Assassination Investigations; and countless newspaper and magazine stories. The author's account of the assassination was compiled from some of the above-named sources, plus the final report of the Senate Select Committee to Study Governmental Operations (Book III); *Military Surveillance of Civilian Politics*; *The Commercial Appeal*; and the *Memphis Press-Scimitar*. The author was a student at the University of Mississippi when King was assassinated. Information about President Johnson's reaction to King's funeral was taken from documents on file at the LBJ Library. For a detailed report on the aftermath of the King assassination, see "Riot Data Review," published by the Lemberg Center for the Study of Violence at Brandeis University.

James Earl Ray's name does not appear in any Sovereignty Commission documents yet examined by the author, which makes the author even more convinced that the Commission was involved in the assassination of Martin Luther King. The Commission had files on *everyone*. The absence of a comprehensive King file means it has been removed.

The author's account of Abe Fortas's nomination to be chief justice was compiled from letters and memos from the LBJ Library; the *Congressional Record* (which contains an extensive discussion of Fortas's suitability for the post); *Fortas: The Rise and Ruin of a Supreme Court Justice*; the *Commercial Appeal*; the *Memphis Press-Scimitar;* the New York Times; and various newspaper and magazine articles. Fortas's attempt to influence Richard Nixon's decision was reported by the *Chicago Sun-Times* (August 15, 1968) and other newspapers.

Information about Webb Burke's background and appointment to the Sovereignty Commission was taken from a *Jackson Daily News* article, "Burke Heads Sovereignty Commission" (August 27, 1968).

Charles Sudduth was interviewed in 1996.

Information about the response of FBI agents to King's death ("They finally got the SOB!") was obtained from *Investigation of the Assassination of Martin Luther King* hearings (Volume 6, 1979).

Descriptions of the books containing U.S. Army dossiers on private citizens can be found in Christopher H. Pyle's *Military Surveillance of Civilian Politics*.

The FBI letter targeting a female worker with Action is described in a memo from the St. Louis SAC to J. Edgar Hoover dated January 30, 1970 (*J. Edgar Hoover: The Man and the Secrets*).

Chapter 9

George Rogers was interviewed in 1996.

David Ingebretesen was interviewed in 1996.

Tennessee Correction Commissioner Harry Avery's firing was reported by the Associated Press and the *Memphis Press-Scimitar* (May 29, 1969).

The author's account of the FBI's involvement with the Muhammed Kenyatta case was compiled from federal court documents and *Facts On File*.

The Jackson State College killings were reported by the *Jackson Daily News* and the *Clarion-Ledger*. Two books, *The Killings at Kent State* and *Lynch Street: The May 1970 Slayings at Jackson State College,* provide excellent, in-depth coverage of the event.

Rick Abraham was interviewed in 1996.

Former Mississippi governor Bill Waller was interviewed in 1996.

The author's account of Byron De La Beckwith's New Orleans arrest and trial was compiled from a variety of sources, including *Ghosts of Mississippi*, the *Clarion-Ledger*, and various other newspaper and magazine articles.

Information about the IRS team assigned to monitor the activities of political activists can be found in the report issued by the Senate Select Committee to Study Governmental Operations (Book III).

Details of Hoover's investigation of the alleged sex lives of Haldeman, Ehrlichman,
and Chapin can be found in Curt Gentry's *J. Edgar Hoover: The Man and the Secrets.*

Information about Wolfson's request for a pardon can be found in the *Congressional
Record* (September 24, 1968).

Mayor Loeb's letter regarding his failure to attend the Fortas function is in the
archives of the Memphis and Shelby County Public Library.

Scripps-Howard issued a news story by Dan Thomasson and Nicholas Horrock on
November 12, 1968, regarding Fortas's link to a real estate shelter in Virginia. On May
6, 1969, Scripps-Howard issued a story by Thomasson on William O. Douglas's connection to the Albert Parvin Foundation.

Details of the Kenyatta case can be found in Muhammed Kenyatta vs. Roy K.
Moore, James O. Ingram, Thomas Fitzpatrick (civil action No. J77–0298 R), U.S. District Court, Southern District of Mississippi.

Chapter 10

In 1985 Hal DeCell became the first weekly newspaper editor in Mississippi to
receive the annual Silver "Em" Award from the Mississippi Scholastic Press Association. The award, which was presented to DeCell by Dr. Samuel Talbert, chairman of the
Department of Journalism at the University of Mississippi, acknowledged DeCell's
"distinguished achievement in the practice of journalism, outstanding public service and
significant contribution to journalism."

Time-Life's "True Crime" series is a good source of information about the legal
woes of Carlos Marcello.

David Ingebretesen was interviewed in 1996.

Fortas's comments to Wolfson regarding the release of his letters can be found in
Fortas: The Rise and Ruin of a Supreme Court Justice.

Chapter 11

By the time of Beckwith's trial, Delmar Dennis had told his story several times to
reporters. According to Dennis, Beckwith had said that killing Evers "gave me no more
inner discomfort than our wives endure when they give birth to our children." When
Dennis testified at the trial, he dropped the words, "inner discomfort," substituting the
words "physical harm" for "inner discomfort."

The Beckwith trial was reported by the *Clarion-Ledger, The Commercial Appeal,*
and various other Mississippi dailies. It is well covered in *Ghosts of Mississippi.*

Rims Barber was interviewed in 1996.

H.T. Holmes was interviewed in 1996.

Harold Ickes did not respond to requests for an interview.

For an analysis of the FBI's investigation of the Martin Luther King assassination,
see the report of the Justice Department's task force dated January 11, 1977.

Select Bibliography

Books

Bartley, Numan V. *The Rise of Massive Resistance*. Baton Rouge: Louisiana State University Press, 1969.

————. *The New South: 1945–1980*. Baton Rouge: Louisiana State University Press, 1995.

Cagin, Seth, and Philip Dray. *We Are Not Afraid: The Story of Goodman, Schwerner, and Chaney and the Civil Rights Campaign for Mississippi*. New York: Macmillan, 1988.

Carter, Hodding (III). *The South Strikes Back*. New York: Doubleday, 1959.

Davis, John H. *Mafia Kingfish: Carlos Marcello and the Assassination of John F. Kennedy*. New York: McGraw-Hill, 1989.

Dickerson, James. *Goin' Back to Memphis: A Century of Blues, Rock 'n' Roll, and Glorious Soul*. New York: Schirmer Books, 1996.

Dittmer, John. *Local People: The Struggle for Civil Rights in Mississippi*. Chicago: University of Illinois Press.

Evers, Charles. *Evers*. New York: World Publishing, 1971.

Editors, The. *True Crime: Mafia*. New York: Time-Life Books, 1993.

Gentry, Curt. *J. Edgar Hoover: The Man and the Secrets*. New York: Plume, 1991.

Gorman, Joseph Bruce. *Kefauver: A Political Biography*. New York: Oxford University Press, 1971.

Harkins, John E. *Metropolis of the American Nile*. Oxford, MS: Guild Bindery Press, 1991.

Jeansonne, Glen. *Leander Perez: Boss of the Delta*. Baton Rouge: Louisiana State University Press, 1977.

Johnston, Erle. *Mississippi's Defiant Years: 1953–1973*. Forest, MS: Lake Harbor, 1990.

Key, V. O. *Southern Politics*. New York: Random House, 1949.

Kurtz, Michael, and Morgan D. Peoples. *Earl K. Long: The Saga of Uncle Earl and Louisiana Politics*. Baton Rouge: Louisiana State University Press, 1990.

Loevy, Robert D. *To End All Segregation: The Politics of the Passage of the Civil Rights Act of 1964*. Lanham, MD: University Press of America, 1990.

Manchester, William. *The Death of a President*. New York: Harper and Row, 1967.

McMillen, Neil R. *The Citizens' Council*. Chicago: University of Illinois Press, 1994.

Meredith, James. *Three Years in Mississippi*. Bloomington: University of Indiana Press, 1966.

Miller, William D. *Memphis During the Progressive Era*. Memphis: Memphis State University Press, 1957.

O'Reilly, Kenneth. *Hoover and the Un-Americans: The FBI, HUAC, and the Red Menace*. Philadelphia: Temple University Press, 1983.

President's Commission on Organized Crime. *Organized Crime and Cocaine Trafficking: Record of Hearing IV*. Washington, DC: U.S. Government Printing Office, 1994.

Pyle, Christopher. *Military Surveillance of Civilian Politics*. New York: Garland, 1986.

Raines, Howell. *My Soul Is Rested*. New York: G.P. Putnam's, 1977.

Ray, James Earl. *Who Killed Martin Luther King?* Washington, DC: National Press Books, 1992.

Russell, Bertrand. *War Crimes in Vietnam*. New York: Monthly Review Press, 1967.

Silver, James W. *Mississippi: The Closed Society*. New York: Harcourt, Brace and World, 1964.

Sims, Patsy. *The Klan*. New York: Stein and Day, 1978.

Spofford, Tim. *Lynch Street: The May 1970 Slayings at Jackson State College*. Kent, OH: Kent State University Press, 1988.

Squires, James D. *The Secrets of the Hopewell Box*. New York: Random House, 1996.

Stone, I. F. *The Killings at Kent State*. New York: New York Review, 1970.

Swados, Harvey. *Standing Up for the People: The Life and Work of Estes Kefauver*. New York: Dutton, 1972.

Theoharis, Athan. *From the Secret Files of J. Edgar Hoover*. Chicago: Ivan R. Dee, 1991.

Tucker, David M. *Memphis Since Crump: Bossism, Blacks and Civic Reformers*. Knoxville: University of Tennessee Press, 1980.

United Press International. *Retrospect 1965*. New York: Ace Books, 1965.

U. S. Government. *Supplementary Detailed Staff Reports on Intelligence Activities and the Rights of Americans*. Select Committee to Study Governmental Operations (Book III, 1976).

―――. *Amnesty*. Hearings Before the Subcommittee on Courts, Civil Liberties, and the Administration of Justice, Committee on the Judiciary, House of Representatives, 1974.

Vollers, Maryanne. *Ghosts of Mississippi*. Boston: Little, Brown, 1995.

Williams, Roger Neville. *The New Exiles*. New York: Liveright, 1971.

Articles

Associated Press. "Sovereignty Group may be Abolished." (March 8, 1958).

―――. "Kennedy Assassinated; Texas Governor Shot." *The Meridian Star* (November 22, 1963).

―――. "Barnett Stumping with Old Script." (April 21, 1967).

―――. "Mississippi Seeks Dismissal of Lawsuit on Secret Files." (October 2, 1980).

————. "Kennedy Tapes Crackle with Ole Miss Tension." *The Commercial Appeal.* (June 24, 1983).

————. "Gov. Coleman of Civil Rights Era Dies in Miss." (September 29, 1991).

————. "Mississippi Civil Rights Files Make Ex-allies Foes." (October 3, 1993).

————. "Sovereignty Commission's Files Unsealed." (June 1, 1994).

Black, Kay Pittman. "Nationwide Search Begun in Connection with Call-Girl Probe." *Memphis Press-Scimitar* (December 20, 1973).

————. "Woman Tells of Recruitment to Prostitution." *Memphis Press-Scimitar* (March 1, 1974).

Branston, John. "A Tale of Two Cities." *Memphis Magazine* (July/August 1996).

Brower, Sinda. "Crowd Cheers Barnett." *The Mississippian* (September 28, 1962).

Brown, David. "Mississippi Citizens Form Councils for Segregation." *Memphis Press-Scimitar* (September 9, 1954).

Campbell, Sarah. "Files Will Open on Civil Rights Targets." *The Commercial Appeal* (September 21, 1993).

————. "Queries Trim Beckwith Jury Pool." *The Commercial Appeal* (January 19, 1994).

Chism, James. "Curfew Ordered After Strife Hits March For King." *The Commercial Appeal* (April 1968).

Dickerson, James. "Rebuilding the CIA a Matter of Trust." *Jackson Daily News* (February 6, 1980).

————. "Winter's Record." *Jackson Daily News* (June 30, 1980).

————. "Official Secrecy." *Jackson Daily News* (February 10, 1981).

————. "Will Governor Winter Change His Tactics?" *Jackson Daily News* (April 14, 1981).

————. "Winter's Voice." *The Commercial Appeal* (April 25, 1982).

————. "Bilbo Would Have Loved 'Great Statue Debate.' " *The Commercial Appeal* (September 13, 1982).

————. "Magnolia Pilgrimage." *The Commercial Appeal* (June 19, 1983).

————. "Politics of Squalor." *The Commercial Appeal* (October 27, 1983).

————. "More Questions." *The Commercial Appeal* (November 2, 1983).

————. "Voter Judgment." *The Commercial Appeal* (November 6, 1983).

Downing, Shirley. "Mafia-style Operations Emerging." *The Commercial Appeal* (December 2, 1989).

Drucker, Peter F. "American Directions: A Forecast." *Harper's* (February 1965).

Drury, Bob. "Mafia Mole." *Playboy* (January 1997).

Editorial. "The Kennedy Strategy." *The New Republic* (February 15, 1960).

————. "The Leadership of LBJ." *The New Republic* (April 18, 1960).

————. "Sovereignty Files: Find Easiest Method to Open Them." *Clarion-Ledger* (September 22, 1993).

Graham, Fred. "The Many-Sided Justice Fortas." *The New York Times Magazine* (June 4, 1967).

————. "Fortas Casts Critical Eye at College Campus Protests." *The New York Times* (May 24, 1968).

Gunter, James. "Unit Is Formed Here to Co-Ordinate Aims of Southern Groups. *The Commercial Appeal* (December 29, 1955).

Halberstam, David. "The Face of the Enemy in Vietnam." *Harper's* (February 1965).

————. "Starting Out to Be a Famous Reporter." *Esquire* (November 1981).

Harrison, Selig S. "Lyndon Johnson's World." *The New Republic* (June 13, 1960).

————. "Kennedy as President." *The New Republic* (June 27, 1960).

Henry, John C. "Bill Would Give Mississippi Highway Patrol Sovereignty Records." *Delta Democrat-Times* (January 6, 1977).

Johnson, Rob. "Tip Says Police Helped Protect Marijuana-growing Operation." *The Commercial Appeal* (August 23, 1996).

King, Martin Luther. "Showdown for Non-Violence." *Look* (April 16, 1968).

Kraft, Joseph. "Johnson's Talent Hunt." *Harper's* (March 1965).

Lemberg Center for the Study of Violence/Brandeis University. "April Aftermath of the King Assassination." (August 1968).

Lewis, Anthony. "Segregation Group Confers in Secret." *The New York Times* (December 30, 1955).

Loggins, Kirk. "Ray's Lawyer Grilled over Hearing Request." *The Tennessean* (August 17, 1994).

Lowi, Theodore. "Ritual and Power: Senator Kennedy and the First Ballot." *The New Republic* (April 11, 1960).

Marsh, Charles. "Rendezvous with the Wizard." *The Oxford American* (October/November 1996).

Means, John. "Dr. King Is Slain by Sniper." *The Commercial Appeal* (April 5, 1968).

Minor, W. F. "Waller Vetoes Funds for Unit." New Orleans *Times-Picayune* (April 19, 1973).

Mitchell, Jerry. "Opening Records Could Create Flood of Lawsuits." *Clarion-Ledger* (July 30, 1989).

————. "Judge Won't Let DA See Secret Files on Evers." *Clarion-Ledger* (November 29, 1989).

————. "Eastland Had Role in Ousting Tougaloo Chief." *Clarion-Ledger* (January 28, 1990).

————. "Jackson Papers Were Tools of Spy Commission." *Clarion-Ledger* (January 28, 1994).

Montgomery, Shep. "Waits Was Father of State Sales Tax." *Delta Democrat-Times* (March 16, 1991).

Oakley, Robert Edward. "The Victims." *Mississippi* (Winter 1967).

Overby, Charles. "A Mental Confrontation." *The Mississippian* (February 6, 1968).

————. "Protesting the Protesters." *The Mississippian* (1968).

Saggus, James. "Governor's Mansion to Become a Fortress." Associated Press (September 15, 1970).

Spence, John. "200 Turn Out to Help Form Citizens Council." *Memphis Press- Scimitar* (November 8, 1961).

Staff writer. "Memphis Again Holds Title as Murder Capital." *Memphis Press-Scimitar* (March 31, 1933).

Steele, John L. "The Political Virtuoso Gathers the Forces to Take on the Job." *Life* (December 13, 1963).

Taylor, Mary Allie. "JKF Administration 'Not New Deal But New Zeal.' " *Memphis Press-Scimitar* (April 4, 1961).

United Press International. "Coleman Appoints Winter to Tax Collector Post." *Memphis Press-Scimitar* (April 4, 1956).

————. "Five Negroes Shotgunned." *The Mississippian* (June 26, 1963).

————. "Once Again Ole Miss Becomes Segregated." (September 25, 1963).

————. "King Raps Mississippi." *The Mississippian* (June 25, 1964).
————. "Fiery Flareup in Political Debate—Barnett, Williams Get Hot." (May 16, 1967).
————. "Dr. King Threatens to Camp in Front of White House." (November 4, 1967).
————. "After Unexplained Delay Waller Reappoints Black." (May 22, 1974).
White, Owen P. "Sinners In Dixie." *Collier's* (January 26, 1935).

Index

Abernathy, Ralph, 123
Allain, Bill, 210
Armistead, Rex, 82, 83
Avery, Harry, 186

Baker, Bobby, 80
Baldwin, C.B., 16
Bankhead, Tallulah, 7–8
Barber, Rims, 218, 224
Barbour, Haley, 159
Barbour, William, 211, 212, 213, 218, 219, 220
Barnett, E.G., 50, 51, 71
Barnett, Ross, 36, 37, 39, 40–41
  sworn in as governor, 43, 44, 49, 53, 59, 60
  member of Citizens' Councils, 62, 65, 66–70, 75, 119
  on Robert Kennedy's visit to Ole Miss, 119
Barr, John U., 4, 12, 23, 54
Barton, Billy C., 52, 53
Battle, Preston, 182–183
Beittel, A.D., 86
Beckwith, Byron De La, 20, 23, 74, 176, 195, 199–200, 213–217
Beckwith, Thelma, 214–215, 216, 217
Bell, B.L., 34–35

Belont, Alan, 12
Bender, Rita Schwerner, 224
Birdsong, Colonel T.B., 92, 93, 117
Blackwell, Unita, 139
Boggs, Hale, 81
Bowen, David, 158
Bowers, Sam, 133, 151
  sentenced, 201
Bramlett, Leon, 210
Bundy, McGeorge, 128
Burke, Webb, 92, 175–176, 177, 185, 196, 197
Burnett, Hamilton, 189
Burnley, William, 131, 140

Cain, Mary, 118
Capps, Charlie, 220
Carmichael, Stokely, 119, 122
  first uses "black power" phrase, 131, 180
Carter, Esther, 99
Carter, Hodding, 31, 61
Carter, Hodding III, 45, 61, 97, 139, 140, 158, 178, 203, 206
Catledge, Turner, 154
Central Intelligence Agency (CIA), 18
Chaney, James, 88, 96, 102, 182, 192
Chastain, Wayne, 222

Citizens' Councils, 29, 41, 53, 54, 72,
    168
  on Martin Luther King assassination,
    168
Clark, Robert, 158
Cochran, Thad, 211
Cointelpro, 19, 32, 117, 138, 191
Coleman, J.P., 15, 19–20, 24–27, 29,
    32, 36, 38, 54, 77, 171, 210
  death of, 210
Collier, Clinton, 122
Connick , Harry, 200
Cook, Eugene, 4,
Coordinating Committee for
    Fundamental American
    Freedoms, 87
Cope, Deloach, 37
Costello, Frank, 11, 14
Cox, Harold, 55, 103, 108
  dismisses felony indictments against
    Neshoba County civil rights
    case, 111
  appointed to appeals court, 149,
    194
Crawford, Russell, 5
Crump, E.H. "Boss," 7–9, 13, 40
  on Jews, 48, 57, 147

Davis, Jimmie, 39
Davis, John H., 12, 55, 113
DeCell, Carolyn, 21, 22, 28
DeCell, Hal, 19, 21–24, 27–29, 33, 34,
    52
  offers reward, 52
DeCell, Hal Jr., 52,
DeCell, Ken, 52,
DeLaughter, Bobby, 213, 215
Dellinger, David, 178
Delta Development Company, 30
Dennis, Delmar, 215
Doar, John, 63, 64, 90, 132, 149, 150
Douglas, William O., 190
Downing, Virgil, 50, 51
Dulles, Allen, 81, 89
  visits Sovereignty Commission, 90

Eastland, James, 3–5, 14–16, 25, 26,
    42, 46, 47, 55, 57, 59

Eastland, James *(continued)*
  on Freedom Riders, 63, 70, 76, 103,
    107
  as informant, 111, 173
  on Fortas, 184, 196–197, 211
  retirement of, 211
Eisenhower, Dwight, 24
Emmerich, J. Oliver, 31, 45
Evans, Medford, 29
Evers, Charles, 91, 102, 121, 126, 133,
    140–141
  on the draft, 167
  on King assassination, 171
  on Robert Kennedy assassination,
    177
Evers, Medgar, 34, 61, 73–74
  murder of, 176, 215
Ewing, Hickman, 222
Ewing, Jim, 214

Federation for Constitutional
    Government, 3, 12, 29, 40, 206
Feikens, John, 49
Ford, Gerald, 81
Fortas, Abe, 10, 11, 25, 26, 40, 43, 58,
    79, 80, 81, 82, 97, 114, 115
  named to Supreme Court, 116,
    144–148
  on scandal, 171, 172, 173, 174, 175,
    187, 188, 189, 190, 207–208
  death of, 207
Fox, John, 74
Friendly, Al, 28

Gartin, Carroll, 29, 36
Gentry, Curt, 190
Glazier, Herman 158
Green, Percy, 27
Goldberg, Arthur, 115
Golding, Boyd, 37
Goldstein, David, 213
Goldwater, Barry, 45
Goodman, Andrew, 88, 96, 104, 182,
    192
Gore, Albert, 171
Gore, Ney, 19, 21, 22–24, 33
Graham, Fred, 146–147
Greene, Percy, 125

Griffin, Marvin, 4
Griffith, Robert, 173, 174, 188
    death threats, 188
Gunter, James, 3, 4

Halberstam, David, 62, 136
Hale, Dennis, 70, 71
Hamer, Fannie Lou, 106
Hampton, David, 217
Harvey, Paul, 31
Haxton, Josephine, 61
Hayden, Tom, 178
Hederman, Rea, 206
Hederman, Tom, 30, 31, 45, 52,
    142–143, 207
    death of, 207
Henry, Aaron, 97
Hewitt, Woody, 17
Hiatt, Fred, 224
Hicks, Leonard, 19, 20
Hilliard, Elbert, 203, 221
Hoffa, James, 56, 76, 77, 79, 114
Holland, W.H., 71
Hollis, Louis, 29,
Holmes, H.T., 218, 219
Hoover, J. Edgar, 11–14, 19, 31, 32,
    45, 56, 81, 92, 102, 129, 161,
    164, 169, 184, 194
Hopkins, Andrew, 42, 71, 74, 75, 93,
    94, 95, 96, 98, 104, 105, 108,
    109, 123, 130
Howie, Bob, 31
Hume, H.H. Reverend, 27
Humphrey, Hubert, 169–170, 179

Ickes, Harold, 59
Ingebretesen, David, 203, 212, 227

Jackson State University, 192–194
    shootings, 192–194
Jobe, E.R., 75
Johnson, Lyndon, 10, 11, 40, 43, 44,
    78
    sworn in as president, 80, 82, 96,
        100, 114, 115
    names Fortas to Supreme Court,
        116, 135, 145, 171, 174, 175,
        181

Johnson, Paul B., 42, 63, 64
    confronts U.S. marshals at Ole Miss,
        82
    sworn in as governor, 83, 105
    orders Commission files destroyed,
        109–110
    grows nervous about use of private
        agencies, 125, 138, 162
Johnston, Erle, 41, 46, 60, 72
    becomes director of Commission,
        75, 86, 87, 91, 92, 98, 101, 105,
        120
    James Meredith shooting, 124, 125,
        130, 138, 148, 157
    shows signs of stress, 160
    collapses at work, 160
Jones, Albert, 41, 50, 72, 73
Jones, Sam, 4, 12
Jordan, James, 150

Katzenbach, Nicholas, 32, 66, 81, 113
Kefauver, Estes, 9, 11, 14, 24, 26, 40,
    57, 58
    hearings on drug industry, 69, 76, 77
    death of, 77
Kennard, Clyde, 34
Kennedy, John F., 38, 40, 43, 44, 45,
    49, 54, 56, 64, 65, 69, 76, 78
    assassination of, 78
Kennedy, Robert, 32, 38, 56, 64, 65,
    70, 76, 77, 89, 92, 113, 118
    visits Ole Miss, 135, 144, 161, 170
    death of, 170
Kenyatta, Muhammed (a.k.a. Donald
    Jackson), 191–192
King, B.B., 15
King, Coretta Scott, 106
King, Reverend Ed, 73, 97, 121, 211,
    212, 217, 218, 223–226
King, Reverend Martin Luther, Jr., 32,
    44, 56, 90, 106, 121, 122
    visits Neshoba County, 124, 128,
        130, 135–138, 155, 156, 161,
        163–167
    in Memphis, 163–167
Kohlmeir, Louis, 115
Kohn, Aaron, 38
    investigates Carlos Marcello, 38

Lambert, A.C. "Butch," 176
Lambert, William, 187
Landingham, Zach Van, 19, 27, 32
Lee, Reverend George Washington, 23
Levitt, Dan, 145
Lewis, Anthony, 4, 115
Loeb, Henry, 166–167, 189
  on Abe Fortas, 189
Long, Betty Jane, 85, 206,
Long, Earl K., 12
Lott, Trent, 211
Louis, Joe, 8

McCarthy, Eugene, 155–156
McCloughan, M.E., 107
McDowell, Cleve, 70, 76, 77, 195,
  225, 226
McFerren, John, 168
McKellar, Kenneth, 7, 8, 9, 13, 25, 40
  on Jews, 57
McShane, James, 64
Mabus, Ray, 212
Macy, John, 114, 116,
Maedke, Janet, 132
Marcello, Carlos, 11, 12, 14, 26, 38,
  39, 55, 57, 79, 113, 114, 168,
  194–195, 203, 204, 206, 209
  goes to prison, 209
Marshall, Burke, 68
Marshall, Thurgood, 45, 55
Martin, John, 48, 49
Meade, Linda Lea, 38
Memphis cartel, 6, 12, 14, 25, 26, 39,
  58, 101, 170
Meredith, James, 61, 62, 64, 65, 66,
  67, 68, 69, 70, 75, 76, 78, 90,
  119
  shot on highway, 122, 143
Milam, J.W., 23
Mitchell, Jerry, 126, 216
Mitchell, John, 188, 193
Mobley, Mary Ann, 149
Moore, Mike, 219
Moore, Roy, 93, 111
Morgenthau, Robert, 187
Morris, William Hugh, 56

Neill, Charles Lamar, 185

Nixon, Richard, 24, 43, 45, 49, 179,
  181, 183, 184, 190
Norvell, Aubrey, 119–120
Novik, Jack, 205
Nunan, Joseph, 7

Oswald, Lee Harvey, 81, 114
Overby, Charles, 152–153, 160, 185,
  207

Paris, Wendell, 106
Parker, Mack Charles, 32–33
Patterson, Joe, 94
Payne, Shirley, 213
Pepper, William, 211, 222, 223
Perez, Leander, 4, 12, 26, 30, 39, 54
Peters, Ed, 213
Pierotti, John, 222
Posey, Buford, 89
Price, Cecil, 88, 89, 93, 95–96, 98,
  111, 122, 151
Procter, John, 93
Pyle, Christopher, 133–134, 137

Rainey, Lawrence A., 50, 51, 93, 94,
  96, 111, 122, 201
Ray, James Earl, 162–163, 166, 171
  captured in London, 182, 183, 186,
  221–223
Rivers, Mendel, 4
Robinson, Jackie, 107
  visits Mississippi, 107
Rockwell, George Lincoln, 143
Rogers, George, 17, 18, 185, 203
Roosevelt, Franklin, 9, 10
Russell, Bertrand, 136
Russell, Richard, 81

Saggus, Jim, 125
Salter, John, 212, 218, 223
  withdraws from case, 223
Sandin, Max, 112
Satterfield, John C., 72, 73, 87
Scarbrough, Tom, 84, 85, 111, 112
  gathers information on Vietnam
    antiwar protesters, 119–121
  James Meredith shooting, 127, 128,
    132, 139, 140

Schreiner, Sam, 125
Schwerner, Michael, 85, 88, 96, 99,
    104, 108, 150, 182, 192, 224
Seaver, Ted, 126
Seigenthaler, John, 76
Sherrill, Robert, 46, 47
Sillers, Walter, 4, 37, 42
Simmons, William J., 5, 29, 42, 52, 55
Smith, Charles, 142
Smith, Hazel Brannon, 31, 60, 73
Smith, Howard K., 83–84
Smith, Mike, 131, 157
Snodgrass, Charles, 117
Sovereignty Commission, Mississippi
    State, 16–19, 21–22, 26, 27, 33
    talk of abolishing, 35
    expands black spy network, 42
    investigates Jews, 51–52
    battle over control, 60, 70, 85
    investigates Michael Schwerner, 86
    makes illegal gun purchases, 88
    private bank account, 99
    uses health department, 101
    uses draft boards, 103, 104, 105
    governor orders Commission files
        destroyed, 107
    names of private agencies used, 112
    targets the antiwar movement,
        119–120
    James Meredith shooting, 157, 160
    campus informants, 163
    link to Selma, 211
    court orders file opened, 227
    files are opened, 227
Spock, Benjamin, 155
Stevenson, Adlai, 24
Stevenson, Coke, 4
Stewart, Potter, 48
Stoner, J.B., 183

Sudduth, Charles, 159
Sullivan, Charles, 36, 77
Sullivan, Joe, 104, 228
Sullivan, John, 87, 113
Sumrall, John Otis, 141

Tarrants, Tommy, 176
Terney, Champ, 76
Thomas, Bill, 186
Thurmond, Strom, 3
Till, Emmett, 22, 23
Trafficante, Santos, Jr., 56
Truman, Harry, 9
Tubb, Tom, 62
Turner, Steven, 37

Wallace, George, 179, 181
Waller, William, 74, 141, 195, 197,
    198, 199
Ward, Jimmy, 23, 30, 31, 60, 126,
    127, 206–207
    death of, 217
Warren, Earl, 146
Waits, Hilton, 17, 33, 37
Williams, Helen Bass, 159
Williams, Reverend Hosea, 221
Williams, John Bell, 4, 25, 27, 142,
    157–158
    sworn in as governor, 175, 177, 178,
        192
Winchester, Jesse, 186
Winter, William, 18, 54, 141, 202,
    205, 230
Wolfson, Louis, 144–146, 172, 187,
    208
Wright, J. Stephen, 205
Wright, Fielding L., 4, 21

Young, Andrew, 123

About the Author

Since his first magazine article was published in 1968, James Dickerson has worked as a magazine editor, newspaper editor, reporter, columnist, book critic, and photographer. During a writing career spanning nearly thirty years, he has worked for five Southern dailies and has published more than 1,400 articles in a variety of media. He is the author of six books, one of which, *Goin' Back to Memphis,* an investigative look at how politics and organized crime have influenced Memphis music for the past century, was a finalist in the 1996 Ralph J. Gleason Awards, granted annually by *Rolling Stone* magazine, New York University, and BMI.